ENGLISH RECUSANT LITERATURE
1558–1640

Selected and Edited by
D. M. ROGERS

Volume 298

HIEREMIAS DREXELIUS
The Angel-Guardian's Clock
[*1630*]

RALPH BUCKLAND
An Embassage from Heaven
[*1611*]

HIEREMIAS DREXELIUS

The Angel-Guardian's Clock

[*1630*]

The Scolar Press

1976

ISBN o 85967 299 9

Published and printed in Great Britain by
The Scolar Press Limited, 59-61 East Parade,
Ilkley, Yorkshire and
39 Great Russell Street,
London WC1

NOTE

The following works are reproduced (original size) with permission:

1) Hieremias Drexelius, *The angel-guardian's clock*, [1630], from a copy in the Bodleian Library, by permission of the Curators.

References: Allison and Rogers 283; STC 7234.

2) Ralph Buckland, *An embassage from heaven*, [1611], from a copy in the library of Lambeth Palace, by permission of the Librarian.

References: Allison and Rogers 180; STC 4007.

Learne to Pray.

Learne to liue.

Learne to Dye.

THE
ANGEL-GVARDIAN'S
CLOCK
TRANSLATED
*out of latin
into English*

At Roven of the
impression of Nicolas
Courant in the streete
of the poterne neere
to the Pallace.

THE TRANSLA-
TOVR'S PREFACE
to his ANGEL-
GVARDIAN.

HOLIE ANGEL, I most hũbly and ingenuously acknowledge my abilities to be farre inferiour to those of my Authour, and my great vnworthinesse to receaue thy helpe and assistance; both which must consequently cause many things in this my Translation to be weakely and inefficaciously exprest. But accept, I beseech thee, O glorious Angel, my intention bent to thy seruice, and (as thou excellently knowest how to do) supply in the hart and minde of the Noble Personage, to whome I dedicate these my endeauours, and of all other Christian Readers, all that, wherein I haue bene defectiue. In confidence whereof, and under the wing of thy protection, I haue presumed to putt my hand to this thy worke.

TO THE RIGHT
HONORABLE AND MOST
Vertuous Ladie,

MAY IT PLEASE YOVR
LADYSHIP.

ADAME, The
greateſt ſcholars
do often caſt back
their eies (for re-
creation ſake) vpon meaner
Authours, then ſuch as exact
and make proofe of their
deeper ſcience. So that I hope
this CLOCK OF THE
ANGEL-GVARDIAN
will not be vnpleaſing to

your Lady:hip's fight. I moſt
humbly preſente it to your
Ladyship beſeeching you to
vouchſafe a fauourable acceptance of the Dedication,
which is all I challenge to be
mine ; hauing throughout
the whole booke ſo confi-
ned my ſelf to my Authour's
ſenſe, yea euen as much as I
might poſsibly, to his verie
words, that it wil be no great
wonder, if my language be
leſſe gracefull in ſeuerall reſpects. But for this I only
pleade, that as the contents
aime not, ſo neither doth the
tranſlation aime to pleaſe or
delight by ſmooth diſcour-

ſes, but to profit by way of reflection and meditation, wherein your Ladyship is moſt conuerſant and beſt ſeene. Which certainly my Good Angel well knoweth, who (as I perſwade myſelf) aduiſes me to this courſe; wherein alſo me thinkes I follow the dictamen of my Authour, who ſeemes to haue bene aduiſed to dedicate the Originall to thoſe of the Sodalitie. Now, whome of the Sodalitie can it be poſsible for me to chooſe more fittly then one , who is not only a member, but an eminent Patroneſſe thereof, and

in this diftreffed countrie a
cherisher of the whole caufe,
which place would be much
more defolate of all côfort,
were it not for the luftre of
your Ladyship's example,
and the exprefsions of your
charitie , which inceffantly
tends to the good both of
mens bodies and foules. To
all which your ladyship is in-
fallibly moued in great part
by your Good Angel. For
his fake therefore be pleafed
to accept cheerefully thi:
poore litle prefent, and con-
ceiue he fpeakes by it,as certainly he doth. And if your
Ladyship shall vouchfafe to

peruse and obserue, what is contained herein, you may be well assured, that he will be in all excellent kindes the verie selffame to your Ladyship, which anie Angel hath euer bene to his Charge; the particulars whereof you will finde to your owne great comfort expressed in this Booke. And I rest confident, that your good Angel will inspire you with an affection to it, since mine (me thinkes) hath incited me to dedicate to you, as a thing pleasing to him. For I abstract herein, from all those innumerable tyes, of dutie, which challer-

ge all that is or can be mine,
to be due to your Ladyship
and which oblige me with
much ioy euer to remaine.

Your Ladyship's.

*Most obedient sonne and
most humble seruant.*

H.

THE
AVTHOVR'S PREFACE,
to his ANGEL-GVARDIAN.

MOST blessed Angel, my best and most louing keeper; I dedicate this my litle booke to all the Angels in heauen; but chiefely to thee I offer it from the bottome of my hart, as proceeding out of my affection bent towards thee. And iustly; since thou hast bound me to thee by innumerable benefits; neither dost thou yet forsake me, though long since vnworthie and vndeseruing. O my most deare Tutour, thou euen as it were compellest me by thy innumerable fauours to liue and die vngratefull. By so much certainly thou prouest thyself the more worthie, by how much the more

wicked thy client is. O most watchfull keeper, thou hast of me an vntoward and sleepie disciple; but such
is thine and all thy fellowes goodnesse,
as that euen to the verie worst of
mankinde you do good. And what
haue I to repay for thy so manie
yeares most faithfull watching ouer
me? better haue I nothing; I will
euen giue thee back thine owne, as a
present. Often hast thou taught me, in
diuerse things instructed me, faithfully admonishing, frequently corre-
cting, day and night defending, and
constantly directing me; in a word,
thou art really without intermission
good towards me. Beholde, I haue
here (the best I can) putt in order
and writing, for the good of manie,
thy Aduertisements, which, as it
were from thine owne mouth I haue
receiued into my weake and confused
memorie; here wilt thou often speake

by

by my words, and I vtter thy meaning. Go on thus, O my moſt deare Tutour, in teaching me, and with me, others, TO PRAY, and TO LIVE; teach vs how TO DIE. To know this, is to be endued with all neceſſarie ſcience : Ignorance in moſt things elſe is more profitable, then knowledge : and if we be well ſeene in this, of what elſe neede we be ſorie to be ignorant ? Teach vs then, O my moſt benigne Angel, how we are TO PRAY, TO LIVE, TO DIE.

THE
ANGEL-GVARDIAN
to his Charge.

Ioh. c.
11.

ARE there not *twelue houres in the day?* apply therefore thy minde hourely both day and night in these three demaunds, which according to thy reach and capacitie I will teach thee to vnderstand. But beginning at the last of thy demaunds, I will first teach thee TO DIE. It is the greatest of all businesses, in which a man can erre but once; but that errour will be eternally punished; neither canst thou beginne to liue to God, vnlesse first thou DIE to thyself. Secondly, I will teach thee TO LIVE. For to

desire

desire to make a good ende, and to liue ill, is a childish and ridiculous wish. Neither can one learne TO PRAY well, if he desist not first from doing ill. Friuolous is his prayer, whose action is wicked. Lastly I will teach thee TO PRAY ; and if thou wilt giue creditt to saint Augustin, *He truly knowes rightly how to liue, whoe knowes rightly how to pray.* Thus will I teach thee TO DIE, TO LIVE, TO PRAY ; and that hourely. I take the dedication of this litle Booke to all the Angels and to me, as a thing done to our honour ; but to whose profitt shall it redounde? yf thou wilt harken to me, my will is, and I commaund thee to dedicate and offer it to the most chast yong men, the children of

B. MARIE

B. MARIE, which are en-
rolled into her Virginlike foda-
litie. Great is the amitie betweene them and vs; neither is
anie thing more deare to vs,
then the moſt chaſt familiaritie,
which we haue with them. According then to the law and
cuſtome of friendship, we will
that all that, which is ours, be
alſo theirs. Yf they loue vs, (as
without doubt they do) they
will louingly embrace our admonitions.

TO THE MOST VER-
TVOVS AND WORTHIE
yong men and others, that are
of the Sodalitie of the most
Blessed Virgin Marie,
Greeting from our
Lord, and from his
glorious mother.

Yee all honour the most blessed *Virgin Marie* mother of *our Lord*; which is certainly a most holie and ancient institution, since this your honour to her or Sodalitie first beganne vnder the holie Crosse of *our Lord* vpon

the

the mountaine Golgotha.
For the firſt of this Sodalitie,
or this Virgin's firſt adopted
ſonne was Sainct Iohn our
Sauiour's beſt beloued;hence
all you of the Sodalitie and
children of this Virgin and
mother haue your begin-
ning; but ſince you are depriued of her preſéce, which
ſaint Iohn enioyed, and that
this great Mother is mounted ſo high aboue all the
Quires of Angels,that rightly the Church ſtileth her *the*
Queene of Angels, it will neither be vnfitting nor vn-
pleaſing vnto you to inſi-
nuate your ſelues into an in-

ward

ward familiaritie with them.
We dare not denie but the
Angels are the deareſt children of that great Mother,
and we ought to eſteeme it
much, if they vouchſafe to
admit vs to be their bretheren. Without all doubt, their
friendſhip is moſt neceſſarie
to them, who deſire to be
eſteemed the children of ſo
powerfull a mother. O yee
vertuous children of the Sodalitie ; I aſſure myſelf, you
deſire to obtaine their friẽd-
ſhip , and you deſire to be
Angels , that you may be
equall children with them;
and for this cauſe I will in-

stantly putt into your hands this *Clock of the Angel-Guardian*; to the ende that if the shrine be to be honoured in respect of the sainct, I make no doubt, but you will be most readie to honour the Angels for their Queene's sake. For easily will he obtaine this Queene to be his Patronesse, who hath the courtiers of heauen his sure friends. I therefore beseech you and euerie one of you, most sincere Children of the Sodalitie, to vouchsafe cheerefully to looke vpon, and receiue this litle Booke dedicated to the Angels, to their king and Queene. Neither will the Angels be honoured by you without benefitt to yourselues. For although this friendship proceede not from their equals, yet will it make you become Peeres with them in heauen. MoNACHIVM, MICHELMASDAY 1621.

Yours in Christ Iesus.

HIER. DREX.

TO THE CHRISTIAN READER.

I Conceaue, O my Reader, the same to be thy desire, which was heretofore the Poet's wish; and I beleeue it to be euerie man's: That, what is sayd or written, might be short and compendious. So do I intende here in few words, with order and breuitie to teach thee Three things, TO DIE, TO LIVE, and TO PRAY well; Which I endeauour to the honour of the holie Angels, and chiefly of the Angel-Guardian. Whosoeuer thou art, that louest the holie Angels, I pray thee despise not this Booke, which will be of so much the greater and more frequent vse to thee, by how much thy loue encreases towards them.

THE

THE
I. HOVRE
OF THE DAY.

LEARNE TO DIE.

*The certaintie of death may
teach it thee.*

BE mindefull, man, that thou art clay; and that (perhaps shortly) the morning will come, til whofe euening thou shalt not liue, or the euening, whofe enfuing morning thou shalt not fee. *It is decreed, that man shall die.* Death will challenge vs and in deed what is ours. Whofoeuer will learne truly

Hebr. 10.

how

how *to die*, it is needefull for him to practife it hourely. Why doft thou admit long hopes and delayes? why doft thou bufie thy minde with great expectations? to morrow perhaps thou wilt be duft and ashes. O man, walke warily. That black Goddeffe Death hangs daily ouer euerie one of our heads; and with a watchfull eye expects the running of the laft graine of fand from the houreglaffe of our life. Yf thou wilt do any thing, do it quickly. Thou shortly shalt pofte hence. Yf thou haft loued Vertue, or committed finne, that will go with thee; and alone from hence accompanie thee. Beare death in minde.

LEARNE TO LIVE.

The law of Patience may teach it thee.

THis vertue rightly deferues to be efteemed by thee, in the firft pla-

ce; it being moſt neceſſary, that thou
be well habituated therein. For euery where in this life thou wilt finde
many things to be ſuffered. S. Bernard ſaith : A good life is to perſeuer
till death in ſuffering euils , and
doing good. Whoſoeuer will not
ſuffer , refuſeth to liue. *Sorrow* and
paine shew vs the way to God. He
that is afflicted , and murmureth not
at it, wanteth not much of attaining
to heauen. It is certainly a great euil,
not to be able to beare an ill turne.
Nothing exaſperateth the anger of a
ſore, more then the impatience of the
hurt perſon. Yf God vſeth often to
wounde, he vſes oftener to cure; eſpecially if one beare his troubles
meekely , and with thankes-giuing,
and hates not him , from whome
they proceede, nor expoſtulates with
God's prouidence, and hath not only
learnt to shew himſelf good in proſ-
peritie. The difficultie of a battle
dures oftentimes the longer, that the
crowne of the victorie may be the
greater. *Patience* is a breaſt-plate of

B proofe.

proofe. Vertue in suffering ouerco-
meth. It is an excellent Canticle,
whilst thou sufferest, to sing: *Blessed be
the name of God*. All impatience gaines
the encrease of a man's owne griefe,
the losse of a promised rewarde, and
the deseruing of a new punishment.
Suffer therefore what thou wouldst
not haue, to the ende thou maist obtaine what thou wouldst haue. For
sufferance doth encrease recompése.

LEARNE TO PRAY.

*An Act of Contrition may
teach it thee.*

O Lord Iesus Christ·, true
God and man, my Crea-
toúr and Redeemer: I am
hartily sory that I haue offended thee, my Lord and God,
whome I loue aboue al things;
and I resolutely purpose neuer
more to sinne , and to shunne

all

all occasions thereof, as also to
Confesse my self, and to performe whatsoeuer pennance shal
be enioined me; and in satisfaction for my sinnes I offer
thee vp thy bitter passion, the
merits of Blessed MARIE that
euer-Virgin, and of all the
saints in heauen, my owne
workes, and my whole life.
And I trust in thy infinite
goodnesse and mercie, that
thou wilt through the vertue
of thy precious bloud forgiue
me my offences, and grant me
so efficacious grace, that I may
be able to leade a pious life, and
serue thee to my ende; who
liuest and raignest with the
Father and the Holie-Ghost
God, and art blessed without
ende.

There

There is contained in this prayer:
1. an Act of Faith. 2. Sorrow to haue sinned. 3. the loue of God aboue all things. 4. a purpose of a future amendement. 5. an offer of ones selfe through Christ. 6. a hope of forgiuenesse through him. 7. a petition for God's grace and assistance.

SHORT ADVERTISEMENTS
touching an Act of Contrition.

COntrition is so precious a thing, that in a moment it is able to expiate a thousand mortall sinnes. It restoreth man to God, and God's grace to man. It gaines eternal blisse, though it happen that he, who hath it, die without oportunitie of Confession. *A sorrowfull spirit, is a sacrifice to God, God will neuer despise an humbled and contrite hart.* The chiefe groundworke of Contrition, is the loue of God aboue all things, and it containes three Acts.

The first is SORROW for hauing offended Almighty God, who is most

worthy

worthy to be beloued & honored of
all aboue all things. Hence it is, that
the good, which is loſt by euery mortall ſinne, is infinit; & greater then all
gaines whatſoeuer. And the euil,
which by euery mortall ſinne is in-
curred, is alſo infinit, and farre greater then all euils. The loſſe therefore
of ſo great a good, and the enduring
of ſo great an euill, should with all
reaſon impreſſe into vs a greater
griefe, then either the loſſe of eſtate
or health, or what elſe ſoeuer, or of
all togeather. To die a thouſand
deathes in this world, is but a ſport,
if it be compared with thoſe *eternall*
flames of hell, to which one onely
deadly ſinne ſubiecteth him.

The ſecond is, A PROPOSE
neither for loue nor feare euer to ſinne againe; and to make ſatisfaction
for any ſinne committed. By this
firme and reſolute purpoſe a man offereth himſelf ſo ready to obſerue
God's commaundements, that he
may ſay: O Lord, I am reſolued to
keepe thy law, and as neere as I can,

O my God, punctually to execute,
what thou haft commanded.

The third is A HOPE OF PAR-
DON , and A PETITION FOR
GRACE , ferioufly to amende ones
life. To Confeffe, and not amende,
is to tempt God ; and it auailes not to
aske pardon for ones finnes , and to
fall againe purpofely into them. The
precious bloud and death of our
L o. IESVS doth giue vs confidence, that if we aske it, we may obtaine the ferious amendement of our
liues after many a grieuous finne
committed.

An accufing of a man's felfe,
with a purpofe of amendment
after a relapfe into the fame
fault, of which he knew
he was to haue had
great care.

O My moft louing God ; I an vngratefull and loft creature as I

am

am, do now returne to thee, after hauing tired myself in forbidden waies.
I now seeke thee to be my friend, whome myself haue made my ennemie. I haue sinned againe, and haue fallen into the same fault. Alas! I haue admitted into my minde those most dangerous thoughts, and haue repeated those most wicked words, & haue fallen againe into that fault, which I knew would mightily displease thee, and bring much domage to myselfe. I foreknew how carefully I ought to haue preuented those things, and yet I haue not taken heede; by meanes whereof, O mercifull God, I haue offended thy Diuine Maiestie, lost thy grace, depriued myself of heauen, and for a base and vile pleasure, am become subiect to damnation. I know, O Lord, that I ought to haue loued thee aboue all things. I acknowledge, O my God, that thy law and honour ought to be more deare to me, then all things created; and yet I loue myself so much to mine owne losse, that I ha-

ue preferred my honour, my profitt,
and my lust, before thy law and honour. Alas, how carnally am I affec-
ted ; and though I should denie it,
yet my workes would proclame it.
The world is not only yet vncruci-
fied in me, but it wholy breathes and
liues in me. Full I am of wicked motions , of filthy concupifcences and
defires; and yet would I feeme ho-
neft and good. My very whole life
is but a meere inconftancie & muta-
bilitie. My exteriour fenfes runne
freely gadding whither they lift. O
how fowle imaginations befiege my
minde ! O how hard and infenfible a
ftone am I, when there is queftion of
doing pennance ! I am as forward to
fpeake, as I am rash and inconfiderate in it. I am deafe to admonitions,
but moft attentiue to fables and foolish difcourfes. Whatfoeuer is faid of
God or heauen, is both ftrange and
wearifome to me. I am fufficiently
vigilant to my worldly profitt, but
altogether dull and droufy at my
praiers. When occafion of banket-

ting is afforded, I haften with a longing to it. But towards Diuine feruice I creepe like a fnaile. To plaies and wanton paftimes I flie as fwift as an eagle; but to goodneffe I fcarce ftirre. I haften to any thing forbidden; to enuie and iealofie I am too much inclined. When I am fcarce toucht, I grow in anger, and ftrike; and my tongue hurts, when my hand cãnot. None iniureth me, againft whome I plott not a reuenge. O God, thou knoweft how the flames of luft are neere me. Here I diffemble and couer it; but to thee, O Eye of the world, all things lye open. There is no fecrett of the hart, which can be hidden from thee. O how often and how great things do I purpofe to performe which inftantly vanifh away in a ridiculous and wicked kinde of obliuion. I haue reafon therefore to grieue for hauing fo often committed things to be repented. And euen this grieues me, that I grieue no more, and that I am not fo very fenfible of mine owne miferie. But now,

B 5 though

though hitherto I haue slowly embraced pietie, and alas haue gladly hastened to vice, henceforth I purpose to do so no more. Now I beginne. no man can perfit his way to heauen, but he, who daily beginnes. I therefore most firmely determine, in confidence of thy helpe, O Lord, most diligently to auoide my former offences and all occasions of sinne. I am now become another man. Assist me, o yee heauenlie saints. O my Lord, my God, create in me a cleane and chast hart; renew, I beseech thee, in me a right spirit, to the ende, that now at length I may amende my life, loue thee with my whole hart; and so perseuer to the ende.

To obtaine the remission of sinnes.

O GOD take pittie vpon me most miserable sinner, who haue done vnworthie things, but do suffer worthily; who haue continually sinned,

ned, and seldome repented, impatiently vndergoing thy chasticements. Thou art iust, ô Lord, and righteous is thy iudgement; great hath bene mine offence, and litle doe I suffer. O merciefull God, thou dost neither afflict vs iniustly nor cruelly. I know, ô Lord, and am most certaine, that our life is not moued by violent and suddaine motions; but gouerned and disposed by thee our God. Thou hast care of all things, especially of thy seruants, who haue placed their desires in thy most holie will and pleasure. I therefore fly for refuge to the Altar of thy Mercie, and most humbly pray thee, not to punish me according to my sinnes, but to forgiue me according to thy mercie. O my God, I refuse not to be scourged, so thou vouchsafe to giue me patience, that I may praise thee in the midst of my torments, and amende my life. Take pittie on me, O Lord, take pittie on me, and assist me, as thou knowest. Thou art ignorant of nothing, and thou art omnipotent, who li-

uest

ueſt world without ende.

Thankes+giuing for all God's benefits.

O Lord; lett all the Angels, Archangels & Principalities bleſſe thee; let them praiſe and glorifie thee world without end.

Let the Powers, Vertues, and Dominations bleſſe thee; let them praiſe and glorifie thee world without ende.

Let the Thrones, Cherubins and Seraphins bleſſe thee; let them praiſe and glorifie thee world without ende.

All you Patriarkes and Prophets, bleſſe you our Lord; praiſe and glorifie him world without ende.

All you Apoſtles and Euangeliſts, bleſſe you our Lord; praiſe and glorifie him world without ende.

All you Martyrs and Confeſſours, bleſſe you our Lord; praiſe and glorifie him world without ende.

All

All you Virgins, and all you ſaints of heauen, praiſe & exalt him world without ende.

O God, let thy deſired bleſſing confirme the faithfull, and neuer ſuffer them to ſtray from thy will, and vouchſafe them grace to reioyce in thy benefits; through Chriſt our Lord.

THE II. HOVRE.

LEARNE TO DIE.

The vncertaintie of the houre of death may teach it thee.

BE mindefull that man is but a ſhadow; and that in the whole world there is no artiſan, who can ſo skilfully make a clock, which can ſhew him the laſt day and houre of his life. *Thou canſt not know future things by anie meſſenger.* Death threa-

Eccleſ. c. 8.

tens

tens thee euerie where; and the diuel is alwaies besetting and vndermining thee ; yet thou goest on dreamingly, and triflest. Why dost thou dispose of yeares aforehand ? and of, I know not how long a life ? There is no time so short, which thou art sure to outliue. It is a pleasing, but a dangerous madnesse, to hope for a long life, and hardly euer to thinke of a good life. It is a businesse of consequence, and long in learning, how to departe with a quiet and indifferent minde, when that houre comes, which is as ineuitable as vncertaine. *Man knowes not his ende ; but as fishes are taken with a hocke, and birdes with a nett ; so are men in an euil houre, when Death comes suddenly vpon them.* Remember that thou art to die.

Eccl. c. 9.

LEARNE TO LIVE.

The law of Obedience may teach it thee.

Whosoeuer resisteth power, resisteth the ordinance of God; and they who resist, worke their owne damnation. Sacrifices were heretofore acceptable to God; but obedience was euer the more welcome. Whosoeuer would haue God heare his praiers, let him harken to his Superiour, and learne to obey him. Sooner is heard the prayer of one obedient, then of a thousand refractarie persons. He that is obedient, heedes not how pleasing and easy the commaundemēt is, but contenteth himself, that it is commaunded; vnlesse it be against God. By other vertues we only fight with the diuel; by patience we ouercome him. When thou hast learned to obey, thou wilt know how to commaunde; and that in heauen.

Rom.c.
13

LEARNE

LEARNE TO PRAY.

*These three petitions being both
exceeding short and good,
may teach it thee.*

1.

Blessed be God in all eternitie.

2.

Take pittie vpon me , O God., according to thy great mercie; although I am, ô Lord, vnworthie of the least of thy mercies.

3.

O my Lord and my God , I offer myself wholy to thy disposing ; thy will be done.

Obseruations to be pondered in these 3. short praiers.

I.

THe first is taken from the mouth of the Prophets Dauid and Zacharias ; the second from the same king Dauid, and the Patriarke Iacob ; the third from Christ's owne mouth, and his Apostle S. Thomas; and these verie same petitions are often reiterated in other places of holie scripture.

1. Reg 25.
Luc. c. 1.
Psal. 50.
Gen. 32
Math. 6.
Ioh. 20

2.

These three litle prayers containe all the perfections of well praying; to witt, the praising of God, thankesgiuing, imploring his helpe, asking his pardon, humbling our mindes, offering ourselues, the worshipping of God, the sacrifizing of our wills, which is the principall effect of loue, and the summe of all good desires.

3.

These three litle prayers are as

three

three golden shaftes, which, when they flie not only from a man's mouth, but from his hart, nothing hindreth them, nor do they ſtay, till they penetrate (if we may ſay ſo) God's owne hart.

4.

Theſe prayers are like bellowes, by whoſe continuall blaſt the fire of a moſt ſincere loue towards God, is continued, fedd, ſtirred vp, and en-creaſed. It is almoſt incredible to de-clare, how gratefull it is to God, and how profitable to man, *by theſe and ſuch like prayers* to ſtirre vp conti-nually, ones minde to God, and vnite it to him.

5.

Of theſe one may ſay moſt truly, *By how much the oftener they be repeated ſo much the better it is.* A thouſand and a thouſand times were not too of-ten, ſo there be an agreement be-tweene the hart and the mouth; and that there be as well the conſent of the minde, as the labour of the lip-pes. For as it is impoſſible, but that

the

the fire will kindle and flash, when
the lighted match falleth vpon the
gunne-powder; so certainly cannot
euen one of these prayers and the
hart of man meete, but that the fire
of diuine loue must needes worke
his effect.

6.

There is no neede alwaies to pronounce or thinke of these three prayers togeather; oftentimes one of
them suffiseth, and chiefly the first,
which some hundred of times may
breake out in the day, especially these three words: *Blessed be God; blessed
be God.* Neither is it alwaies needefull to vtter them vocally (though it
be good) but it suffiseth to repeate
them in ones minde.

7.

These deuout prayers to God are
most conuenient for men , who are
full of businesses, sick, afflicted or dis-
tressed , from whome it were hard to
exact long prayers; but then wholy
to omit praying, were impious, and
forbidden by Christ; *Because we must.*

continually

continually pray, and not desist. This law therefore is excellent for all sorts of people. By how much more our businesse doth vrge, paine, or smarte; by how much more irkesomenesse, griefe, sicknesse, or affliction doth presse; so much the more ardently should we cry out: *Blessed be God: blessed be God in all eternitie*; or *Take pittie vpon me, ô God*; Or this, which is most excellent: *Let thy will be done, let it be done; thy will, O Lord, and not mine.* This is with great ardour to be repeated; and most of all, when we perceaue the obstinacie of our owne wills.

8.

There are some, who often both in hart and mouth repeate them; and can auouch, that they finde, that the seldomer they vse them, the worse it is for them, and the oftener, the better. Certainly it is a wonderfull thing, what manie holie men haue felt by the meanes of such Iaculatorie prayers, as these; and as it were by often bursting forth into deuotion

towards God. These are winged prayers, which carrie vp the minde, and
place it in tranquillitie; and by a
gentle blast of loue do kindle it, and
do so vnite diuine and humane loue,
that at length it seemes bitter to a
man, to desire anie thing contrarie to
God's will. S. Chrisostome (as Nicephorus saith of him,) at his last gaspe
burst forth into these his last words:
Glorie be to thee, ô Lord, from all things. It
was an excellent cry of the people in
the Ghospel: *God hath done all things
well. Therefore Blessed be God in all eternitie.*

9.

None ought to be dishartened,
though at first these prayers seeme
neither pleasing nor profitable, since
nothing can in the beginning be per-
fited. Vse and continued reiteration
will render this manner of prayer
both easie and profitable; so that this
office be not of the tongue alone,
though of the hart alone it may be.
Yf the voice be present, let not the
hart be absent. Workes, which pro-

Lib.13 c.37.

Mar.7

ceede

ceede ioyntly from them, cannot
but make our prayers to God, fruit-
full to vs.

A deuout aspiration to all the Angels.

O Yow Angels, Archangels,
Thrones and Dominations,
Principalities and Powers, Vertues,
Cherubins, and Seraphins, and all
yee Saints of heauen, intercede for vs
now and in the houre of our death.
Amen.

THE III. HOVRE.

LEARNE TO DIE.

Differred pennance may teach it thee.

Remember that man is like graffe; and (if thou canft) differre not the amendement of thy life frō yeare to yeare, from moneth to moneth, from weeke to weeke, nor from one day to another. To morrow pennance may be too late; beginne therefore to day. It is a great teftimony of health, to vnderftand ones difeafe; & a great parte of goodneffe confifts in defiring to do good. It is moft dangerous in a difeafe, when the patient hath loft the feeling of it. And alas, what is more miferable, then a wretch not commiferating his owne cafe.

Make

Make haste about thy businesse; thy
death approches, not lamely , but
with a swift foote ; and it will instantly ouertake thee; suspect that it
will be to morrow ; and grieue, and
amende thyself to day. This(saith S.
Augustin)draweth manie into perdition, that they still cry : TO MOR-
ROW , TO MORROW; and the
doore is quickly shutt against them.
Beare this therefore still in minde;
THOV ART TO DIE.

LEARNE TO LIVE.

The law of Temperance may
teach it thee.

THou oughtest *to suffer* many
things , but certainly *to abstaine*
from more. Sinne watcheth still at
the doore; which vnlesse thou ope-
nest, it will not enter. Temperance
appoints a meane in all things. It
commaundeth , that a man be sober
of diet, that he be cloathed , but yet

accor-

according to his condition; that he carefully obserue *a meane* in all things, *leaſt any thing be ouermuch.* Nothing is safe, which exceedes a meane. It is an excellent meane to be obserued by thoſe, who naturally couett, not to deſire what they would, but what they ought; and it is better & a farre greater contentment, to ly vpon ſtraw with a quiet conſcience, then in a bed of golde, & withall to be agitated with troubles in our mindes. A glutton takes the modell of his life from the kitchin and his pallat; but to a temperate man ſobrietie affordes a patterne. Fortune yeildeth ſumptuous fare; but Temperance prouides it be frugally vſed. To a temperate man God and reaſon are lawes; but an intemperate man hearkens to nothing but to pleaſure and his belly.

LEARNE TO PRAY.

The litle Office of the Angel-guardian may teach it thee.

The little Office of the Angel-guardian. At Mattins.

℣. God hath giuen his Angels charge ouer thee ; that they keepe thee in all thy waies. ℟. Amen.
The verse.
O Lord, open thou my lippes. ℟. And my mouth shall shew forth thy praise.
℣. O God, incline to mine ayde;
℟. O Lord, make haste to helpe me.
℣. Glorie be to the Father, and to the sonne &c.
℟. As it was in the beginning, both now and euer, world without ende, Amen. Alleluia.
From septuagesima to Easter, in steede of Alleluia *is saide* : Praise be to thee, O Lord, king of æternall glory.

THE

THE HYMNE.

WE sing of Angels-guardians
of man kinde
Whome God our heauenly Father
hath assign'd
For our assistance, least the mortall
foe
Our soules by craft and malice ouerthrow.

Antiphone. O holy Angels, our Guardians, defend vs in the combat, that
we perish not in the dreadfull iudg-
ment.

℣. In the sight of the Angels I will
sing to thee, O God. ℟. I will adore
at thy holy temple, and I will confesse to thy name.

Let vs pray.

O God who by thy vnspeakable
prouidence vouchsafest to send
the holy Angels for our custody;
graunt to thy humble suppliants
to bee alwaies defended by their
protection, and to enioy their
euerlasting societie; through

C 2   our

our Lord Iesus Christ thy sonne &c.

AT PRIME.

℣. God hath giuen his Angels charge ouer thee ; that they may keepe thee in all thy waies. ℟. Amen.

℣. O God, incline to my aide;

℟. O Lord, make haste to helpe me.

℣. Glory be to the Father &c. Alleluia.

THE HYMNE.

THe trayterous angel seing himself destroy'd

Fall'n from the honour , which he once enioy'd

Inflam'd with enuy striues to dispossesse

Of heauenly ioyes, whome God hath chosen to blesse.

Antiph. O holy Angels our guardians &c. *as before.*

℣. In the sight of the Angels I will sing to thee, ō my God. ℟. I will adore at thy holy temple, and I will confesse to thy name.

LET

Let vs pray.

O God , who by thy vnspeakable prouidence vouchsafest to send the holy Angels &c.

AT THIRD.

℣.God hath giuen his Angels charge ouer thee &c. *as before.*

℣. O God, incline to my ayde;

℞. O Lord, make haste to helpe me.

℣. Glory be to the Father &c. Alleluia.

THE HYMNE.

O Yee watchfull Guardians still
  attend

And euer from all harme your charge
  defend;

Keepe both our soules and bodies
  from annoy

Who your so firme protection do
  enioy.

Antiph. O holy Angels our &c.

℣. In the sight of the Angels &c.

Let vs pray.

O God, who by thy vnſpeakable prouidence vouchſafeſt to ſend the holy Angels &c. *as before.*

AT SIXTH.

℣. God hath giuen his Angels charge &c.

℣. O God, incline &c. ℟. O Lord, make &c.

℣. Glory be to the Father &c. Alleluia.

The Hymne.

O Chriſt, in whome Angels their glory finde
Gouernour and Creatour of man-
　　kinde;
This fauourable grace to vs extend,
That we may to th'eternall heauen
　　aſcend.
　　Antiph. O holy Angels our &c.
℣. In the ſight &c. ℟. I wil adore at &c.

Let vs pray.

O God, who by thy vnspeakable prouidence vouchsafest to send the holy &c.

AT NINTH.

℣. God hath giuen his Angels charge &c.

℣. O God, incline &c. ℞. O Lord, &c.

℣. Glory be to the Father &c. Alleluia.

THE HYMNE.

S End downe from heauen the Angel
Of peace, the great saint Michel;
That coming often at our n eede
All things may prosp'rously succeede
Antiph. O holy Angels our Guardians &c.
℣. In the sight &c. ℞. I will adore &c. *Let vs pray.*
O God, who by thy vnspeakable prouidence &c.

AT EVENSONG.

℣. God hath giuen his Angels charge &c.

℣. O God, incline &c. ℟. O Lord, make &c.

℣. Glory be to the Father &c. Alleluia.

THE HYMNE.

L Et Gabriel the Angel strong
Defend & saue vs from all wrōg
And visiting vs frequently
Defend vs from our ennemie.

Antiph. O holy Angels our guardians &c.

℣. In sight of the Angels &c. ℟. I will &c.

Let vs pray.

O GOD who by thy vnspeakable prouidence &c.

AT COMPLINE.

℣. God hath giuen his Angels charge &c.

℣.

The verse.

COnuert vs , o Lord our Sauiour;

℟. And auert thy anger from vs.

℣. O God, incline. ℟. O Lord, make
&c.

℣. Glory be to the Father &c. Alleluia.

THE HYMNE.

COme also Raphael the diuine
Angel of God, the medicine,

By whome our soules, which are infected

May healed be, our deedes directed.

Antiph. O holy Angels our &c.

℣. In the sight &c. ℟. I will adore
&c.

Let vs pray.

O GOD, who, by thy vnspeakable prouidence , &c.

THE COMMENDATION.

THese Houres, ô Angel-Guardiã,
for thy sake

I haue rehears'd, them with fauour
take;

Protect me in the dangerous agony

Of death, and bring me to felicity.

C 5

O Angel of God
My keeper who art,
Committed to thee
By the diuine part
Defend me this day
Enlighten my hart, Amen.

THE IIII. HOVRE.

LEARNE TO DIE.

The vaine & fruitlesse wishes of the dāned, may teach it thee.

Remember that man is but like a bubble; and ponder seriously, what the damned would giue for one little houre of our time, and thou art so prodigall in spending slouthfully so manie. Liue still mindefull of death. Time flieth; and nothing swifter then yeares. The law of death is rigorous and ineuitable: we must all die. As soone

as we are borne, we become fub-
iect to this tribute : that we muft die.
Death will difcouer what we haue
profited in our life; therefore,whilft
thou maift, endeauour to profite
and to do good workes; there is one,
whoe will rewarde thy labours.
Thou maift be fure God doth perpetually and attentiuely beholde thy
workes;& as he knowes the number
of thy haires,fo will he keepe reckoning of thy thoughts, either that he
may rewarde them or punish thé, &
that eternally. Beare death in minde.

LEARNE TO LIVE.

The law of fidelity towards
God may teach it thee.

BY how much more thou oughteft to diffide in thyfelf, fo much
the more oughteft thou to confide in
God, in whome in all things, and
alwaies all truft is to be repofed.They
who truft in our Lord, fhall be like

mount

mount Sion neuer moued. Confide in God, and that with as free and generous affection as thou canst. Why dost thou feare? God will prouide. Our Lord doth gouerne thee, and nothing shall be wanting. Why art thou troubled, though thy enemy should draw thy limbes asunder, yet God numbreth the haires of thy head. Feare not therefore the losse of thy limbes, when thou art assured of the number of thy haires. S. Augustin sayth; Giue credit to me in this, that the life of good men is so throughout all affaires and moments of time ruled and ordered by God, that all things will redound to their good. He sailes securely, who casts his ancker vpon God's prouidence; and trusts to him in all things.

Genes. 22.

Serm. 4. de festiu. Mart.

LEARNE TO PRAY.

The Letanies of the Angels may teach it thee.

L Ord haue mercy vpon vs.
Chrift haue mercy vpon vs.
Lord haue mercy vpon vs.
Chrift heare vs.
Chrift gratioufly heare vs.
O God the Father of heauen ; haue mercy vpon vs.
O God the fonne Redeemer of the world; haue mercy vpon vs.
O God the Holy Ghoft, haue mercie vpon vs.
Holy Mary Queene of Angels ; Pray for vs.
Holy S. Michell , who ftill defendft the people of God; Pray for vs.
Holy Michell, who didft thruft Lucifer downe from heauen, with all his rebellious cōpanie; Pray for vs.
Holy Michell , who didft throw headlong into hell the accufer of

our

our bretheren; Pray for vs.

Holie Gabriel ,.who didſt lay open the viſion to Daniel; Pray for vs.

Holie Gabriel, who didſt foretell the birth and miniſterie of S. Iohn; Pray for vs.

Holie Gabriel, who wert the meſſenger to announce the Incarnation of the Diuine Word; Pray for vs.

Holie Raphael, who didſt leade Tobias ſafely to and fro ; Pray for vs.

Holie Raphael, who didſt diſpoſſeſſe Sara; Pray for vs.

Holie Raphael , who didſt reſtore ſight to Tobias; Pray for vs.

Holie Seraphins.	Pray for vs.
Holie Cherubins.	Pray for vs.
Holie Thrones.	Pray for vs.
Holie Dominations.	Pray for vs.
Holie Vertues.	Pray for vs.
Holie Powers.	Pray for vs.
Holie Principalities.	Pray for vs.
Holie Archangels.	Pray for vs.
Holie Angels.	Pray for vs.

You that ſitt vpon the high and eleuated Throne of God; Pray for vs.

Yee that ſing continually to God:

Holie,

Holie, Holie, Holie, Pray for vs.

Yee that diſſipate darkeneſſe, and illuminate our mindes; Pray for vs.

Yee that denounce diuine things to
men; Pray for vs.

Yee that haue receaued the cuſtodie
of mankinde frō God; Pray for vs.

Yee who euer beholde the face of our
Father in heauen; Pray for vs.

Yee that reioice at the repentance of
a ſinner; Pray for vs.

Yee that brought forth Lot from the
middle of ſinners; Pray for vs.

Yee that aſcended and deſcended by
the ladder of Iacob; Pray for vs.

Yee that did deliuer the law to Moiſes
on mount Sina; Pray for vs.

Yee that did denounce ioy to mankinde at the birth of Chriſt; Pray.

Yee who ſerued Chriſt in the deſert;
Pray for vs.

Yee who carried Lazarus into Abraham's boſome; Pray for vs.

Yee who ſate in white at the ſepul-
cher of Chriſt; Pray for vs.

Yee who after the Aſcēſion of Chriſt
appeared to his Diſciples; Pray for.

Yee

Yee who ſhall go before Chriſt with the ſigne of the Croſſe, when he comes to his iudgement ſeate; Pray for vs.

Yee who ſhall gather togeather the Elect from the midſt of the wicked; Pray for vs.

Yee who ſhall ſeparate the euil men from the midſt of the iuſt; Pray for vs.

Yee who carrie vp the praiers of ſuppliants to God; Pray for vs.

Yee who aſſiſt the dying; Pray for vs.

Yee, who leade to heauen the ſoules of iuſt men purged from all ſpott of ſinne; Pray for vs.

Yee who do miraculous and prodigious things through the power of God; Pray for vs.

Yee who are ſent to ſerue thoſe, who are to receaue the inheritance of their ſaluation; Pray for vs.

Yee who are appointed ouer kingdomes and prouinces; Pray for vs.

Yee who often diſſipate whole armies of ennemies; Pray for vs.

Yee who often deliuer, the ſeruants

of God, from prison & other dangers of life; Pray for vs.

Yee who often haue bene comforters to Martyrs in their torments; Pray for vs.

Yee who are wont with a peculiar care to cherish the Prelats of the Church, and those Princes, which are cherishers of it; Pray for vs.

O all yee holie Orders of blessed Saints; Pray for vs.

From all dangers through thy holie Angels; Deliuer vs ô Lord.

From all heresie and schifme; Deliuer vs ô Lord.

From plague, famine, and warre; Deliuer vs ô Lord.

From suddain and vnprouided death; Deliuer vs ô Lord.

From eternall death ; Deliuer vs ô Lord.

We sinners; Beseech thee to heare vs.

For thy holie Angels sake ; we beseech thee to heare vs.

That thou spare vs ; we beseech thee to heare vs.

That thou pardon vs ; we beseech

thee to heare vs.

That thou vouchſafe to gouerne and
preſerue thy holie Church: we beſeech thee to heare vs.

That thou vouchſafe to preſerue our
Apoſtolike Prelat and all Eccle-
ſiaſticall Orders in holie Religion: we beſeech the &c.

That thou grant peace and vnitie to
the Emperour and all Chriſtian
Princes: we beſeech the &c.

That thou vouchſafe to giue and preſerue the fruits of the earth : we
beſeech the &c.

That thou vouchſafe to giue eternall
reſt to all faithfull departed : we
beſeech thee to heare vs.

Lamb of God, that takeſt away the
ſinnes of the world: Spare vs ô Lord.

Lamb of God, who takeſt away the
ſinnes of the world : Heare vs ô
Lord.

Lamb of God, that takeſt away the
ſinnes of the world: Haue mercie
vpon vs.

O Chriſt, heare vs.

O Chriſt gratiouſly heare vs.

Lord.

Lord haue mercie vpon vs.
Chrift haue mercie vpon vs.
Lord haue mercie vpon vs.
Our Father &c.

A Pſalme compoſed of diuers Pſalmes.

PRaiſe yee our Lord all yee in heauen, praiſe him in the higheſt.

Praiſe him all yee his Angels, and all his vertues.

Praiſe yee our Lord all yee his Angels powerfull in vertues.

Executours of his word, and diligent obſeruers of his commaund's.

Bleſſe yee our Lord, all yee his vertues, and yee his miniſters., which performe his diuine will and pleaſure.

My ſoule, bleſſe our Lord, and forgett not his benefits, who redeemes thy life from vtter ruine, & crownes thee in his mercy and compaſſions.

Becauſe he hath giuen his Angels charge ouer thee, that they keepe thee in all thy waies.

They

They will carrie thee in their armes, leaſt thou trippe with thy foote
againſt a ſtone.

Thou ſhalt walke vpon the ſerpēt
and baſiliske, and thou ſhalt treade
downe the lyon and the dragon.

The Angel of our Lord will come
amongſt thoſe that feare him , and
will preſerue them from all danger.

Glorie be to the Father &c.

℣. In the ſight of the Angels I will
    ſing to thee, O my God.

℞. I will adore at thy holie temple,
    and I will confeſſe to thy holie
    name.

℣. Lord, heare my prayer.

℞. And let my cry come vnto thee.

Let vs pray.

OMnipotent and mercyfull God,
who haſt vouchſafed to ſtrengthen vs with Angelicall cuſtody,
grant, we beſeech thee, that being ſe-
cured by ſo great a protection , we
may be freed from euil thoughts in
our mindes, and from all aduerſities
of body ; through our Lord Ieſus
Chriſt thy ſonne, who liueth and rai-

gneth God in vnitie with the Holie-
Ghoſt, world without, ende, Amen.

THE V. HOVRE.

LEARNE TO DIE.

Death's continuall praying
ⱱpon mankinde, may
teach it thee.

Emember that man is
Vanitie; and that thou
art not only to die,
but doſt daily & hou-
rely die. The begin-
ning of this life is alſo
the beginning of death. The firſt
houre, which giueth life, doth both
maime and waſt it. Death ſhares with
thee in this verie day, in which thou
liueſt. Whatſoeuer thou doſt, regarde
thy ende. Short are the daies of man;

and

and God numbres his houres. The
bounders of his life are appointed,
which he fhall not ouerpaffe, alas he
cannot! And not only can he not
ouerpaffe them, but euen knowes
not, how neere they are to him. Wilt
thou be freed from fuddain death?
thinke then continually vpon death.
That is euer to be learned, which
cannot be tried, whether we know
it or not. Meditate vpon death : for
no man doth vnprouidedly die, who
thinkes ftill he is to die. Thinke then
on death.

Iob.c.
14.

LEARNE TO LIVE.

The law of Iuftice may teach it thee.

IT is the office of vertue to hate In-
iuftice, and all the companions thereof: fuch as are treacherous deceipts
and iniuries. Receaue them rather,
then inferre them. It is not the law
of the world, but Chrift's law, that

to him , who fnatches away thy
cloak , thou fhouldft alfo adde therevnto thy coate to relieue him. And
what doth it auaile thee to haue monie in thy purfe, and a fting in thy cō-
fcience. Loffe is ftill to be preferred
before an vnlawfull gaine. *What will* Mat.c.
it auaile a man, though he gaine the whole 8.
world , and loofe his foule? But in thefe
times , fuch is the practife of life and
manners, as that the name of Iuftice
is religioufly obferued; but Iuftice it
felf is vrefted to euery man's fenfe
and profitt. Many defire to be efteemed iuft ; but few ftriue to be fo. It is
a great parte of Iuftice , that thou do
not thyfelfe , what in others thou ef-
teemeft vitious. Learne Iuftice , you
mortall men , and contemne not the
Deitie.

LEARNE TO PRAY.

Thefe prayers may teach it thee.

O GOD who difpofeft the mini-
ftery both of men and Angels in

wonderfull order, grant propitiously, that our life may be guarded on earth by them, who faithfully serue and attend on thee in heauen.

O most louing God, whose immense goodnesse and wisedome doth wonderfully appeare in all thy holie Angels; I humbly beseech thee, that by their Angelicall suffrages for me, thou wilt gratiously receiue all my workes, and grant that they may redound to my saluation ; through Christ our Lord.

O eternall God, I humbly beseech thy goodnesse, that through the prayers & merits of all thy Angels & Archangels, what is wanting of my loue to thee, may be recompensed by their most ardent loue towards thee; through the same our Lord Iesus Christ thy sonne, who liueth and raigneth with thee and the Holie Ghost world without ende. Amen.

THE VI. HOVRE.

LEARNE TO DIE.

The daily burials of many, may teach it thee.

REmember that man is but durt; and how manie there be, who, I will not say this day, but euen this houre are to be called frō this life before the Tribunal seate of the highest Iudge; and how many of them are damned; And thus not only often, but continually thinke of thy mortality. Nothing can equally auaile thee towards the gaining of Temperance in all things, as the frequent reflecting vpon the breuity and vncertaintie of this life : *Reioyce not at the death of thy enemy, knowing that we are all to die.* Attende therefore to thyself. Whosoeuer hath a begin-

Eccl. c. 8.

ning, may alfo feare his ende. *We shall
all paſſe that way.* Some shall leade,
but euerie one of vs shall follow, according to the order, wherein death
shall call. Looke to thyself; for to die
daily, is the gaining of life. Remember therefore to die.

LEARNE TO LIVE.

*The law of Mercy may teach
it thee.*

Mat.9 TRuth it felf faith ; *I deſire mercy,
and not ſacrifice.* It is fitt to helpe
the needy, and not the rich. He ſpil-
les, who poures into a veſſell already
full. And that is rather preſerued,
which is putt into empty veſſels. The
meales afforded to the hungry redound more to thy praiſe, then plen-
tiefull banketts made to gluttons.
Moſt wonderfull it is, that in the full
aſſembly of thoſe, who shall riſe from
death at the day of Iudgement in
ſight of all the Angels, Chriſt will

not

not fay, that Abel was the firft Martyr; that Abraham excelled in obedience; that Noë preferued the world; that Moifes gaue the law, or that Peter, firft afcended the Croffe of Iefus; all thefe things, I fay, the chief Iudge will paffe ouer in filence, and only proclaime, who it is, that hath fed the hungry, clothed the naked, and lodged pilgrims. Obferue, that whatfoeuer is giuen to the poore, is but lent; for whatfoeuer is fo beftowed, will be returned with moft rich and abundant rewarde. The gainefulleft trade and moft knowen to the keepers of heauen-gates, is almes-deedes; but of all almes the moft precious and chiefeft is, TO LOVE OVR ENEMIES.

LEAR-

LEARNE TO PRAY.

Prayers in commemoration of
S. Michell the Archangel
may teach it thee.

1. O Lord , we befeech thee , that
the glorious interceſſion of S.
Michell thy Archangel may euer and
euerie where protect vs, and bring vs
to life euerlaſting: through Chriſt our
Lord, Amen.

O moſt glorious Prince, O Michell
the Archangel , be mindefull of vs,
and intercede for vs to the ſonne of
God, here and euerie where, for euer.

Reioycing through the commemoration of bleſſed S. Michell thy
Archangel, we humbly befeech thee,
O Lord, that what we cannot obtaine through our owne deſerts, may be
ſupplyed by his interceſſion; through
Chriſt our Lord.

THE

THE VII. HOVRE.

LEARNE TO DIE.

*The irrecouerable loſſe of time
may teach it thee.*

Emember that man is
but like a ſparke; and
that not only thy
words, but thy time
doth flie away, and is
neuer to be recalled more then a houſe conſumed with fire. The loſſe will
fall vpon thee; and no pretious ſtones
can be compared to the price of thy
loſt time. All gemmes and pearles are
to be valued but as ſtraw in compariſon of the worth of time. Neither is
there anie more hurtfull theft, then
to ſteale time from ones ſelf, either
by doing euil, or doing nothing. There be waies to recouer all things but

D 3   only

only time. It would be thought a
great loſſe , to looſe a thouſand
pounds, and a greater to looſe ones
good name; but no loſſe like that of
time. For the more it is waſted in vaine, the more frightfully will death
approch to vs; whereof thou muſt be
continually mindefull.

LEARNE TO LIVE.

The law of mildeneſſe may teach it thee.

Ecl 3. O Sonne performe thy workes with
mildeneſſe , and thou shalt be beloued
aboue the glorie of men. Whatſoeuer
thou ſaiſt or doſt, aboue all things let
thy words and countenance be good.
Bleſſed be the meeke. The heauenlie
cittie Ieruſalem is not a ſpoile for
warriers, but a hopefull inheritance
of the meeke. They are meeke , who
giue way, and reſiſt not an euill and
wicked turne, but requite euil with
good. There be ſome, who are milde;

but

but it is fo long as all things proceede according to their owne wills.
Stirre vp afhes, and prefently you
perceaue the fire, that is to fay, an offered iniurie doth inftantly reueale
what otherwife lies hidden in a
man's hart. It is a great propertie of a
good courage, to know, how to be
appeafed, and that one be not ignorant, how to fubdue his owne paf-
fions; and how with a milde and
cheerfull countenance to difgeft iniuries and offences done to him. A
truly milde man is tractable like
wax, meeke like any doue, foft and
fupple like oyle.

LEARNE TO PRAY.

*Prayers to thy Angel-guardiã,
to the Mother of Chriſt, and
to Chriſt himſelf, may
teach it thee.*

1. *TO THY ANGEL-GVARDIAN.*

ALL haile, O holie Angel of God,
O noble Prince , my faithfull
kceper, to whome the Diuine, goodneſſe hath deliuered me to be preſerued , after God; how much do I owe
thee for thy charitie , with which ſo
many yeares and by ſeuerall meanes,
thou haſt faithfully and clemently
aſſiſted me, and doſt daily procure the
health both of my bodie and ſoule ? I
commende myſelf to thee this day,
that thou being my captain, I may be
preſerued vnhurt by the malignant
enemie , and that I may perſeuer in
the grace of God, firme and conſtant

to my laſt gaſpe, and may praiſe with thee in heauen Chriſt our Lord for all eternity.

2. To the Bleſſed Virgin Marie. Twelue Salutations likened to ſo manie ſtarres.

ALl haile, honour of the world and euerlaſting lamp.

All haile, eye of the world, gate of heauen, and glorie of Seraphins.

All haile, moſt pure mother, whome wicked thought neuer durſt inuade.

All haile, great and portending miracle of the world.

All haile, moſt adorned pallace of the higheſt King, magazine of life, and field full of all odoriferous fragrancie of the Holie-Ghoſt.

All haile, O hidden treaſure of grace; who didſt alone beare the, Word, which beareth all things.

D 5

All haile, O admirable veſſell of election; all haile, O mother of the Sonne, daughter of the Father, and ſpouſe of the Holie-ghoſt.

All haile, cleare cloude; haile O pillar of fire, which ſheweſt the way to the people of God through the deſert of this world.

All haile, moſt pure fleece, wett with the dew of heauen, by whome and in whome the Paſtour became a Lamb.

All haile, O ſcepter of learning, temple of deuotion, the moſt ſumptuous treaſurie of all guifts.

All haile, O Paradice of new Adam; all haile, O golden Vrne, which containes the heauēlie Manna.

All haile, light of the faithfull, container of the infinite, the altar of chaſt ſoules; all haile eternall and ineffable ioy.

The names of the Fathers, from whome we haue receaued these starre-like salutations.

CYrillus *Alexandrinus*, *Epiphanius*, *Elias Cretensis*, *Fulgentius*, *Gregorius Nicomediensis*, *Gregorius Neocesariensis*, *Hildefonsus Toletanus*, *Origenes*, *Proclus*, *Sophronius*, *Theodoretus*, *Methodius Olympius*.

To these *as it were* 12. *Apostles, S. Bernard (as was S. Paul) deserues to be added. S. Bernard could not containe himself, but thus cries out to the* MOTHER OF OVR LORD *from the verie bottome of his hart.*

All haile, O Queene Virgin ; All haile, O Ocean most full of pearles and precious stones.

Neither was this sufficient, but i *uising the whole world to the verie*

ration of this Mother of God, he sayth
thus: *Let vs honour Marie from our whole
harts ; becaufe fuch is his will, who would
haue vs to receaue all by Marie.*

3. To Chrift.

O Good IESVS : I ferue thee too
imperfitly , I praife and loue thee
too coldely. Alas, how farre am I'frō
the true denying of myfelf, from true
humilitie, patience, and charitie. I befeech thee to fupply for what is wanting in me, and to offer thy diuine
hart to thy Father for me. O Lord
IESVS Chrift, let me loue thee only
for thyfelf, and let me loue nothing
but in thee. O Lord IESVS Chrift,
encreafe my labour and paine , fo
thou encreafe alfo my loue; O Lord
IESVS Chrift, grant to me, that I
may be only delighted in thy moft
holie will and pleafure, and that aboue all things I may reft therein.

ᙦᙦᙦᙦᙦᙦᙦᙦᙦᙦᙦ:ᙦᙦ:ᙦᙦ

THE VIII. HOVRE.

LEARNE TO DIE.

The feare of the Iudgement,
which hangs ouer thy head,
may teach it thee.

Emember that man is duſt ; and
aske thy conſcience , if God
ſhould call thee at this inſtant before
his Iudgement ſeate, whether it were
readie to giue vp an accompt : Say
not : *to morrow* ; for God hath promiſed mercy to thy amendment :
but hath not promiſed *to morrow* to
thy delay. Alas, alas, how miſerable
are we all ! what a thinge of nothing
is whole man ! what a play and
May-game is any thing which is ſaid
to be in this world ! Go to therefore,
and bid farewell to humane things,

and

and prepare thyself to giue vp thy laſt
accompt. Thou art called to the tri-
bunall-ſeate of God; no delay will
ſerue, no euaſions, no puttings off;
thou muſt gett thee hence. Leaue
thy tergiuerſations; thou muſt giue
accompt. Excuſe not thyſelf; for as
thou haſt done, ſo ſhalt thou be iudged. Remember to die.

LEARNE TO LIVE.

*The law of Truth may teach
it thee.*

Eccl.
37.
Pſal.
30.

Let truth go before all thy workes.
For God requires tryth. Let not
thy tongue know, how to ſweare or
lye. Endeauour ſo to tell truth, as if
thou didſt thinke, whatſoeuer thou
ſayſt, thou wert readie to ſweare it. It
is not the part of a ſincere and honeſt
man, to haue one thing hidden in
his breaſt, and another readie at his
tongues ende. Truth, as it is euerie
where the mother of ſanctitie, ſo

is it

is it euerie where to be beloued;
and no two things are so consonant,
and of so neere an affinitie, as *Ver-*
tue and Truth. Truth is oftentimes
oppressed, but neuer so ouerwhelmed, but that at length it is discoue-
red. It is often wrestled withall, but
neuer ouercome. A louer of vertue
needes feare no reprehender; for he,
who reprehends, is either an ennemie, or a friend; yf an ennemie insult,
he is to be borne with; if a friend erre, he is to be tought; or if he can
teach, he is to be harkened to. To
counterfit, polish, faine, smooth, or
paint truth, is to destroy it. To lye, *Sap.c.*
is to kill ones soule; *for the mouth, that* ᵗ·
lieth, killes the soule.

LEARNE TO PRAY.

A prayer containing acts of Di-
uine loue, may teach it thee.

13. A C T S   O F L O V E
T O W A R D S G O D.

O My moſt Louing God ; I
am brought to thee as to
the chiefeſt good, by my hart's
intire affection. 2. I reioice in
thy immenſe goodneſſe, 3. and
am highly glad , that all the
Angels and Saints of heauen
praiſe thee. 4. O my Creatour,
how much do I deſire , that all
men may acknowledge thee,
honour thee, and ſerue thee
alone. 5. O how much doth it
repent me , of all my ſinnes ; 6.
and therefore I reſolue moſt
firmely hence forwards to ob-

ſerue

ierue thy law in all things. 7. I
will seeke all my comfort in
thy holy will. 8. I will be a-
gainst euerie thing, that may
displease thee. 9. O my God, I
consecrate to thee all things,
that are mine. 10. I will gladly
suffer all aduersities for thee.
11. I will euer be most content
with that, which thou permit-
test or disposest. 12. O goodnesse, encreasse in me thy loue.
13. O charitie; I will liue to
loue thee.

An explication of the former praier.

Since all the praise of vertue consists in action, these by Diuines, for
the most parte are assigned for the
acts of loue tending to God.
1. To desire with an earnest affection, to see and enioy God as *the*

Chiefest

Chiefest Good.

2. To dedicate to God all his goods and graces ; and that for no other ende, but becaufe they are his ; as is, wifedome, goodneffe, power, and the like.

3. To reioice hartily, that God is ferued by his Angels, his Saints, and by all good creatures.

4. To defire only, that all good things may be employed to God's diuine honour and glorie.

5. To grieue in ones minde, for all iniuries committed by himfelf and others againft God.

6. Serioufly to refolue to obferue exactly all God's lawes.

7. To propound to himfelf, God's onlie will in all things , to be followed by him.

8. To refift all things, which one knowes would difpleafe God.

9. To offer all things, that are his, with a free fubmiffion to God.

10. To meete all aduerfities with a readie and cheerefull minde, which are to be fuffered for God's fake.

11. To acknowledge and extoll euerie where the prouidence of God.

12. To confeſſe that he is but litle
anſwerable to the fauours receaued
of Almightie God and to procure en-
creaſe of loue towards him.

13. Continually to implore and beg
a happy perſeuerance in the loue of
God.

*Touching theſe acts of diuine loue,
two things are chiefly to be
noted.*

1. The deadlie wounds of a man's
ſoule , which nothing cures but
loue or *ſorrow* , for to vſe the tearmes of Deuines, there are two onlie
acts , which can recouer the loſt
grace of God ; the act of Charitie,
and the act of Penance ; the one
whereof includes the other. The
Publican chiefly by griefe , and S.
Mari. Magdalen by loue , wiped
away all peſtiferous ordure from
their ſoules and cleanſed them;
Manie ſinnes are remitted her, becauſe

she

Mc. 7. *she loued much.*

2. The chief act of diuine loue, is, seriously and from ones hart to desire to obey all Gods precepts. *He, who hath my commandments & keepeth them, is he, who loueth me. This is charity and loue to God, that we keepe his commandements.* Euerie man is bound to this act of diuine loue, through a three-fold danger. First, when one is grie-uously sett vpon by the diuel, or is inuited to vice by other allurements; as for example: when one sees gold lie without a keeper, his ennemie within his power, or when he sees an offered occasion of satisfying his lust; and then the diuel doth with a great force suggest thus; wilt thou ouerslip so faire an occasion? behol-de, here is gold, beholde here is a fitt time to reuenge thyself; beholde, de-lights are prepared for thee; if thou be not a very coward, enioy the o-portunitie, while thou maist, and vse it. Here it is altogeather necessary, that a man, who abhorres mortall sinne, should thus witnesse his loue

Ioh. c. *14.*

Ioh. c. *5.*

to God:

to God : O my Lord and God ; thy
law and thy honour are dearer to me,
then anie profitt, then anie filthie or
forbiden pleasure, yea then the whole world. Now vnlesse he, who is in
this ieopardie, shall behaue himself
thus, he looseth God, parteth from
his grace, and cannot hope for heauen. Therefore he must then loue
God, or he will be ouercome by the
diuell. Yf one should aske a man giuen to theft, or to corporall pleasurs: Sir, loue you God ? he will affirme, he doth. But know you the
Ten Commandements ? he will say:
I know them. Do you remēber also
the sixth ? he will answear : he doth.
Whether do not you perceaue all lust
to be forbidden by it ? he will say, he
doth; for he cānot denie. And what?
dare you notwithstanding so wan-
tonly and so often sinne expressely
againſt this commandment ? thy
womẽn therefore, thy stolen loues,
and tny pleasures are farr more deare
to thee, then God's law, or then God's
honour. There resteth not therefore

one sparke of diuine loue in thee, while thou perseuerest in these courses, and impure loues. *For this is the loue of God,that wee keepe his commandments.* Why is it, saith S. Augustin, that we will say, we loue the king, when we hate his law? and most truly saith S.Gregorie:He truly loues God, who according to his commandments abbridgeth himself of his pleasurs, and flieth from vnlawfull desires. He certainly loueth not God, who contradicts him in folowing his owne appetites. Secondly, this danger doth also oblige one to the act of diuine loue, when a man prudently feareth himself, least, by reason of the place, whither he is to go,or the person, with whom he is to be conuersant, he may grieuously sinne; then certainly it is needefull,that he enflame his minde with the loue of God, and that he stregthen himself in such manner,that he may pronounce with the kinglie Psalmist: *I will search thy law, O Lord, and will keepe it in my hart.* The last perill both of bodie & soule

Psal. 18.

requires

requires the fame encreafe of the loue
of God, which I haue faid before, that
when one perceaueth the houre of
death to draw neere, he be tranfpor-
ted with loue towards his Creatour;
& that, not through feare of punifhment or hope of rewarde, but becaufe he acknowledges, that he owes
this in all refpects to the *Chiefeft Good*.
Certainly in this houre of death, this
act of loue is moft intirely to be obferued : *Thou fhalt loue the Lord thy* **Luc.**
God from thy whole hart , from thy **c. 10.**
whole foule , with all thy forces , and
with thy whole minde. Charitie neuer **1 Cor.**
faileth ; therefore let vs encreafe in chari- **11.**
tie and loue towards him in all things. **Eph 4.**

A proteftatiõ to God, to be made
at the leaft once a weeke.

O My God , if I haue faid or done
any thing through vnwarineffe
or otherwife, contrarie to thy diuine
pleafure, I do proteft before thee and

the whole court of heaué, that it hath
bene done againſt my will ; or if
with my will, O Lord, take pittie,
and recall me againe, who haue erred;
lift me vp, who am fallen; and leaſt it
ſhould happen ſo againe, moſt mercifull God, I aske thee, through thine
owne goodneſſe, that thou vouchſafe
to preuent it with thy benedictions,
and to poſſeſſe and gouerne me as
wholy thine. I ſubiect my free will
ſo to thee ; I deſire it may be compelled and ouercome, leaſt it rebell a-
gainſt thee or thy will, or leaſt it cō-
mitt the leaſt offence. I only deſire,
O my God, what thou wilt ; and I
only repugne againſt that, which
thou willeſt not, let this be my onlie
deſire, to ſeeke thy will, and to do it
in all things. Yf I aske anie thing,
O Lord, do not giue it, if it derogate
from thy honour, and repugne to thy
will. I now know, O ſoueraigne
Goodneſſe, that only hurts me, which
diſpleaſes thee. I therefore beſeech
thee, through the interceſſion of all
Saints, graunt me the hatred of my-

ſelf,

ſeif , and the loue of thee in all
things.

Aſpirations all full of loue to God.

I LOVE thee, O my God, and I
yet deſire to loue thee more ardently; my hart is altogeather lique-
fied with that flame of loue. Nothing but thou, can make me happy.
And when , O my God , and when
ſhall I haſten hence to thee?

THE IX. HOVRE.

LEARNE TO DIE.

*The infinite number of thy debts
may teach it thee.*

REMEMBER that man is but froth; and that thou art all drowned in debts. Thinke vpon all thy sinnes, & bring them into one heape ; so manie lasciuious thoughts, so manie words not only idle, but also cōtumelious, dishoneft, or of detraction ; so manie wicked deedes, which no flourish or difguife can excufe. Looke then vpon thofe heapes of thy offences, and thou wilt be forced to confeffe : I am a great debter, of manie thoufands of talēts. And alas, if death fhould deliuer me

ouer thus indebted to my aduersarie,
certaine it is, that I should neuer gett
out of prison, til I had satisfied to the
last farthing. Thinke of this matu-
rely; and be frequent in pardoning
others, but neuer thyself. They who
know that they alwaies sinne, do
likewise continually grieue. Wilt
thou not be sad? then liue well. Blessed is that man, who liues euer and
euerie where, as though he spent euerie day like the last, which will neuer
returne. Remember to die.

LEARNE TO LIVE.

*The law of Chastitie may teach
it thee.*

THE *fruits of the Spirit are* **Charitie,**
*continencie, and chastitie; for there is
nothing of what weight or moment soeuer,
worth a continent soule.* Let not anie one
boast of a chast minde, if he haue an
vnchast eie; nor glory in a chast body,

Gala:
5.
Eccl
16.

E 2   if his

if his thoughts be vncleane. Holie Iob did therefore make an agreemēt with his eies, that he might also performe it with his thoughts, saying: *I haue made a couenant with mine eies. For otherwise, saith he, what part should God aboue possesse in me?* Take the exposition from blessed S. Hierome: In whatsoeuer vertue, saith he, thou excellest, and in whatsoeuer workes thou art most eminent, if thou lacke the guirdle of Chastitie, they will all auaile thee nothing. And belieue me, O creature, if the pestilent desire of lust do burne, and thou resist it not, thou art but a lost man. Thy bodie, thy soule, thy riches, and thy good name, are all perished; bid farewell to heauen, and die. Therefore hinder it in the beginning, and strike this serpent in the head, least the taile sting and poison thee.

Iob.c. 11.

LEARNE

LEARNE TO PRAY.

S. Francis his prayer may teach it thee.

MY GOD AND MY ALL.

Radition teacheth, that S. Frācis passed ouer foure whole nights, only in thinking vpon, and often repetinge those words ; and that not only once, but manie seuerall times; *My God and my all* : with great contentment & delight of minde. I will repeate this a thousand times , and thinke vpon it as manie more ; neither cā I either say or meditate vpon a better subiect then this ; *My God and my all*. Let others seeke after other things , and desire them ; I will only seeke God, & desire God ; *O my God & my all*. I will relinquish all my right, & all other riches, honors & pleasures to others ; let me only enioy God and I haue all. I freely leaue all the

E world

world to others. I enuie not his goldē mountains, nor those that are full of precious stones. I thinke not vpō any other delights ; to me *my God is all.* There is nothing so good, nothing so faire, nothing so pleasant, but this supreme Good is still better, is fairer, & more delightfull: *My God, and my all.* How oftē do seuerall desires inflame me ; and how often do I burne with such wishes ? so that one while I am as it were snatched into the fire, another time into the water, like that lunatike yong man. But what are the goods, which I so infinitly desire? are they of this or that kinde of costlie fare ? no, my God is my foode and all this to me. Is it this or that kinde of recreations or pleasures ? no, my God is all my ioy, my pleasure, and my all. Is it this or the other dignitie ? my God is my honour, my dignitie, & my all. What is there then at length, that I can desire, which God is not to me, since he is all? he is my bankett, my delight, my treasure ; God is all and more then all. For though I might

feede

feede vpon thofe delicaties, which I
defire; though I might haue thofe delicious draughts, which I thirft after;
though I might enioy thofe pleafurs,
with the defire whereof I burne, and
thofe honours, to which I afpire;
what is it to be fed with fuch delicaties? what is it to enioy fuch pleafures?
& to obtaine fuch honours? *My God is*
my all. To enioy thee, & to be refre-
fhed by thee, is the moft perfect refec-
tion, & the enioying of all good. *My*
God & my all. But fay that labour pref-
fe, grief afflict, cares diftract, men trouble and vexe; nothing of all this not-
withftanding is to be feared, or to be
thought euill; yea though they affalt
one all at once, if God enrich vs with
that chiefe good : *My God and my all.*
O mercyfull God; o Goodneffe itfelf;
to me thou art in labour reft, in paine
pleafure, in cares tranquillitie; thou
art a bullwarke moft fecure againft
anie inuafion, thou art a refuge from
all euill; Thou art A L L whatfoeuer
I can thinke vpon; therefore when-
foeuer hereafter I defire any thing, or

E 4   what-

whatsoeuer I desire, thou shalt be that
to me : *My God and my all.* Leaue, ô
man, the following of impure riuers,
since thou hast so cleare a fountaine,
as is the most iust God; and therefore
wantest nothing of whatsoeuer thou
canst desire to haue.

*Certaine short choice prayers to
Christ our Lord.*

I.

GRANT me, I beseech thee, O
Lord, that I may alwaies obey
thee readily , and serue thy Maiesty
with a sincere hart.

2.

O Omnipotent and eternall God;
grant that I may auoide all Dia-
bolicall infection; and compell me,
though rebellious, to be pliāt to thee.

3.

I BESEECH thee, o Lord , that thy
grace may alwaies both preuent &
follow me, and may make me continually attent to all good workes, O
sweet Iesus; who liuest world without ende ; Amen.

An

An vniting of the will of man in suffering adversities, sicknesse, and death, with the will of God, which inflicts them.

O My God and my loue ; farre be it from me to be vnwilling to accept what thou desirest, or to desire what thou wilest not ; thy will is my will : yea now it is no more mine, because it began to be thine. And thine is to be followed by me, because it began to be mine. I am obliged to desire the same, which thou desirest ; and really, O Lord, so I do. Wilt thou that I be sick ? I vndergoe it willingly. Wilt thou that I be impouerished ? that I pine away? that I be afflicted with griefes? destitute of côforts? agitated by aduersities? yea and that I die ? To all these I also submitt. Wilt thou that I haue parte in heauē? I desire it. Wilt thou that I be côdemned to hell ? alas, sweet Iesus, my walke went that way, and I was euen sorie, that thy goodnesse would not suffer

me to follow my owne pleasures,
which were to leade me to it; thy will
was opposite to mine, and thou didst
grieue, that I would not then striue
to shunne it; and if it were possible,
as it is not, that I might choose, either
that I should be saued, or damned, to
the ende that thy most holie will
should continue firme & established.
I proclame, it were better, that I were
damned, and so that be done, which
thou, O God, shalt desire. But, O eternall Goodnesse, I know, that thou
wouldst not my death, who wert therefore willing to subiect thy sonne to
death, because thou desirest not mine.
Beholde the wounds, beholde the
bloud, which hath bene sacrificed for
me; thou wouldst not pardō thy sonne, that so thou mightst spare thy seruant, whome thou cãst therefore pardon, & wilt take pittie vpon him. O
immense & dreadfull Maiestie, haue
mercie vpon me. Pardon me; I haue
sinned, and cannot denie it; but thou
art able to forgiue whatsoeuer I haue
cōmitted. I am thy worke, who desire

to see

to fee and praife thee, my Creatour, in all eternitie. It is certainly in thy power to deftroy me, as it is in the potter's power to breake an earthen veffel, which vnder his hands proues moft vntoward and vnpliable; and long fince I haue deferued it; yea euen to be caft into the flames of hell; but fince thy goodneffe is greater then my malice can be, pardon me, o Lord, pardon me; & let me liue ftill, louing thee, who am fhortly to die, & let my laft breath ferue me to cry thus out: *O Lord, haue mercie vpon me.*

Annotations touching the conformitie of humane will, to the will of God.

I.

THroughout the whole fcripture nothing is found more commendable, then the vnitie of man's will with the diuine will. Chrift, as he knew beft of all men, how to pray, prayed thus: *Father, not my will, but thine be done.* Neither did he teach vs to pray

otherwife,

otherwife , then *Thy will be done in earth , as it is in heauen.* A thoufand other places of holie fcripture teftifie the fame. 2.

To attend to the will of God in all things, is an epitome & fumme of an excellent and moft peaceable life.

3.

Whofoeuer fquareth all things according to the only will of God, liues as it were, aboue the cloudes fecure and free from all the rage of tēpefts; the greateft teftimonie of friendship is *willingneffe*; & *to will* the fame in all things with God , makes God our friend. 4.

Whatfoeuer things are done in this world, are either euil & finnes againft God, or not euil, becaufe they are not finnes. In the former, God's permiffion appeares admirable , and in the later, his diuine ordering of them.

5.

Epictetus doth therefore wifely warne vs faying : Require not that things be done as thou wilt ; but if thou be wife, wifh they may be done

Ench. c.13.

as

as they are done; for so all things shall happen succesfully to thee. But Tho. à Kempis saith it more wisely : A spirituall man doth quickly recollect & accommodate himself, according as things happen. And most wisely Salomon : It will not moue, (saith he) nor make a iust man sad, whatsoeuer happens to him. For why should he be sad, who acknowledgeth in all things God's high prouidéce, & most holy will?

Lib. 2 c. 1.

Prou. c. 12.

6.

In all fortunes, prosperous or crosse, in all tribulations or temptations, in whatsoeuer stormes, it is excellent and most safe, to propound to ones self the onlie will of God to be followed; and to reduce all things, which are either to be done or suffered, to the onlie will of Almightie God. Whosoeuer is arriued to this perfection, will walke securely.

7.

Ludouicus Blosius witnesseth, that no exercise is more vsefull either in sicknesse or death, then intirely,

rely to submitt ones self to God's diuine will, and to embrace with the armes of *Humilitie* and *Charitie*, the immense goodnesse & mercie of God.

∽∽∽∽∽∽∽∽∽∽:∽∽:∽∽

THE X. HOVRE.

LEARNE TO DIE.

The vsuall Psalme of the dead, may teach it thee.

REMEMBER that man is but as aire; & what all those, who now are dead, cry out to thee, namely, that YESTERDAY WAS MY IVDGEMENT PAST VPON ME, AND TO DAY WILL THINE PASSE VPON THEE. *Be mindefull of my iudgemēt, for such shall also be thine.* This is the common psalme of the dead, which inuites vs all to the graue. We are all to come thither; not at once, but successiuely & shortly one af-

ter

Eccl. 38.

ter another. The vniuerſall law is to
be borne, to grow towards our ende
and to die. *We all die, and are as it were*
waters ſliding on the earth, neuer to retur-
ne. Therefore that, which of neceſſity
is to be once done, is often to be
thought vpon, ſo that thou muſt make vp thy pack. For death is at hand,
who will ſhew thee the way. It is a
iourney, which cannot be preuented
either by entreaties, or by any price or
art. Thou muſt go, and paſſe from this
world into another. Yf thou feareſt
eternall death, ſee that thy vices dye
before thee. Remember to dye.

Reg. 2.
c. 14.

LEARNE TO LIVE.

The law of Humilitie may
teach it thee.

HVmilitie preceedes glorie. Whoſoeuer would heape vertues togeather without humilitie, throwes duſt
againſt the winde. A truly modeſt
and humble man deſires not to ſeeme
ſo, but to be ſo really. Whenſoeuer he

Prou.
15.

is afflicted and defpifed, he fays to himfelf: THOV ART WORTHIE OF ALL THIS. He, who tends to great things otherwife then by humilitie, defires rather to fall, then to rife. He euen defires to perifh, who runnes headlong vpon pride and a vaine oftentation of himfelf. *By how much thou art greater, humble thyfelf fo much the more in all things.* And indeede, why doft thou loue fpecta-tours vpon earth, fince thy theater is prouided in heauen? why doft thou gape after a fruitleffe praife, fince eternall glorie is promifed thee? And not withftanding all this, many follow the fhadow of humilitie, but few humilitie it felf. An infatigable patience and a generous contempt of ones felf, fhewes a true humble man. And of this thou maift be moft certain, that how much leffer thou art in thy owne eyes, fo much greater thou art before God; and fo much more eftimable to God, by how much the more vile to thyfelf.

Eccl. 3

LEARNE

LEARNE TO PRAY.

*A recommendation of the foule
into the hands of the Creatour , may teach
it thee.*

INto thy hands , O Lord , I commende
my ſpirit. O Chriſt , I now being
well and in health , recommende
myſelf to thee , that thou maiſt take
me thus offered , at the time when I
ſhall not be able to recommend myſelf , though I ſhall then be in diſtreſ-
ſe and miſerie. I feare that time, when
I ſhall be liuing and yet not ſenſible
of it. We often ſee them , who are at
the verie gate of death, to breath and
liue , and yet they know it not. O
Creatour of the world , who will receaue a ſpirit then ſtriuing for life,
trembling to departe from the frind-
lie priſon of the bodie, if thou exclude it ? O moſt patient Chriſt, remem-

ber

ber that thou thyſelf didſt complaine
in thoſe extremities and lamentable
ſtraightes, as if thou hadſt bene forſaken, & that thou didſt commend thyſelf to thy Father, cry out, and giue vp
the ghoſt. Therefore do I now cry to
thee, that thou, ô my Redeemer, maiſt
receaue my ſpirit, whenſoeuer it ſhall
departe out of the body, by what diſeaſe or accident, in what time and
place ſoeuer. Remember, ſweet IE-
SVS, that thou didſt ſpread thy armes
abroad vpon the croſſe, openedſt thy
breaſt, & didſt hang downe thy head.
Beholde my ſoule forſaken by all
creatures ſeekes refuge, and caſts itſelf into thoſe armes, and inſinuates
itſelf into that breaſt of thine. Admitt it, I beſeech thee, all wretched as
it is; and driue it not out of the body,
till the wrath of God be pacifyed.
There ſhall it bee ſecure and lye hidden ſafe from all infernall darts. Into
thy hands therefore, O Lord, do I
commend my ſpirit; yea thy ſpirit; for
thou didſt both create and redeeme
it; it is a veſſell made by thee, and
there-

therefore, O God, defpife it not.

Afpirations to Chrift for a happie ende.

ENter not into iudgement with thy fer-uant, O fweet IESVS, becaufe euerie man aliue fhall not be iuftified in thy fight. *Pfal. 142.*

Remember not, O deare IESVS, my iniquities, O let thy mercie anticipate me, becaufe I am become extreamely poore. *Pfal. 78.*

O moft milde IESVS, illuminate mine eyes, leaft I fleepe at anie time a dead fleep; and leaft my enemie obiect to me : I haue preuailed againft thee. *Pfal. 12.*

O Lord IESVS Chrift fonne of the liuing God, interpofe thy holie paſsion, thy croffe and thy death, betweene my foule and thy iuft iudgement.

O moft louing Lord IESVS Chrift, through the vertue of thy bitter Paſsion, commaund that I be admitted into the number of thy Elect.

An

An ardent Aspiration to all the Angels.

O You most blessed Spirits and holie Angels of God ; succour and preuent me in all extremities : and when I shall not be able to implore your assistance , forsake me not.

⸎⸎⸎⸎⸎⸎⸎⸎ : ⸎ ⸎ ⸎ ⸎ ⸎ : ⸎ ⸎

THE XI. HOVRE.

LEARNE TO DIE.

Death's suddain treacheries may teach it thee.

R EMEMBER that man is a dreame ; and when thou goest to rest, thinke how many haue begunne to sleepe , and so continued till suddain death ouertooke them. So

Sitara

Sisara *sleeping till death, expired.* How *in.i 4* manie in health haue gone to bed, and haue bene found dead in the morning? how many in the middle of their discourse at table and in merriment haue bene ouertaken by death? There are a thousand wayes leading to death. One poore poisonous herbe, one neglected litle sore, a wheale scant to be perceaued, a tile from a house, a cherrie-stone, a fish-bone, a small haire, and the very aire itself being but a litle corrupted, killes a man. Cunning and treacherous DEATH hath a thousand waies to bereaue vs of life. Therefore euery day is both carefully to be begunne and ended. It is an excellent order to beginne the day with God, and with him to ende it; nor anie sooner to go to rest, then his accompt may be so ended, as though he thought to die. For he is too rash, that dares presume to sleepe, hauing offended and not pacified God. Beginne still to sleepe, as though some bodie did thus whisper thee in the eare: *This night shall*

they

Luc. 11 *they take away thy soule from thee.* Remember to die.

LEARNE TO LIVE.

The law of Charitie may teach it thee.

Rom.
c. 8.

TO *those that loue God, all things redound to their good.* Blessed, O
Lord, is the man, who loues thee, and
his friend in thee, and his enemie for
thee. The cause of louing God, is God
himself; the maner, is to loue without
measure. Where thy treasure is, there
is thy hart and thy loue. Wilt thou
finde out, where thy treasure lies?
marke what thou louest. Wilt thou
know what thou louest? attend to thy
thoughts. Where thou hidest thy treasure, thither wilt thou oftenest bende
thy thoughts. Where God is forgotten, there is he not a man's treasure;
neither doth he loue God, who hates
man. Knowest thou S. Paul's maxi-
me? Yf I *want charitie, saith he, I haue*

nothing, though I haue all things els.
And : *Aboue all things , fee yee haue cha-* R*om.* 8
ritie. Therefore though thou beſtow
thy granaries, full of corne , and vi-
nyeards full of wine vpon the poore,
or if thou giue mountains of gold, or
houſes full of precious ſtones in almes , yet with all this if thou malice
but euen one creature , thou haſt giuen nothing. For thou canſt neuer
haue concord with Chriſt , if thou
haue diſagreement with a Chriſtian.
Chriſt's whole law is included in
foure letters : L o v e . Loue God, and
thou haſt kept all his Commaundements.

LEARNE TO PRAY.

A prayer for the happie fini-
shing of thy life , may
teach it thee.

O Chriſt I e s v s , waſh me cleane
frō all my ſinnes with thy bloud,

and grant, that my foule paſſing out
of my bodie, may appeare cleane before thy tribunal. O ſweet IESVS,
forſake me not in thoſe laſt ſtraites,
in that laſt combat with death, on
which all ETERN. TIE depends. O
my Redeemer, I commende my ſpirit
into thy hands. O my God let thy
moſt holy will be done in me for all
eternity.

Tó Chriſt crucifyed.

I Adore thee, IESVS Chriſt, and
bleſſe thee, becauſe by thy Paſſion thou haſt redeemed the whole
world. Sauiour of the world, ſaue
me, who through thy croſſe and with
thy bloud redeemedſt me. Draw me
to thee, ſweet IESVS, who ſaidſt:
When I ſhall be aſcended from earth,
I will draw all things to me. I beſeech thee through thy precious
bloud, which thou wert willing to
ſhed for me a ſinner to waſh away all
mine iniquities. O my Creatour and
Redee-

Redeemer Chrift Iᴇsᴠs. I deliuer myſelf wholy into thy hands ; reiect me not; I come to thee, repell me not, caſt me not away from thy face, and take not from me thy holie ſpirit, leaſt mine iniquitie deſtroy, whome thy goodneſſe hath created.

An aſpiration to all the Angels, which may be made by a man readie to yeelde vp his laſt breath, yet mindefull of the iudgement hanging ouer him.

O All you moſt pure Spirits and holie Angels of God, caſt your eies vpon me ; here I lye ſighing and groaning, becauſe the hand of God hath touched me. No mortall mã can, yee only may help mee. The day of Iudgement is alreadie appointed me. Alas I am to appeare before the higheſt God, to yeeld an accompt of all my thoughts, words and deedes : yee know, o holie ſpirits, that I vile worme of the earth haue ſtriuen daily to ſay or doe ſomething in your honours

F O foi-

O forsake me not in this extreame necessitie, in this my last moment, vpon which my whole ETERNITIE depends. Now is that houre at hand, in which my whole safetie or euerlasting perdition consists. O prostrate your selues before the King of kings for me, and I beseech you, reconcile me to my Iudge. I now expect my last sentence ; obtaine that it may mercifully tend to life, and that through your prayers and merits, I may auoide euerlasting death, which I haue long since deserued. Preuent, O holie Angels of God, preuent and succour mee. Now will the Iudge Christ IESVS come ; haue mercie vpon me, O IESVS haue mercie vpon me for all thy holie Angels sake, I beseech thee, IESVS HAVE MERCIE VPON ME.

THE XII. HOVRE.

LEARNE TO DIE.

Death's suddain inuasion may teach it thee.

REMEMBER man is nothing; and euen as theeues vse not to warne a house, which they meane to breake into or vndermine, telling the houre they meane to come either at 12. 1. or 2. of the clock in the morninge; so is it not death's custome, to admonish by certaine messengers, that he will come at such a day, or such an houre. Death is euerie where and alwaies at hand. Watch therefore, O you mortall men, daily and hourely. *Yee know, that the day of God will come like a theefe in the night.*

F 2   Iacob

1 *hof.*
fal 2.

Iacob being to die, drew vp his legs vpon his bed, and died. Recollect, O man, thy minde; Recollect thy spirits; thou must shortly departe; thou must go into the house of ETERNITIE. Remember to die.

LEARNE TO LIVE.

The Law of familiaritie with God may teach it thee.

Iac. 4.

APproche *to God , and he will come neere thee.* It needes not to be feared , that this familiaritie will grow too great; for how much more a man is familiar with God, so much more will he reuerēce him. The coniunction of mindes, and participation of counsells makes friends. No man is made a friend to God, but by his most pure conuersation. Here, o man, I most earnestly entreate thee , to make all thy cause knowen to God thy best friend. Goes it well with thee? consult with God of this thy
good

good fucceffe ; goes it ill with thee ?
Do in like manner ; and refolue of
nothing without him. Deliberate of
all things with this thy friend;fpeake
as confidently with him as with thy
felf. Almightie God is the moft pleafing and faithfull of friends ; but it is
only to a foule feeking him. As often
as thou art leffe mindefull of God, returne inftatly, & cry out : O my God!
o thou the moft louing of all friends,
I haue loft the day , becaufe I haue
loft thy prefece, I haue neglected the
memorie of thee. I know, he who is
a friend, loues at all times ; and eftee-
mes nothing more pleafing , then to
be with his friend. True friendfhip is
euerlafting.

LEARNE TO PRAY.

A dailie and practicall examen
of thy confcience , may teach
it thee.

S Aint Gregory faith ; that one expects God with fo much the

F 3   greater

greater securitie, by how much more
carefully he daily examineth his
owne côscience. S.Auguftin putting
vs in minde of this dutie faith: Afcend
into the tribunal of thy minde againft
thyfelf, and call thy guiltie felf before
thee; but place not thy felf behinde
thee, leaft God difcouer thee before
thy felf. It is the opinion of all wife
men, that a dailie examen of a man's
côscience is a moft profitable praier.
Manie affigne it 5. heads. There is
none can teach this manner of praying in fuch fort, as it may not feeme
difficult to fome. But it will be moft
eafie, if thou pray thus, and obferue
only this, that thou ftay a while after
the two firft litle prayers, and rumi-
nate how thou haft fpent the day.

*Yf thou wilt therefore pray thus, the
difficultie will be foone ouercome.*

I.

O *infinite Goodneffe*, I giue thee
thanks for all the benefitts, which
this day and throughout my whole

life

life thou haſt beſtowed vpon me.
Praiſe and gloriebe to thee through
infinit millions of ages.

2.

O *immenſe Maieſtie* , grant that
whatſoeuer hath this day diſpleaſed
thee in me , I may intirely call to
minde.

3.

Here call to minde all the thoughts ,
words and deedes of the precedent day,
and thinke in what thou haſt offended
God.

4.

O *endeleſſe Mercie* , pardon me in
what I haue ſinned againſt thee this
day. I burie it in the bottomeleſſe
pitt of thy mercie; and through the
death of thy ſonne I beſeech thee,
pardon me , in whatſoeuer I haue
at anie time offended thee.

5.

O *eternall wiſedome* Chriſt IESVS,
I purpoſe firmely neuer more to
ſinne.

Th.

This is the dailie examen of ones con-
science , to which this may
be added.

O eternall Father , through the life
and death of thy sonne , through all
thy goodnesse I beseech thee , grant
that I may perseuer in good, and die
in thy grace.

O deere and sweet IESVS , through
those last words, by which thou didst
commend thy spirit to thy Father,
receaue my soule in the ende of my
life.

O God the Holie-Ghost , haue mercie
vpon me now and in the houre of
my death.

THE HOVRES OF
THE NIGHT.

*WE HAVE GONE
ouer* THE HOVRES OF THE
DAY ; *there reſts now thoſe of
the* NIGHT *, which as it is more
quiet then the day , ſo is it more
fitt for meditation. Therefore
thoſe , whome we taught by day
to pray , we will now teach by
night to conſider , and meditate.
Yet will we firſt aſſigne the rea-
ſons , why the Angels ought to be
honoured by vs with ſo much
due loue and ſeruice ; and that
vpon a great deale of cauſe.*

F 5   THE

THE CAVSES WHY
the holie Angels are chiefly to be honoured before other Orders of Saints.

The 1. cause is the holie scripture.

THE DIVINE Scripture is full of testimonies and praises of the most happie estate of Angels; and of the manie benefits, which they bestow vpon vs.

The 2. cause is ancient Histories.

Ancient histories plainely relate how great offices Angels do for vs.

3. The number of Angels.

The number of Angels is almost infinit to vs, and only by God to be numbred; so that he gaines innumerable friends, who entertaines frindship with them.

4. Angels are the vice-gerents of God.

As well in the ancient as new law, Angels performe manie things in the place of Almightie God. Oftétimes

times doth God promise to send his
Angels : My Angel shall go before
thee. The Angel shall send forth &c.

5. *The Angels are most addicted
to vs;*

They are most bountiefull towards
vs ; and by all their offices, they procure and make vs in short time like
themselues.

6. *They are our aduocats
without number.*

With one act of honouring so manie
millios of blessed Spirits, we gaine an
innumerable companie of Aduocats.

7. *The testimonies of their Aduersaries.*

The arch-hæretikes themselues
Luther and Caluin write most vene-
rably of Angels. Caluin, although he
denie all other Saints, he expressely
teacheth, that Angels may be inuo-
ked as our aduocats and pleaders for
vs.

8. *Dailie experience.*

Teaches manie men, how continually and faithfully Angels watch
in our behalfe.

5. In-
stitut.
c. 1c.

9. The will of God.

God hath giuen the Angels charge, to looke carefully to our faluation, and to keepe vs in all our waies.
The Church is a theater for Angels,
in which they admire God's wifedome, and help & affift vs in our ignorance. Angels beftow infinit benefits
vpon vs. Let vs therefore performe
thoufands of offices of honour and
feruice towards them.

THE
I. HOVRE
OF THE NIGHT.

LEARNE TO DIE.

Confider with thyfelf : Am not I alfo at length to deceafe and die ? Wherefore do I not then prepare myfelf?

LEARNE TO PRAY.

I. O SOVLE OF CHRIST fanctify me. O body of Chrift faue me. O bloud of Chrift, inebriate me. 2. O water flowing from the fide of Chrift, cleanfe me. 3. O paffion

of

of Chrift, ftrengthen me. 4. O
fweet Iefus, heare me. 5. Within thy wounds hide me. 6. Per-
mitt me not to parte from
thee. 7. From the malignant
enemie defend me. 8. In the
houre of my death call me. 9.
Command me to come to
thee. 10. To the ende that with
all thy faints I may praife thee,
in all eternitie.

This is a short Praier; but it doth prefente
ten notable documents, to be pondered
in the exercifing of vertue to
which the feuerall num-
bers point.

1. Frequent Communion. 2. Often
Confeffion. 3. Meditation vpon the
Paffion of our Lord. 4. Continuall
prayer. 5. The feare of Iudgement. 6.
Perfeuerance. 7. Fortitude in temptations. 8. Remembrance of death.
9. A defire of the heauenlie countrie.
10.

10. Meditation of Eternitie. *And the-*
se with 2. other documents , will I expli-
cate to thee in the 12. houres of the night.
Let vs then beginne in this houre.

LEARNE TO LIVE.

LET THY LIFE BE a fre-
quēt Communion. Vnlesse thou | *Ioh.6.*
eate the flesh of the Sonne of man,
thou shalt haue no life in thee. He
loues not his friend , who hates his
presence ; nor loues he Christ , who
shunnes his feast.

THE II. HOVRE.

LEARNE TO DIE;
and meditate.

What will be done with me after my
death? whither will my soule go?
it is vncertaine. Wherefore
then do I liue carelessely
as if, I were already
certaine of
heauen?

LEARNE TO LIVE;
and let thy life be.

Psal.
3.

A FREQVENT Confeſſion.
Waſh me againe from my ſinne.
The beginning of good workes, is
the confeſſion of euill. We ſinne daily; at the leaſt very often; and a ſinne
not waſht away by Pennance, drawes vs on by the proper weight thereof into another ſinne.

LEAR-

LEARNE TO PRAY;
and confider.

A True prayer ought to come
more from the hart, then from
the mouth or lippes. For Ifidorus
faith, that God attends not to the
words of our prayers, but to the hart.
I will therefore, ô man, teach thee
by litle and litle to pray from the
hart, that is, to meditate, and confider
attentiuely any diuine thing. He
prayes beft, who côfiders in this māner the bufineffe of his faluation; and
Ifaac vfually prayed after this man-
ner. *He went out in the, field to meditate,* | Gen.
the day being then in declining. There is | 24.
nothing, which continuall practife
may not render moft eafy. The firft
thing I committ to thy confideration, fhall be the queftions, which a
good while fince, thou haft defired to
propound; now thou maift do it; and
it fhall be thy part to aske, and mine
to anfwear.

Three litle Queſtions.

1. O my Angel; why did not God for the fallen Angels become an Angel, as for fallen man he was made man?

Alas, aske not this queſtion ; for thou wilt neuer ſufficiently vnderſtand the R V I N E of Angels, and fall of men; till thou haſt left being man, & ſhalt liue among Angels, who can expreſſe in words, or euē by thought ſufficiently ſearch into that ordinance and decree, by which the moſt milde God did banniſh out of heauen for all eternity ſo many millions of moſt noble & beautifull ſpirits; who is that Monarch amongſt men, who would condemne a great number of kings and Princes children , to the ſword, & being brought vpon a ſcaffold would commaund their heads to be cutt of for a fault, which in many mens iudgements were very ſmall? & what are many a thouſand ſonnes of Emperours to one only Angell? but yet did the ſupreme Goodneſſe it ſelf

refuſe

refuſe to pardon ſo many millions of Angels. And what was the offence? one only thought , ONE VNWIL-LINGNESSE.

Our king doth truly watch as well to Iuſtice as to Mercie , that he may pardon, and puniſh. God created ſo many beautieful Angels;yet he knew from all eternity,that they would be moſt wicked diuels.But as God, ſaith S. Auguſtin, is the beſt Creatour of good natures, ſo is he the iuſt orderer of euill intentions; to the ende that when they abuſe their good natures, he may make vſe of their euill intentions.The ſeates of theſe apoſtat-Angels are now decreed for men, if they will make them theirs by liuing wel. So is the ruine of Lucifer an occaſion of a greater glory to mankinde. Origen ſaid well : yf I were of that power , that I could ouercome Lucifer,I ſhould thē obtaine his throne in heauen.For by how much the ſtrōger & more crafty the diuell is, whome a man ouercomes, ſo much the higher ſeate will he obtaine amongſt the

Angels

Angels in heauen. It auailes thee nothing to know, which man is to be placed in the seate of the Prince Angel. Know thou this, that he will be there most high, who hath bene here on earth most humble.

2. O my Angel ; shall there be as manie men saued, as there were Angels cast downe headlong ? there be some bookes, which constantly affirme it; and not without reason.

And this question would I also thou shouldst omitt. I had rather thou shouldst make pious and deuout demaunds, then curious questions. But the vice of mankinde is CVRIOSITIE. Most truly saith the Wise man: *I haue only found this, that God made man with his face vpwards, and he embroiles himself with infinit questions.* Aske thou rather, with what wings thou maist be carried vp into the companie of Angels. Thou hast learned out of the scriptures, that there are Nine Quires of them ; the lowest are Angels, the next Archangels, aboue these, are Principalities,

Eccl.7

Powers,

Powers, Vertues, Dominations, Thrones, Cherubins, and Seraphins. Do thou deſire to be inſerted amōgſt one of theſe? But thou wilt aske, how thou maiſt attaine to it. Bleſſed Mechtildes being taught from heauen, ſpeakes of this point according to this ſenſe: They who ſerue the needy, the poore, and pilgrims for God's ſake, make themſelues way to arriue to the 1. Quire of ANGELS. To the 2. Quire of ARCHANGELS, do they attaine, who giue themſelues to prayer and the meditation of diuine things. They belong to the PRINCIPALITIES, who driue out of themſelues all concupiſcence, and luſt. They are to be eſteemed amōgſt the POWERS, who command and gouerne others with due watchfullneſſe, loue and care. They are to be numbred amongſt the VERTVES, who preferre pouertie before riches, and ſubdue themſelues wholy to patience and obedience. To the Quire of DOMINATIONS do they aſpire, who with moſt deuout deſires, con-

Reuel. c. 54.

forme

forme their owne wills to the diuine
will of God, in all things. They are
to be ftiled THRONES who by continuall meditation of diuine things
make their hart a feate worthy of
God. They fhall be mounted as high
as CHERVBINS, who by preaching,
ingraft in the mindes of others, what
they fee in God by meditation , and
what they learne by this laborious
reft of the minde. They are to be en-
rolled amongft the SERAPHINS,
who loue God with their whole
harts, and are inflamed with the loue
of their enemies for God's fake. Yf
they loue any thing eife, they loue it
in God, and are only moued with iniuries cõmitted againft him. And this
is the way to thofe high Hierarchies.
3. And why, ô my beft keeper, haue
none of the holie Angels (that I
know of) euer poffeffed the bodies
of men, which oftentimes diuels and
fugitiue angels haue aduentured to
do, & fince many thoufands of diuels
haue entred into the parts of one
man's body , as if it had bene fome

publike

publike tauerne, hardly to be driuen
out, but with much force. Why may
not the holie Angels with greater aduantage to vs doe the same?

Man is a temple consecrated to the
Deity. Angels both out of reuerence
& loue wil not aduenture to enter into
their Prince's closett. It is the part of
an impudent seruant, his maister looking vpon him, either to sitt vpon his
seate, or ride vpon his horse. Angels
are not ashamed to confesse themselues seruants. So it happens, that since
God hath so ennobled man's originall, with the admirable coniunction
of Diuine and Humane nature, Angels will not haue it lawfull for
themselues to doe any thing with
man, which may hinder them from
being called the seruants not only of
God, but of man, and will contriue
nothing against man, but by the cõ-
mandement of our Lord & God. The
bannished Angel being God's corri-
ual doth all things with fury & cruell
impudencie, vnlesse God forbid him.
But sometimes God permitts him to

punish a man, who denies to receaue
God. For whosoeuer denies to receaue God, is of necessitie to admitt this
guest from hell. There are not two
closets in man's hart; there is only
one, in which either God is enter-
tained, or the diuel admitted. For
certainly vnlesse that place be giuen
to God, it is the diuel's. So where-
soeuer sinne raigneth; thence is ba-
nished all vertue.

THE III. HOVRE.

LEARNE TO DIE;
AND MEDITATE.

With what diseafe, at what time, or in what place will death affault me? Thefe things are foretolde to no man; wherefore then do not I expect death in euerie place, and euerie moment?

LEARNE TO LIVE.
LET THY LIFE BE

A CONTINVALL MEDITA-TION VPON THE PASSION of our Lord Iefus Chrift, who fuffered in flesh. *Be you armed with the fame meditation.* He is free and fafe from all enemies, who knowes how to burie himfelf, within the wounds of our Lord Iefus. Neither doth a generous and deuout fouldier feele his

Pet.4

G   owne

owne wounds , whilſt he beholdes the wounds of his Captain & leader.

LEARNE TO PRAY;
AND MEDITATE.

Three times 9. short meditations drawne compendiouſly out of Holie Scripture, by which manifeſtly appeares , either the Angels benigne loue, or their iuſt anger towards vs.

1. *THE ANGELS do free out of priſon.*

AN Angel bringing the Apoſtles out of chaines and fetters , who had bene impriſoned by the High-Prieſt , ſaith : *Go yee , and ſtand in the temple ; preach to the people all the words of life.* No man is either to be harkened to , or feared , when God commaunds the contrarie.

2 *They preſerue in the midſt of flames.*

The three Hebrew yonge men in the midſt of flames were preſerued vntoucht by an Angel. Innocēcie is

Act. 5.

Dan. 13.

alwaies

alwaies late to the guiltlesse. Flames are but like dewes; and lyons, like lambes.

2. They protect from the sword.

An Angel freed Isaac being layde vnder his fathers sword vpon the point of suffering : *And beholde, an Angel of God cryed from heauen : Abraham, Abraham ; who answered : Here I am Then said the Angel to him: Strike not thy sonne , nor do him any hurt* Genes. c. 22. That is the most commendable obedience , which is performed in things of most difficultie. Gen. 22.

4. They guarde amongst the Lyons.

An Angel defended a Lamb from being touched, though he were cast amongst seauen hungrie and rauenous lions , which Daniel confirmeth of himself, Cap. 6. *My God sent his Angel , who closed the mouthes of the Lions , and they did me no hurt.* Chastitie guarded by the Angels, liues securely amongst the Lions , as in the midst of Lambs. Dan. 6.

5. They

5. *They preserue in the waters.*

Exod.
2.

An Angel protected Moises from destruction, being floting vpon the riuer Nilus in a baskett made of twigs. He may safely vse his cloake for a ship through the maine seas, who hath an Angel for his pilot.

6. *They loosen chaines & fetters.*

Act.
12.

An Angel like a penetrating sunne-beame, called vp Peter being asleepe & bound with two chaines, saying: *Rise presently, putt on thy garment, & fol-low me.* Angels haue the keyes of all lockes, and penetrate all things. He cannot be in prison, whome an Angel assures to be at libertie.

7. *They preserue from fire.*

Gen.
19.

Two Angels leading forth Lot out of Sodome, said to him: *Looke not back, nor stay in anie region hereabouts; but saue thy self vpon a hill, least thou also perish.* The most hurtfull poison to a good man, is wicked companie. Be alwaies conuersant with those, who may make thee better.

8. *They defend from the punishment of death.*

An

An Angel freed the chast Susanna
from death , when she was alreadie
led forth to the execution, by the spirit of the most innocent yonge man
Daniel, who thus cried out publikely to those impure olde men; *There
stands the Angel of God with a sword in
his hand, that he may cutt you off by the
middle, and kill you.* No man in vaine
confides in God ; but by how much
the lesse he hath humane help in
maine and imminent dangers , so
much the more is he sure to haue diuine help at hand.

Dan.
13.

9. *They diuert an imminent*
destruction.

An Angel like an Emperour's
herald hindring a present destructiō,
cried out : *Hurt yee not the earth , nor*
the sea , nor the trees , vntil we haue
marked out the children of God in the
fore-head. And euen emptie vessells
are to be honoured , being so marked.

Apoc.
c. 8.

1. *Angels resist obstinacie.*

AN Angel with a drawen sword
assaulted Balaam riding vpō his

Num.
12.

G 3   asse,

asse, and said to him? *I am come to oppose thee, because thy way is peruerse, and contrarie to me.* And soe he commaunded him to returne the way he came. Man is subiect to erre, but it is requisite, that being admonished, he amende.

2. *They reprehend disobedience.*

Iud. 2.

An Angel rebuked bitterly all the people of Israel, saying: *You haue not bene willing to hearken to my voice; And why haue you done this?* After which speach, there followed, not only a generall lamentation of all, but also a great amendment of manners. He doth ridiculously deplore his offences, who by and by falles againe into the same sinnes.

3. *They punish Pride.*

Act. 12.

An Angel strook Herode being in his robe Royall, sitting vpon his throne, and making a speach to the people, *because he had not giuen honour to God; and therefore he died consumed by vermine.* Pride is hatefull euen to the proude man himself; how should it then please the Angels?

4. *They*

4. *They overthrow the enemies tents.*

One onlie Angel made an effusion of a great sea of Assyrian bloud. *An Angel of our Lord ouerthrew the tents of the Assyrians, and destroyed them all.* One ill-spoken tongue, such a one as that of Senacherib, drawes into destruction both itself, and innumerable others.

Eccl. 48.

5. *They kill manie by plague.*

One Angel by three daies pestilence killed 70000. Israelits. And when the same plague was in Ierusalem, *our Lord taking compassion, commaunded his destroying Angel saying: It suffiseth ; thou maist now holde thy hand. And Dauid lifting vp his eyes, saw an Angel standing betweene heauen and earth , with a naked sword in his hand. Then he and the Elders all clothed in sackcloth fell with their faces vpon the ground.* 1. Paral. 12. God is as milde towards those, who grieue for their sinnes, as he is seuere against sinners.

6. *They*

6. *They ſtrike terrour in warres.*

An Angel like a horſe-man all in whit, glittering in golden armour, went before Iudas Machabeus marching towards his enemies, & gaue ſuch courage to his ſoldiers, who followed him, that like lions they aſſaulted their enemies, and were readie to paſſe through walles of iron. Vnder ſuch a captain, whatſoeuer the number of ſoldiers be, the victorie is moſt certaine.

2. Mach c. 11.

7. *They oppoſe themſelues in their friends behalfe.*

The Angels in the mountaine Dathain ranged in battle, were ſo formidable and terrible an armie, that Elizeus ſaid to his ſeruant, who trembled at the verie ſight thereof, *Feare nothing, for there are more of the enemie, with vs, then with them; And behold a mountain full of horſe-men and firie chariots enuironed Elizeus.* Let Xerxes his great armies come and inuade me, let all the troupes of diuels

4. Reg 6.

come

come againſt me ; I ſhall be ſafe,
whilſt one onlie Angel defends me.

8. *They appoint captains in warres.*

An Angel ſaluting Gedeon ſaid: *Iud.6.*
Our Lord conduct thee , moſt valiant
man , proceede in thy way of fortitude,
and thou ſhalt deliuer Iſrael out of the
hands of the Madianits ; know that I
haue ſent thee , and will be with thee.
There is no man, but he is ſtronge
through the power of Angels , if he
deſire it.

9. *They foretell future ruine.*

An Angel of mightie ſtrength
tooke vp a huge millſtone in the
ſight of S. Iohn , and caſt it into
the ſea , crying out with a lowde
voice : *That great cittie Babylon ſhall be* *Apoc*
caſt downe with ſuch force, as it ſhall neuer *8*
appeare againe. Take you heede , O
Babilonians ; for this verie ruine attends you.

1. *ANGELS endue men with*
eloquence.

A N Angel touched the lippes of *Eſay. 6*
Eſay the Prophet , with a firie
cole from the altar. It is an eaſie mat-

G 5   ter

ter for one to speake eloquently in a great Auditorie, whē he hath studied Rhetorick vnder such a master.

2. They cure the sick

Ioh. 5.

An Angel did often in the yeare, for the good of the sick moue the water at Ierusalem, which stoode within the porch of Salomon : in such sort, that whosoeuer had gone into it after the motion, went out healed. This is no ordinarie Phisitian, who by onely troubling the water, cureth the sick.

3. They refresh the wearie.

3. Reg. 19.

An Angel awaking Elias the Prophet, who slept vnder the shade of a Iuniper-tree, sett before him a loafe of bread and water, saying: *Arise and eate; for thou hast yet a great way to goe.* All the delicacies of kings are to be esteemed nothing in comparison of bread and water, which such a sewer brings from heauen.

4. They suffer themselues to be ouercome by such as are deare to them.

Gen 21.

An Angel wrestling with Iacob the Patriarch suffered himself to be ouer-

come,

come, and saued his conquerour from the intended threats of his brother. While we liue, we must wrestle and fight: and happy art thou, if in wrestling thou die, for being dead, thou art sure to be crowned.

5. *They quickly comfort the afflicted.*

An Angel calling Abraham's seruant Agar from dispaire sayd : *What dost thou, Agar ? feare not.* And at the same time he shewed her a fountain at hand, which might remedie her desperate case. He is wretched and most vnhappy, who hath not bene tempted by vnhappinesse and aduersities.

Gen. 21.

6. *They exhort to do well.*

An Angel exhorted S. Philip saying: *Rise and go towards the south &c.* The Angel was desirous, that occasiõ might be giuen, that Candaces the Treasurer of the Ethiopian Queene, might be instructed in trueR eligion. An occasion to do good to others, is not only to be sought for, but oftentimes to be suddenly layd hold on, as it were, by force.

Act.

7. *They come from heauen to earth.*

Angels as well in the olde as in the New Law descend to earth, and ascend to heauen, in performing dutie and seruice. *Iacob saw in his sleepe, a ladder standing on earth, the top whereof touched the heauens, and the Angels ascending and descending by it.* Christ foretelling the like desire of Angels to goe to and fro, said : *You shall see the heauens open, and the Angels of God ascending and descending.* He certainly desires to erre, who neglects to learne the way to heauen of these heauenly messengers.

Gen. 29.

Ioh. I.

8. *They encourage those that pray.*

The wife of Manuë related simply to her husband. *A man of God, said she, came to me, hauing an Angelicall face, and yet very terrible.* And when the Angel againe shewed himselfe to them both, being asked, what his name was, answered : *Why aske you my name, which is wonderfull.* God doth both terrifye and comfort the good, and his will is, that all redounde to their benefitt.

Iudic. 13.

9. *They*

*9. They loue moſt ardently, and fight
for thoſe, that are chaſt.*

The moſt chaſt Iudith attributes
the preſeruation of her chaſtity being
in the power of that Aſſyrian deſ-
troyer Holofernes, vnto her Angel-
Guardian, ſaying : *Let God liue ; for his
Angel hath kept me ; and our Lord hath
not ſuffered his hand-maide to be defi-
led, either going hence, abiding there, or
returning thence.* Obedience is moſt
deare to Angels ; deare is Patience,
and humilitie ; but aboue all things,
moſt deare is Chaſtitie.

Iud. 13

THE IV. HOVRE.

LEARNE TO DIE;
and confider.

Are not manie taken out of this life by fuddain death? and whither go they? Wherefore then do I promife myfelf fo peaceable, fo flow, and fo gentle a death?

LEARNE TO LIVE;
and let thy life be

Luc 18   A CONTINVALL PRAIER; *becaufe it behooues vs alwaies to pray, and neuer giue ouer. Meditation teaches one, what may be wanting; and by praier is obtained, that it be not wanting.*

LEAR-

LEARNE TO PRAY;
and meditate.

Of the nature and number of the holie Angels.

CHAPTER I.

CONSIDER the wonderfull excellencie of the nature of Angels, by which an Angel may be termed a perfect man, and a man, an imperfect angel, Angels liue most happily; voide of all corporall dregs, and free frō all corruption; and moreouer they are endued with the full & hidden knowledge, of all things, except only the secret of man's hart. *Thou only knowest the harts of the sonnes of men.* And yet, God knowes, it is an easie thing for Angels to penetrate into the secrets of a man's hart. They finde out many things by signes; or without signes they see all things in God, who sees and knowes all things. All the

2. Paral. 6.

miste-

mysteries of Nature lye opē to them;
neither do they by difcourfe draw
one confequence from another; but
euen in one moment, they apprehend
innumerable things togeather, being
confirmed in Diuine grace; with their
vnderftāding they euer beholde God,
and that without any vaile ; and as S.
Paul faith : *We shall fee him face to
face.* They being moft full of diuine
loue , doe ardently loue God with
their wills. Thefe you may rightly fti-
le morning-ftarres , or moft cleare
funnes. Yf euery Saint in heauen exceede feauen times the fplendour of
the funne; how much more will thofe neereft courtiers of God fhine
with immenfe and glorious beames?
They are truly moft pure looking-
glaffes , in whome the eternall Wifedome, Goodneffe, Power, and loue of
Cant.2 the Creatour is cleerely feene. Thefe
Cant. 8 are thofe whiteft lillies , amongft
whome the heauenly fpoufe is fed
and delighted aboue all pleafures.
Thefe are thofe mountaines, which
bring forth aboundātly the beft and

fweeteft

fweeteſt odours. Theſe are, as it were,
that moſt pleaſant field, where are to
be found millions of flowers ; and
which is moſt wonderfull, there are
not two of them of the ſame coulour, forme, or odoriferous ſmell.
Such is the opinion of S. Thomas
of Aquin. Yet thoſe opinions are not
to be reiected, which apply this
otherwiſe.

1. Part
qu. 50

CHAPTER II.

THeir number is ſo great, that as
Nazianzen faith truly of it : It is
ſufficient to make a new world of
creatures greater farre in number,
then this of ours. For as the heauens
exceede all that in greatneſſe, which
they containe within them ; ſo do the
heauenly ſpiritts exceede in number
all other things; and it is very plainely
to be gathered out of the holie Scriptures, that neither vnderſtanding can
comprehend, nor tongue declare
their number. Iob asketh : *Are his
ſouldiers to be numbred ?* The Lacede-

Orat.
de Na-
tiuit.
Domin

Iob.c.
25.

monian kings vſed to haue abou
their perſons 300. choice ſouldiers.
The Macedonian kings had a thouſand men to guarde their perſons.
All theſe were numerable. But no
number can be aſſigned to the ſouldiers of God. Daniel endeauoures to
calculate them in his 7. Chapter
ſaying : *A thouſand thouſands did ſer-*
ue him , and ten hundred thouſand thou-
ſands did attende vpon him. Whereby
the Prophet did , as it were , affirme the number of Angels to be
infinite. So doth clearely Saynt
Gregory ſay , that the number of
the heauenlie cittiſens was by Iob
accompted infinit; and by Daniel it
was aſſigned , to ſhew , that their
number was innumerable; but innumerable to man only ; to which opinion the Royall Prophet ſeemeth to
aſſent ſaying : *The chariot of God is*
drawen by ten thouſand. Chriſt in the
garden of Oliuet reprehending Peter's too much forwardneſſe ſayth:
Thinkeſt thou not, that I can aske my Fa-
ther and he will ſtraitwaies ſend me more

Pſal.
72.

                                              then

then twelue legions of Angels ? as if he
would say:O Peter, I want not thyne
nor thy fellowes helpe; Let the Apoſtles ſwords remaine in their ſcab-
bards,ſince I refuſe to be reſcued by
Angels; For if I would be helped by
others, I would already haue demanded of my Father 12. legions of Angels, as well as I haue 12. Apoſtles;
which had bene, as S.Hierome calcu-
lateth,ſeauēty two thouſand Angels;
Albertus Magnus reckones it after
the ſame manner,ſaying; that in one
legion there are 6000.Angels.Chriſt
our Lord might therefore haue bene
defended ſufficiently by 72000.ſoul-
diers in the mount Oliuet,ifſo he had
bene pleaſed. S. Luke ſaith, that at
the birth of Chriſt our Lord , there   *Luc 2.*
was heard a multitude of heauenly
armies, & Angels. He calles the Angels ſouldiers, as holy Iob doth; to
ſhew , that they be euer moſt ready
and prepared for battle, to defend the
honour of their heauenly king;
which Zacharias alſo teſtifieth in
his 9. Chapter. I will enuiron my

house

house by those, who going and coming, do fight for me. These souldiers
are so deare to God, that from them
he tooke his Title, calling himself,
not from his goulden and celestiall
palace, nor from the riches of Land,
and sea, nor from the dreadfull Em-
pire of all sublunarie things, but from
his heauenly souldiers: THE LORD

Hebr.
2.

OF HOSTES. The Apostle S. Paul
is of the same opinion saying to the
Hebrewes: *Yee approch to the cittie of the*
liuing God Hierusalem, and to the presen-
ce of many millions of Angels. And the
Apostle S. Iohn, who was priuy to all
secrets, sayth: *I heard the voice of many*

Apoc.
5.

Angels enuironing the Throne, and their
number was thousands thousands. These
are ineuitable proofes, that the number of Angels is greater then we can
conceaue or expresse. Dionysius, S.
Paul's disciple, and S. Hierome affirme, that the multitude of Angels is so
great, that we can hardly define the
number, though we multiply it to
the infinit. And some of S. Thomas of
Aquin's disciples affirme, that the

opinion

opinion of their maifter was, that the Angels of heauen were more in number, then the ftarres in the heauens, the birdes in the aire, droppes of water in the fea, graines in the fandes, flowers and leaues of graffe on the earth, yea more then there are atomes, and laftly more then all the indiuiduall creatures in the whole world. S.Gregory Nazianzen's words importe the fame, when he fayth: there are infinit thoufands of Angels, and S.Bernardin of Siena, and S.Ambrofe Bifhop of Milan fay: There be fome, who thinke the number of Angels to be 99. times greater then the number of men. And that this opinion is confirmed by the 15. chapter of S.Luke, where mention is made of a fhepheard, who left 99. fheepe, to go feeke one, which was gone aftray. And iuft fo (fay they) did Chrift forfake the Angels, and came downe into the defert of the world to reclame mankinde from errour. S.Hilary is of the fame opinion; and S.Brigit fayth: There be fo many thoufand

t. de creat. hom.c. 18. Tom. 4 fer.49. Epiftol. ad Ant

c 8. in Math. 4. Reuel. c.

thoufands that ferue Almightie God,
that if all the men frō the firſt Adam
to the laſt man, were numbred, there
might be affigned to each man, more
then ten Angels-guardians. This fee-
mes certaine and agreable to diuine
teſtimonies, namely, that the number of Angels is farre greater then
that of men. But how many Legions
there be, and how many millions,
Pfal. *He knowes veſt, who numbreth the mul-*
146. *titude of ſtarres, and calies each by his na-*
me. The Angels them felues fee in
God, as if it were, in a glaſſe, their
owne number; but thefe fecrets are
not yet to be reuealed to mortall
men.

CHAPTER III.

LEt vs therefore clippe the wings
of our curiofity, and differre the
knowledge thereof, till we arriue in
the world of the Bleſſed ; In the meane time, let a deuout hope comfort &
ſtirre vs vp, to tende thither, with all
our whole defires; where we may not

onely

onely know the number of Angels,
but being in the midſt of them, we
may alſo ſee and beholde them. Let
vs in the meane time continually cō-
template the moſt repleniſhed court
of our high king, though it be but a-
farre of; to which the words of Salomon may well be applied. *The dignity
of a king conſiſts in the multitude of his people.* It is therefore moſt fitt, that the
king of kings in the immenſe kingdome of heauen, maintaine a moſt
copious family: which Dauid won-
dring at cried out: *God, who is glorified
in the councell of Angels, is great and
terrible aboue all who are about him.* It is
a wonderfull thing; in this world a
king is defended by his guarde, but
there, the king defends his guard. The
ſtrength of our kings is in the number and valour of his ſoldiers; but
that great king giues ſtrength to his
ſouldiers; and that which is moſt
ſtrange, is, that the immenſe company of thoſe heauenly forces are vnited togeather with ſuch loue, as
though they had but one will & one

Prou.
14.

Pſal.
88.

vnderſtanding. O how vnlike is the
ſtate of heauen to that of this world!
here euery place is full of ſtrife and
diſſenſion ; amongſt the leaſt com-
panies there be factions ; all ſeemes a
continuall warre ; for on euery ſide
is nothing but iarres. But giue eare
to the Angels, and conſider, what
they proclame : Let there be an eſtabliſhed peace on earth ; but let that
peace be amongſt men OF GOOD
DESIRES.

THE V. HOVRE.

LEARNE TO DIE;
and consider.

What makes death most terrible? a wicked conscience. Wherefore then do not I procure it peace, and make it become good?

LEARNE TO LIVE;
and let thy life be.

A FEARING THE SVPREME IVDGE. We shall all stand before the tribunall of Christ. Therefore every one of vs ought to take an account of himself. Euerie thing hath a time. Now is the time of Mercie; then will be the time of Iudgement. That day will be a day of wrath.

Rom. 14.

LEARNE TO PRAY;
and meditate.

How, Angels are painted, with what clothes & habits in what formes & shapes.

H CHA-

CHAPTER I.

ANgels are well reprefented like beautifull yong men. They are yong; for no olde age, no difeafe, nor number of yeares corrupt them. S. Marke fpeaking of the womē, which would haue annoynted Chrift, faith: *Entring into the monument , they faw a yong man fitting on the right hand.* Their beautifull fhape doth fo dimme and eclipfe the formes of the moft beautifull men, as the funne doth the ftarres. The beauty of the Angels is no fraile thing ; it is not fpoiled with wrinkles, or gray haires; it knowes neither pride nor lafciuioufneffe; it is euerlafting and euer-flourifhing. Now let our loue to Angels moue vs to a double confideration : 1. Yf the loweft and leaft Angel do fo excell all humane creatures, as that there is no comparifon, what pleafure will it be to fee fo many millions of Angels, not a farre of, nor as it were, through a mift, but with a perfect and

Mar. 6.

eternall

eternall light, neuer satisfyed with this most delightfull spectacle, notwithstanding that this will be the least parte of our Beatitude. Let it be our care, daily to grow yong; not in yeares, but in chast desires and holie purposes. The spirit of deuotion is daily to be renewed; and the age of a lazie languishing is to be shaken of. We fall thousands of times. Let vs rise as many. King Dauid made himself daily become yonger, saying : *I haue now begunne , now , and euen now.* What I haue neglected for ten, twentie, thirtie, fourtie yeares, I will do this day, this houre, this verie instant. So shall we daily renue our age, and become ten, twenty, thirty, fourty yeares yonger. S. Charles Borromeus to one of his, asking, what way did best leade to heauen, gaue this document: Proceede so in thy iourny to heauen, as if euery day thou didst but beginne a new.

CHAPTER II.

De nat.
Domini
c. 4.

THE habits of Angels are painted glittering, and for the most parte, white as snow, S. Augustin saith; that the Angel, which was sent to the B. Virgin, appeared to her with a shining countenance, a glittering garment, and an admirable gate and motion. And why should not most innocent, and pure Spirits weare white clothes? This comely candour becomes them; neither ought they to be painted with black or sad garments, seing they ouerflow with pleasures, their life being a perpetuall ioy. The Angels, who brought the first newes that night when Christ was borne, could not but appeare in ioyfull shape saying : *I declare to you a great ioy.* Yet Angels are often seene in armes; and whereas our souldiers are couered from top to toe in iron, they are so with golde. The historie of the Machabees relates, that when Lisia was readie to giue any assault,

lib.
c. 11.

                                    and

and Iudas Machabeus went to luc-
cour his owne forces with fresh men,
there also appeared a horseman in a white
garment, & golden armour going before
them & charging his lance. Againe, when
he fought againſt Timothee captaine of the Aſiatike armie, *there appea-*
red from heauen fiue horſe-mē with golden
bridles conducting the Iewes, whereof
there were two, who holding Machabeus
in the midſt betweene them, and enui-
roning him with their armour, preſerued
him, and caſt dartes, and thunder-boltes
againſt their enemies.

2. lib. 10.

Certainly it is no noueltie for
Angels to ſerue in warre without
pay. Happie are thoſe tents, which
enioy but one ſuch ſouldier. And
what a ſlaughter did one onely Angel
make in one night in the tēts of Sen-
nacherib? One ſuch ſouldier from
heauen did there kill, neere 19. thouſand men. And S. Chriſoſtome twelue
hundred yeares ago, ſaw a ſtatue of
waxe made in remembrance of that
Angel, who filled the tēts of the Aſſy-
rians with ſo manie dead carcaſſes,

Orat. de le-
giſlat. veter.
& no.
Teſt.

and beheld it with teares in his eies,
and a hart-feeling of the cafe. Thus
the Angels both in warre and peace
make proofe of their obedience and
inuincible force; and do not only
carry in their hands a walking-ftaffe
like pilgrime, but alfo a truncheon
like Captains and Commaunders.
They offer both peace and warre, as
heretofore Quintus Fabius in the
Court of Carthage, gathering vp the
skirts of his gowne, faid to the fena-
te: LOE, WE BRING YOV HEE-
RE PEACE AND WARRE;
CHOOSE, WHETHER IT
PLEASETH YOV. So do Angels
bring peace to fuch as are well dif-
pofed; and warre to libertins and re-
bells. Angels haue befides bene very
often feene all in white; not for that
they may not vfe garments of other
coulours, as I know not what Seue-
rus Antiochinus dreamed, as though
purple were forbidden them, as it was
heretofore to the Roman women,
which is a ridiculous fable. But candour pleafeth the Angels both in

their

their garments and mindes;and surely it becomes them to be candide,
who are in perpetuall feasts , daily
nuptialls, a continuall ioy , and eternall triumph. But we haue a litle too
much enlarged ourselues touching
THEIR FACE AND GAR-
MENTS. Let vs now come to their
WINGS; which is the third Chapter
of this Meditation.

CHAPTER III.

THE diuine Dionysius Areopagi-
te saith, that Angels are painted
with wings ; because they partake
of nothing that is composed of the
base dregs of this earth , and to the
ende, that we might know , that no
bodily weight can hinder them from
being in a moment , where they
will. They also attend neere to God
with so great sweetnesse of loue,
as they seeme to hang in the aire
with an euerlasting delight. Saint
Chrisostome speakes of wings

Homil
3. de
incor-
nat.
Dei

H 4   in

in Angels, and affirmes, that the Archangel Gabriel is rightly painted with wings; not becaufe God created him winged, but that we may thankefully remember the flight, which he made from heauen into the B. Virgin's clofet at Nazareth, where the Angel performed his embaffadge and in God's place demaunded the affent of the Bleffed virgin to the reparation of the world. Yf we compare the fwift wings of birds, the fudden flight of arrowes, and of the windes thefelues, the courfe of ftags or tigres, the flight of eagles, the fwiftnes of the clowdes, the whirling about of the celeftiall globes; if we compare, I fay, thefe with the wings of Angels, they will feeme but flow motions & full of delay. Angels will foone ouertake, & diuert their courfes, and euen the windes themfelues; For that great king of heauen hath fwifter meffengers, thẽ all thefe, who in a moment do moft obediently go that way, which the will of God appoints for them. The kinglie Pfalmift

wondreth

wondreth at this saying : *O my Lord*
my God, thou art greatly magnified, who
walkest vpon the feathers of the winds,
and makest thy Angels Spirits, and thy
ministers burning fires.

CHAPTER IV.

Painters sett out Angels with
gemmes, and adorne their heads
with garlands of crosses, because it is
agreable to reason & to Holie Scripture. Ezechiel speaking of the most *Ezech*
beautifull of all Angels saith : *All* *c. 28.*
kinde of precious stones enrich thy gar-
ments. Obedience is a noble gemme;
and because Lucifer was disobedient,
he lost all his precious iewels. Con-
stantine the Great, (as S. Damasus
witnesseth) in the Church of S. Iohn
Lateran, which was anciently called the Church of Cõstantine, besides
innumerable other ornaments of
golde and siluer, placed foure great
Angels of siluer, which shined with
glistering light of manie precious
stones : and each of them' weighed

500. pound weight of filuer, which
was a Royall prefent. Angels beare a
croffe in fronte, becaufe at the laft
day they fhall carry it to the place of
Iudgement, as the Trophy of their
Lord. Chrift foretold it in Saint Mathew : *And then shall appeare the signes
of the Sonne of man.* Angels will be
the enfigne-bearers, who loue the
croffe of their Lord, not becaufe they
were preferued from deftruction by
the Croffe, as we were (though there
be writers of extraordinary note,
who fay, that Chrift did meritt both
grace and glory for the Angels, but
becaufe their king hath ouerthrow-
en the diuel by the croffe. Therefore a Seraphin would not be feene
by S. Francis otherwife then crucified;to the ende that he might admonifh vs by that fpectacle, that all our
loues ought to tend to IESVS crucified : and that we may breathe forth
in our foules : MY LOVE IS
CRVCIFIED ; yea and wee ought
daily to crucifie ourfelues. For the
golde of diuine loue is not more

certainly

certainly tried by any touchſtone
then by the Croſſe. IN LOVE NO-
NE CAN LIVE WITHOVT
GRIEFE.

CHAPTER V.

ANGELS are painted with naked
feete, walking vpon the cloudes. This is not vnvſuall to God's
Embaſſadours to caſt of thoſe clogs
of their feete. Moiſes did it. So did
Eſaias; and the Apoſtles, as alſo many
other holy men, whoſe mindes were
already placed in heauen. They felt
no want of ſhoes, who had inured
themſelues many yeares to go barefoote; as S. Nicolas of Tolentine, and
many other Chriſtians haue done heretofore. The Angels walking vpon
the cloudes inſtruct vs how we
ought with a quiet minde, to ouercome aduerſities. A cloud is but a
light thing, only a thickned va-
pour, which the winde blowes to
and fro. All diſtempers of thunder

and

and lightning are debated in the cloudes, which send downe into the inferiour parts those fierie issues of lightnings. Beyond the cloudes there are no tempests. Those whose *conuersation is in heauen* adhere to God by so firme a loue, that no calme of prosperitie, nor tempest of affliction can draw them thēce. Their care is onely for God, and their conscience; all things else they esteeme lesse then nothing. The black clowdes of impatience, enuie, or anger, trouble not them; they are aboue the clowdes; & they treade vpon them, by the commaunde and rule of their minde. And this is to walke with Angels vpon the cloudes.

CHAPTER VI.

THE Prophet Daniel saw a gyrdle of the Angels not made of silke, but of beaten golde. This gyrdle is the note of Chastitie. *They shall be*, saith Christ, *like the Angels of God.* And S. Gregorie saith: We binde our loines, when by continencie

Hom. 15. in Euäg.

we

we correct and bridle neithe luit;
and the Angels doe not onely binde
their loines with their gyrdle , but
their breaſt alſo; to ſhew,that chaſtitie côſiſtes not onely in the bodie,but
alſo in the minde. But alas , how often do we feele the want of both theſe girdles ? There are certaine gameſ-
ters , who when they haue conſumed
and waſted all their money,are yet ſo
tranſported with the deſire of play,
that they alſo venture their clothes;
and for the moſt parte,the gyrdle is
the firſt,which they thinke they may
better ſpare then their hatt or cloake,ſo whoſoeuer admitts Concupiſcence into his companie as a play-
fellow , he hath alreadie loſt ſhame;
and the wretch doth one while couet
this , and another while that. Now
he runnes after this pleaſure, and by
and by after another ; and is by ſo
much the leſſe ſatisfied,by how much
his minde is,more poſſeſſed with fil-
thineſſe. Concupiſcence is a moſt
skillfull gameſter ; it plottes one deceipt after another ; it intices by faire

termes,

termes , and enueagleth with a shew
of sweetnesse , and retaines, as though
it had glewie hands, and passeth from
a suggestion to a thought , from a
thought to a desire , from a desire to a
delight , from a delight to a consent , from a consent to a fact, from
a fact to a custome , from a custome to despaire of amendment, from
despaire to a defence of sinne , from
a defence of sinne to a boasting of it,
and lastly from a glorying in it, to
damnation. This is fine sport ; and
after manie things lost in this play,
the next is the gyrdle of ones breast,
or chastitie of minde ; which being
lost , a man is prone to be prodigall
also of the gyrdle of the loines , or
chastitie of bodie. Belieue me , the
world seekes to bereaue thee of both
these gyrdles. O chastitie (saith
Ephrem) mother of the best delight,
and a kind of an Angelicall life. O
thou truly happie Virginitie , which
striuest with Angels for glorie , and
dost euen conquer them in vertue,
though not in felicitie. There is an

odori-

odoriferous roote , which we call
Angelica , antidote to the plague.
This Chaftitie may well be called
Angelica , which doth not fuffer the
venime of the hart,fuch as are impure
cogitations to take roote , but refifts
and beates back this plague of the
minde , and hath alwaies the Angels
to befriend it. S. Auguftin faith :
By how much more one is pure , the
more is he kept and enuironed by
Angels ; who through a fimilitude
and likeneffe , which they haue with
chaft men , delight to be conuerfant
with them. Angels hate vngyrdled
perfons ; neither can they loue their
companie , who take vpon them all
manner of bafeneffe. I will here repeate that of S. Hierome : In whatfoeuer vertue thou excelleft , or in
whatfoeuer workes thou art moft
eminent , if thou wante the gyrdle
of chaftitie , all goes to the ground.
Chrift admonifhing vs of this in S.
Luke faith : *Let your loines be gyrt.*
This is the FACE ; *thefe the garments,*
wings precious ftones gyrdle, and pofture,

Lib. 1.
de
Virgin

Luc 13

in

in which the Angels are painted.
All which, vnleſſe wee be blinde
and deafe, may be a ſilent, yet eloquent exhortation to vs, how we
ought to forme our manners.

THE VI. HOVRE.

LEARNE TO DIE;
AND CONSIDER:

*How do I deſire that death should finde me
in manners and in life? why therefore
do I not become ſuch a one as I deſire
to bee?*

LEARNE TO LIVE.
Let thy life be a meere ſtudie,
how to perſeuer.

*Bee faithfull till death, and I will giue
thee the crowne of life. It is a greater
worde, to execute good purpoſes, then
to make them. It is of litle validitie to
beginne well, vnleſſe thou alſo ende
well.*

LEARNE

LEARNE TO PRAY,
AND MEDITATE.

*The Angels songs and their
functions.*

CHAPTER I.

HOlie *Iob in his* 38. *chapter demaunds
thus* : *Who will bring asleepe or
make rest from motion the heauenlie harmonie?* We leade such a life , that sad-
nesse doth still succeede ioy , and im-
mediatly ensueth it. And a sweet melodie doth so rauish our eares , that
we thinke a sirene sings with great
sweetnesse. But how long do we so?
At length satietie , tediousnesse, and
lothsomenesse expelles the former
sweetenesse. And while we greedily
harken to a musicall consort, and our
eares listen hungerly after it, if it once
cease, all the contentment of the eares
vanishes away , and so doth that
sweetnesse ende, while we still would

Iob 38

willingly

willingly listen; and our eares are so
much the more troubled at the silence, by how much more they were
delighted with the sweetnesse of the
harmonie. The Angels sing otherwise in heauen; they beginne & neuer
ende; they neither grow wearie, nor
cause loathing; after thousands of
yeares this melodie will be as acceptable as it was the first houre we beganne to heare it. No mortall eare can
attaine to the sweetnesse of this harmonie; but the immortall & blessed
possesse it euer. But what do the Angels sing? who euer heard them sin-

Esa. 6. ging? Esayas hath heard them, and
describeth the words of that heauenly
dittie. *The Seraphins did cry out one to*
another: Holie, Holie, Holie, the Lord
God of hostes; the whole earth is replenished
with his glorie. This is the holie dittie
of three Partes, which those diligent
and vigilant Creatures vtter, whome
the Angel in the Apocalips saw and

Apoc. hard crying out: *Holie be the omnipotent*
4. *Lord God, who hath bene, is, and shall be.*
Let some one I pray you cōpare these

noDle

noble Quiristers of God & heauenly
Courtiers, with so manie impious
men on earth, or diuelish spirits in
hell, who with vnspeakable execra-
tions and continuall blasphemies do
perpetually breath forth venime a-
gainst Almightie God. Alas, how vnlike is the Psalme of the Blessed, and
that of the damned.

CHAPTER II.

SAint Iohn also that eye of our
Lord, and the dearest to him of
all the Disciples, hearing the cōsorts
of Angels in heauen, saith: *I saw and
heard the voice of manie Angels and of
beasts, and elders about the Throne, and
they were in number thousands of thousands, crying out with a lowd voice. The
Lamb, which hath bene slaine, is worthie
to receaue vertue and diuinitie, wisedome & fortitude, honour & benedictions.*
And in another place he relates,
what, in that highest tower of eternall pleasure, he had seene & heard.
And all the Angels stood compassing the

Apoc.
5.

Apoc.
7.

Throne,

Throne, the Elders and the foure Beasts; and before the Throne they fell on their faces , saying : Benediction , splendour, wisedome , thankes-giuing, vertue , and fortitude , be to our God , world without ende , Amen. Neither is there anie doubt to be made , but that the Angels with the innumerable companie of the Blessed , do sing that most ioyfull song *Alleluia.* O heauens! o habitation of all beautie, and ioy, who would not thinke the sweetest conforts of men as tedious and irkesome, as the rude bellowing of beasts, when he thinkes of thee ? and not onely of thy most sweet melodie, but of the verie summe of eternall delight ? O death ! come and change me from this valley of mourners , to that Tower of Angels.   Draw me from the companie of men, that I may be partaker with the Angels.

CHAPTER III.

THE Angels office is fiue-folde: they are *Singers, Suppliants, Em-*

bassadours,

baſſadours, *Protectours* , *and warrel.ke*
Conductors. Their fitſt and chiefe dutie
is , to loue God ; and neuer to ceaſe
from prayſing him. They ſo loue
God , that they burne with zeale
towards him. They ſo loue God,
that they extoll him with an euer-
watchfull and vnwearied harmonie
of praiſe. Beholde , here are the
Courtlie Quiriſters , who with continuall readineſſe attend their Lord
and God, who doth ſo much eſteeme
this office , that he would haue the
higheſt and moſt noble of his Angels
to be ſingers, Eſay teſtifieth, that the
Seraphins ſing before their Lord that
diuine and ſweet ſong : HOLIE,
HOLIE , HOLIE ; and like larkes
they aſcend whilſt they ſing. This is
an argument of their deſire and moſt
feruent affection , that they do more
& more ardently loue God, and ſo do
they as it were approch neerer and
neerer to him ; and in the meane time
in ſigne of great reuerēce they couer
their feete , and bow downe their
heads before him. For to all thoſe

that defire to praife God, thefe things
are moft neceffarie, REVERENCE,
and LOVE. The higheft Angels performe this; what then ought we to
do who are moft abiect wormes:
King Dauid exhorteth vs faying:

Pfal.
2.

Serue yee our Lord in feare, and praife
him with trembling. Praife without
loue proues colde, and loue without
reuerence is too familiar. God will
be beloued, but chaftly and reuerently.

    Another office of the Angels is to
be SVPPLIANTS. They offer to God
men's prayers & good wifhes, which
the Angels themfelues teftifie; among
whome one of the chief faith to To-

Tob.
12.

bias: *I haue offered thy prayers to God.*
And the fame another of the Angels

Act.
10.

affirmed to Cornelius the Centurion:
Thy Prayers and almes-deedes haue
afcended in the fight of God. That
moft vnderftanding man of hidden
myfteries, and God's chief fecretarie
S. Iohn faith, that he faw the fame,

Apoc.
8.

There ftood (faith he *) an Angel befo-*
re the Altar hauing a golden cenfer in

                                              bis

his hand ; *and much incense was given him , that he might presente the prayers of the Saints.* After this manner the holie Fathers learned to speake out of diuine Scriptures ; but in steede of citing them all , I will onely alleadge what S. Bernard saith. Angels , saith he , are wont to assist those , who pray, and to be delighted in those , whome they see lift vp their cleane and vndefiled hands in their prayers. The Rabbins, who are full of fables, do also here inserte their fictions , expounding the first chapter of Genesis. They say , the faces of the firmament are birds , which carrie vp all things to God. This fiction doth inuolue in it something of truth; but we giue more credit to Iacob the Patriarck's eyes though they were shutt and bereft of light ; He saw Angels ascending and descending in a diligent kind of office, as though they were the messengers betweene heauen and earth, and the Princelie Postes, who

Serm. 3. Super: Missus est.

Gen. 28.

do as

do as it were bring letters from heauen into this vale of miserie ; and
carry hence their answers back with
them, which they receaued from men.
They are spectatours of our calamities, hearers of our sighes and grones,
and witnesses of our teares, and
praiers. But what is that ascending
and descending? what are these obla-
tions of our prayers? do they relate
to God what before he knew not? I
pray thee, creature, when thou pray-
est to God, and in thy prayers dost
deplore thy wants, and imbecillities,
dost thou then explicate any thing to
God, whereof he is ignorant: He
knew all this, before thou beganst;
and he knew it from all eternitie.
Should we therfore not pray? it is
ridiculous and impious so to thinke.
Imagine then the same of Angels ; it
hath pleased God, that it should be
done in such sort, that his Diuine
Maiesty : might take the more notice
of it, when the inhabitants both of
heauen and earth ioyne their endeauours in worshipping of him. And

there-

therefore God made them *all mini-string Spirits.* And to giue vs surer testimonies of his power and goodnesse, he saith : *I will send my Angel, who shall go before thee, and keepe thee in all thy waies, and bring thee into the place which I haue prouided.* S. Bernard assigning another cause saith : Who will grant me, that my prayers may be manifested before God by you, O gratious Princes ? not to God, who knowes the verie thought of man, but to those Spirits, which are endued with vertue, and are freed from the bondage of flesh. For which there may be also another reason alleadged, because Angels ioyne their prayers with ours, and temper the coldnesse of our prayers, with the fire and feruentnesse of theirs. Hilarius saith : The Diuine nature of God needes no Angels ; but our imbecillitie needes them. God is ignorant of nothing we do ; but our childishnesse and weakenesse in asking or deseruing, requires such suppliants as these to concurre with vs. But why

Hebr I.

Exod 23.c

Serm 7. in Cant

in Pf 129

I are

are they fayd onely to offer our
prayers, and not the reft of our workes? Becaufe of good workes prayer
is the beft, and the originall of all
others. I will adde this, that from
Angels we learne to pray, according to
S. Bernard, who faith, that men teach
to feeke God ; the Angels, how to
adore God ; and the Holie Ghoft a-
boue, teaches how we may finde
him. But we will not omitt, that almes-deedes are prefented vp to God
by Angels, and not prayers alone. So
witneffeth Holie fcripture. But how
do they exhibite our prayers, fince
they fee not our thoughts? They eafily fee by the vifion of God for what
it is we pray, as alfo by other circum-
ftances of our carriage. For who is he
that prayes, and doth not at the fame
time either figh, knock his breaft, lift
vp his eies, or the like, though he
vtter no words. It is an eafie thing;
for thofe wife fpirits to attaine the
knowledge of what lies in our harts:
and though they fhould obferue nothing in vs, yet certainly, as I was
faying.

saying. They see in God, who is the
mirrour and wonderfull glasse, in
which all things are represented, and
chiefly those things, which appertai-
ne to their charge. S. Gregory saith:
What is it, that cā be hidd from them,
who know him, that knowes all
things. At the same time, but in seuerall places Tobias & Sara prayed; she
at Rages a cittie of the Medes, and he
in Niniue a cittie of the Assyriās; not-
withstādeing at the self same time both
their prayers were receaued by God,
as the Booke of Tobias witnesseth.
Holie Raphael the Angel of God is sent,
that he may carefully looke to them both,
because at the same time their prayers
were recited in the sight of God. Who recited them? who recommended them
being recited? and who offered them
being recommended? if not the Angels. And certainly this is to all good
men a great comfort, that in heauen
they haue their Oratours, and pleaders of their cases and actions.
Whatsoeuer they suffer or do, whatsoeuer they pray or bestow, is by the

Lib. 4.
Dial.
c. 33.

Tob. 3.

recom-

recōmendation of Angels made more
acceptable to God.

The third office of Angels is ; they
are EMBASSADOVRS ; and that in
matters of greateſt weight. When the
ſonne of God became man , when he
died on the croſſe , when he reuiued
in the Sepulcher, and when he departed from vs and aſcēded into heauen,
the Angels were readie and prepared
to all obedient offices. God wanted
not their help and endeauour : but
this he did out of his owne goodneſſe,
that our mindes might conceaue,
what a great care he had of our ſaluation. Our moſt louing God is wont
ſo daily to aſſiſt our endeauours , that
he oftētimes euen complies with our
cuſtomes , and affordes manie great
teſtimonies of his loue, by condeſcending and accommodating himſelf to
our capacities.

The fourth office of Angels is,
they are PROTECTOVRS. The
kinglie Pſalmiſt ſaith : *God gaue his
Angels charge ouer thee , that they might
keepe thee in all thy wayes.* In pathes,not

Pſal.
90

in

in precipices; thy Angel ſhall looke
to thee but yet walking, not flying;
he that will perish, let him perish. For
as euery man, ſo euery region, prouin-
ce and kingdome hath his Angel-
guardian; and ſo in euery kingdome
are two kings, in euery Dioceſe two
Biſhops; but the kings and Biſhops,
which are of heauen, do not expoſe
themſelues to humane eies.

The 5. office of Angels is, that
they are CONDVCTOVRS in warre; and ſuch Generalls, that when
they liſt, they haue the victorie on
their ſide; they fight without cãnon,
without victuals, without troupes,
and voide of bag and baggage; and
with the leaſt breath they diſperſe armies how great ſoeuer. When *Ioſue*
was in the field of Iericho, he lifted vp his
eies, and ſaw a man ſtand againſt him, hol-
ding in his hand a naked ſword; & going
to him, he asked : Art thou of ours, or of
our enemies. He anſweared : I am of nei-
ther of both ; but I am chiefe of the army of
our Lord ; and now I come. O moſt bleſſed of our Lord, comming alreadie

Ioſue
5.

the tempests of warre blow vp whole prouinces. God promising his people faith: *I will send a forerunner to thee, an Angel, and I will cast forth &c.* Now also do many troopes of euil men assault good men; but happy is he, who fightinge against whatsoeuer enemie, hath for his champion though is be but one of these Legionaries, and not a whole legion.

THE VII. HOVRE

LEARNE TO DIE;
and consider.

Yf I were at this present houre to die, what would I do? why then do I not now the same?

LEARNE TO LIVE;

Let thy life be a Tower of fortitude in temptations. Resist the diuel and he will flie from you. Behaue yourselues manfully, and your harts will be strengthened, all you who can fight in our Lord.

Iac. 4
Psal.
30.

A

A man doth most profit, where he gaines most ouer himself.

LEARNE TO PRAY;
and meditate.

The offices of the Angels towards men.

CHAPTER I.

THE Angel-guardian receaues vs into his custody, when we are first borne. Our good God seemes to giue vs to vnderstād & see, as it were, painted forth by the Archangel Raphael, the chiefe benefits, which Angels conferre vpon men. He leadd Tobias the yonger, and brought him back safe to his parents. This most faithfull familiaritie betweene the Angel and Tobias was thus first begunne. *Tobias going forth found a beautiefull yong man, as it were prepared, and readie to walke.* An infant doth scarcely come forth of his mother's wombe, but beholde an Angel is

Tob. 5.

I 4   pre-

present with him, whome God, assigned from all eternitie to be his Guardian. A worthie witnesse whereof, is S. Hierome saying : Great is the dignity of soules, since euerie one hath from his first natiuitie, an Angel, ordained by God to take charge of him: here is that beautiefull yonge man, a companion to vs in our pilgrimage. S. Mathew describing the splendour and beauty of one of these yong men saith. *His aspect shined like lightning, and had his garment white like snow.* This yong man stands prepared and readie to walke, and to leade one the way to heauen.

Cap.18 in Math.

Mat.8 cap.28

CHAPTER II.

T HE Angel obligeth his faith & carefull custodie vnto vs, by the salutation of Tobias the elder saying: *Ioy be alwaies to thee.* This certainly is the Angel-guardian's wish ; of this hath he care, and this doth he take to hart, that we may neuer be but ioyfull, euen when teares flow from our

eyes,

eyes, when griefe or sorrow is seated in our countenance, yea and amongst the greatest torments. *Whatsoever happens to a sad man, will not make him sorrowfull.* Yea though the heauens should fall, yet will the ruines thereof not dismay him. Dost thou heare, Tobias? *Let ioy be alwaies to thee,* though thy wife vexe thee, thy kinsfolkes deride thee; yet *Let ioy be euer to thee.* S. Paul commends the same to the Thessalonians: *Reioyce yee alwaies.* But what cause haue we of ioy? especially of continuall ioy? The Angel obligeth his faith to thee saying: *I will leade and bring thee back.* This is the true cause of sincere ioy: the Angel obligeth himself vnder his hand and seale, *to be alwaies our conductour,* to performe to vs the office of a faithfull companion. Let vs trust to his promise; for he will not deceaue vs. He will leade vs, so we do not wrestle nor resist; he wil bring vs back, so we be earnest to follow him.

Prou. 22.

Thess 4

I 5 CHAPT.

CHAPTER III.

THis, which is aboue mentioned, may be of comfort to vs, feing that both while we enioy this life, or are departing out of it, we want continuall confolation. There is neuer wanting what to fuffer, euerie day and houre (nay I may fay euerie moment) there is a worme, which gnawes, pulles vp, and fometimes deuoures both the flower, and fubftance of all our ioy and contentment. Yea though all things be peaceable and fauourable to vs, and that the vniuerfall world be gouerned to our côtentment, the verie feare alone of loofing it, is a fufficient motiue to vexe and trouble our felicitie. And thus we are neuer wholy deliuered from euill; either we are bodily fick, or grieued in our mindes. This is the law and neceffitie of our life; to the which is annexed all kinde of griefe. The Angels therefore diftille downe into vs the perpetuall dew of comfort, and

fay

say *Haue courage ; now is the time at hand* , when you shall be cured and freed from all this , by *Almightie God* : despaire not of your saluation ; it is at hand; it wilbe perfected by one onely expiring, and you shall possesse ALL ETERNITIE amongst the Blessed. But yet the Angel doth not alwaies stop and drie vp teares, but sometimes procures them, as he did to the refractarie people of Israel, to whome he obiected their rebellious obstinacie; yet true it is , that these heauenly Priests are alwaies more ready to comfort & exhort , then to threaten; and they euer inspire vs , and crie out thus. *Take courage : for now is the time at hand, when God will cure you of all diseases and afflictions.*

CHAPTER IIII.

THE Angel discouereth the drift of the diuell heere , and saith to Tobias : *I will manifest them to thee , with whome the diuel can preuaile.* How manie admonitions do we daily receaue from this our beſt tutour? how often doth he ſweetely warne vs? Take heede of this, and, omitt the other; fly thence, & haſten from Cupid's darts. Fly, fly, thence doth danger and thence doth deſtruction grow to hang ouer thy head; ſtrengthen thyſelf on the ſide, where thou art weakeſt, approche not hither; a ſnake lurkes here, touch not this ſtone, a Scorpion lyes hiddē vnder it; caſt away this, which thou ſeekeſt, it is not gold, but durt; it is not light but ſmoke; walke here carefully, leaſt thou fall into ſome trappe; forſake this pleaſure; for it will be grieuouſly puniſhed. Thus doth he hundreds and thouſands of times admonish vs; and manie hundreds and thouſands of times do we afforde but deafe eares to his warnings, wretches that we are; we ſhall ſuffer for this affeſted deafneſſe, we ſhall not be heard, when we be readie to periſh, who refuſed to heare him ſo often warning vs, that we might not periſh.

CHAPTER

CHAPTER V.

HE defends from the assault of the diuell. Tobias cried out that a huge whale was at hand to deuoure him; to whome the Angel speaking saide: *Take hold by his gilis, and draw him to thee.* Tobias did so tremble at the sight and approch of this huge sea-monster, that he thought himself al readie deuoured by him; but the Angel so freed him of feare, and so animated him by his speach against the whale, that he, who had horrour to see the whale, did presently not feare to touch him. The Apostle S. Iames most prudētly saith: *Resist the diuell, and he will flie from you.* The diuel is like a crocodile, which, as they say, being fled from, and not seene followes and killes; but being followed & seene, flies and dies. Therefore, my Tobias, take holde of the gylls of the whale; Resist the diuell, & oppose thyself stoutly against him, and thou shalt putt this fearefull

Iac. 4.

croco-

crocodile to flight; but otherwise if thou seeke not to preuent him, thou must looke for the same from him. Hearken to thy companion and thy assistant Angel; if thou fight assisted by him, thou shalt surely ouercome. Neither did he only free Tobias from the whale, but also kept him vnhurt, from the diuell. *Then did the Angel Raphael apprehend the diuel, and sent him back to the higher Egipt.* So doth this our best Tutour hinder the diuel, that we may not receaue more hurt from him then from a dog tyed in chaines, which may barke, but cannot bite, vnlesse one come neere to him.

CHAPTER VI.

AS the Angels holde vs for their bretheren, so do they tenderly loue vs. *O brother*, said the Angel to Tobias, *if it please thee, let vs proceede.* And another Angel, by a probable coniecture congratulates with vs in the Apocalips: *Now*, saith he, *saluation is obtained, since the accuser of our*

bretheren

Apoc. 12.

Apoc. 12.

bretheren is cast downe. Obſerue, O
Pilgrim, the courteous ſpeeches of
thy brother : *Therefore if it pleaſe thee,
let vs proccede.* He deſires thee to walke along with him towards that heauenly country , and to accompany
thy deſire thereto. What trauelier
caſteth not his eie to the ende of his
iourny ? and though his corporall eie
cannot ſee it, yet his minde is bent
that way ; and when he ſees it neere,
his hart leapes for ioy ; his eies haſten thither, where his feete ſtriue to
ſtande. So , O brother , L E T V S
P R O C E E D E ; and let our minde be
there , where in ſhort time we hope
our bodies will follow. Let vs loue
our owne reſt and quiett ; but that
reſt only , which , when all tumults
ſhall be ended, we ſhall enioy in heauen.

CHAPTER VII.

THE Angel Guardian defendeth
his charge from all dangers.
Tobias being returned , related

to his father, how many benefits that
holy man (for so he called him) had
bestowed vpon him, from how many
dangers he had defended him. For,
saith he, he silenced and put to flight
the diuell; yea he deliuered and freed
me from being deuoured by a fish.
How assured friends are those heauenly Princes to vs? who is it, that
hath not found it often in most difficult and vncertaine things. How
often had we broken our armes,
and legs, nay our neckes, had we
bene depriued of the help of these
our friends. Yf we cast vp the accompt right, we shall perceaue, that
euery where is perill of shipwrack:
as manie pores as we haue in our
bodies, so many doores there are,
by which death on a sudden may
creepe in we neither sweate nor
coole without danger; we neither
sitt downe to the table, nor go to
bed in securitie, meate killes a glutton, and famine the hungrie; warre
deuoures this man, and perhaps
the ruine and fall of his owne

house,

houfe , buries another. On horfe-
back , vpon the fea , in woods or
in plaines , at home or abroad, dangers are incident to vs ; and vnder
each ftone , lies a fcorpion ; But
our Angels-guardian watch in our
behalues.   Thefe defended Ionas in
the whales bellie , S. Paul from the
waues of the fea , Daniel in the
denne of lions , Moifes in his cradle , Iudith in the enemies camp;
and thefe knew well how to preferue the three Hebrew yong men
in midft of flames ; without the
help of thefe , we our-felues had a
hundred times perifhed ; of which
I myfelf am a witneffe ; For hauing
neuer learned to flie , yet falling
headlong from the top of a high
paire of ftaires downe to the ground,
and being caft headlong, the coche
ouerturning, from the top of a mountaine into the riuer Danaw , I efcaped
at both times without anie hurt ,
To fay nothing of other dangers,
euen from thefe I could neuer haue
bene freed without the help of the

Angels.

Angels. And I can witnesse, that I haue hundreds of times, euidently perceaued their present help. And I belieue it also to be most true, and manifest, by others confessions. Certainly we haue the Angels our intire friends, and then most present and carefull, when the greatest dangers assault vs.

CHAPTER VIII.

Tob. 5.

THEY teach others to do well. Raphael gaue Tobias the gall, which he had drawen out of the fish, and saide: *Annoint his eies with this gall of the fish which thou carriest with thee, and know thou, that instantly his eies shall be opened; and thy father shall see the light of heauen.* The Angel had not only obtained for his Tobias money from Gabel, from Raguel his daughter, and all his inheritance, but also taught him an art, how to restore his father's sight. And most truly saith Nazianzen : Man hath nothing in him so like to God, as to do good to

others

others. We all know, that no man is borne for himself alone, and that we are not to liue only for ourselues; whereof the most Wise-man doth admonish vs saying : *Let thy fountaines be brought forth , and in the streetes diuide thy waters* And that Samaritan, who formerly had bene a woman of no good fame, yet when she had receaued of Christ better lawes and rules , how to liue , she instantly brought her neighbours to heare the same sermons and instructions. It is worthy of great praise to be able to boast with the Wise-man : *Looke vpon me, and view me; for I haue not laboured for myself alone.* No man doth a good turne with out a rewarde, though it be to the most vngratefull ; for by how much the lesse pay or praise he receaues from man, so much the more rewarde he may expect from God. Let vs learne of Angels to do well, to the ende we may become Angels.

Pro. 5.

Iob. 4.

Eccle. 33.

CHA-

CHAPTER IX.

THE Angel-guardian inciteth to all kinde of vertue. The Angel Raphael recommends the defire of praying, fafting, and almes-deedes; not as a marchant fetts forth his wares, but he propounds it fo, as that it may be knowen by the profit, which it affordes faying : *Prayer, fafting and almes deedes are more profitable then to hoarde vp goulden treaſures; for almes-deedes free from death and purge finne, and canſe vs to finde mercie and eternall life ; but they that commit iniquitie and finne, are enemies to their owne foules.* The Angel could not poſſibly, in a leſſe volume, teach vs all vertue. Theſe three vertues include all good actions : Prayer reſtores vs to God ; Fafting caufeth vs to become ourfelues; and Almes-deedes make the poore, who are the friends of God, to become our friends. Prayer is like an eagle, which carieth the minde vp to God;

Tob.
12.

but

but without the two wings of fasting and almes-deedes, or of temperance and mercy, she in vaine striues to rise, but falles downe before she can ascend. To pray much, and not to refraine from gluttony, and to deny to giue to the poore, is as friuolous as to wash a black More. *Prayer is good, so that it be accompanied with fasting and almes-deedes.* Franckencense vnlesse it be laide on hote coles, neither perfumes nor striues to ascend; euen so doth Prayer freeze, which abstinence and due frugality, which mercy and pious liberality doth not commend and adorne.

CHAPTER X.

TOBIAS gathered togeather all sorts of good; and recounting to his father in order, how many benefits he had receaued of his cōpanion, & to the ende that he might compendiously lay many things before him, he saide; We *are replenished by him with all good.* So might Cornelius

Tob.12
Act.10

say

fay of his Angel, who laide open to
him the way to his faith , and vnto
heauen by a moſt familiar diſcourſe:
he hath bene replenished by him with all
good. So may each of vs ingenuouſly
& truly confeſſe of our Angel-guardian : *I am replenished by him , with all*
good. For what euill do theſe heauenly Courtiers teach vs , theſe moſt
chaſt pure flames , which both by
example and admonitions do day
and night beate into vs this one
thing : *Loue God ; for all things elſe are*
not to be loued , but for God. O man, loue thy Creatour , who hath loued
thee ſo much to his owne paine and
coſt. Let vs then harken to theſe our
moſt wiſe teachers ; *we shall be reple-*
nished by them with all good. What can
we deſire , which by them we ſhall
not obtaine ? do we ſeeke friends?
we cannot finde any more faithfull.
Do we want counſellers ? they are
moſt vnderſtanding , and ſee all
things. Do we deſire Aduocats? theſe
are moſt eloquent. Do we deſire
champions ? Angels are moſt powerfull.

ful. Do we wilh for benefactours? we can neuer haue any more liberal then thefe, By them we fhall be repleniſhed with all good.

CHAPTER XI.

THE Angel-guardian defends his charge in deaths laſt combat. Raphael bidding fare well to his Tobias faide: *It is now time to returne to him, who fent me: Peace be with you, and do not feare.* There is no doubt, that the Angels were prefent with poore Lazarus, who had no other phiſitians nor chirurgeons, then dogs: The Angels were they, who carried him to our good father Abraham's bofome, as Saint Luke witneſſeth. *That poore man died, and was carried by the Angels into Abraham's bofome.* We neuer want the Angels help, when death aſſaults vs. Then E T E R-N I T Y lies open before our eies; then doth a colde fweat, the wounds of a fearefull confcience, and all forts of ſtraites and miferies poſſeſſe & preſſe

Tob
12.

Luc
16.

vs; thē doth the diuell, who is furious
and mad, affault vs, leauing no kinde
of wickedneffe vnattempted, to trie,
whether in that laft houre he may
fubdue our foule. For being affured,
that all the reft of ones life he could
hope for no victorie, leaft now all his
former attempts might be fruftrated,
in that houre he tries all conclufions,
and is moft vigilant to finde occafion
either to fright or deceaue vs. But haue courage and a quiet minde, O yee,
who are dying, be you yong or olde;
for your defender and protectour is
not abfent; you fhall not be ouercome, if you defire to be defended.
Thoufands of wolues may come
about vs, but they fhall not bite vs,
being protected by this Paftour. Many millions of diuels may affault vs;
but one Angel can fufficiētly defend
vs. Looke, O thou man, whither this
Champion of thine, pointes his fingar: it is at Chrift crucified; thither let
thy eies, thither let thy fighes & grones euer tend. Here learne patience,
hither ftriue & ftirre vp thy felf with

all

all truit and confidence; to this thy Lord, dead for thee vpon the Crosse, offer thyself with all submission ; say hundreds of times, and againe repeate them by millions of times, *O Lord, thy will be done; thy will be done; let it be done, let it be done.* I am ready to liue, to languish or to dye; as thou wilt. True it is , my sinnes trouble me; but thy precious bloud comforts and restores me; as thou wilt, sweet IESVS, so let it be done. Reflect continually vpon these things, and committ thyself to the Angels, and to the king of Angels. He can hardly perish, who tends by these waies to ETERNITIE.

CHAPTER XII.

THE Angel-guardian doth also serue , and help his charge after his death. It is very probable, that the Angels sometimes afforde comfort to those, whome the purging flames of Purgatory prepare for heauen; And it is affirmed by diuine testimony, that in the last day of Iudgement, the

K   Angels

Angels ſhall gather euery man's duſt & aſhes togeather, ſo that euery Angel ſhall gather againe togeather the bones and aſhes of thoſe men's bodies, whereof formerly in this life he had care. And ſo will they at laſt, awake vs out of our long ſleepe, either to the eternall feaſts & nuptialls of Paradiſe, or to the euerlaſting torments of hell-fire. *God himſelf, at the voice of an Archangell will deſcende from heauen.* One and the ſame will be the voice of all the Angels, to the friendes of the ſupreme Iudge. *Bleſſe yee the God of heauen before all the liuing, who* are preſent and to be iudged; *confeſſe yee to him; becauſe he hath ſhewed you his mercy.*

THE VIII. HOVRE.

LEARNE TO DIE;
AND MEDITATE.

What would I, that I had donne and suf-
fered in the former yeares of my age
paſt, if death were now at hand? Whe-
refore then do I refuſe to do, and ſuffer
the like now?

LEARNE TO LIVE.

Let thy life be a reflexion vpon thy ende.
And be you prepared, becauſe in the
houre, which you thinke leaſt, the Sonne
of man will come. It is the moſt power-
full and ſoueraigne medecine againſt all
vice, continually to beare in minde ones
death. What thou ſhalt then do or haue
neede of, will preſently occurre to thee,
when thou reflecteſt vpon death.

LEARNE TO PRAY.

The dutifull offices of Angels towards Chriſt.

CHAPTER I.

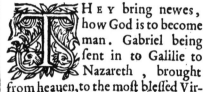

THEY bring newes, how God is to become man. Gabriel being ſent in to Galilie to Nazareth , brought from heauen, to the moſt bleſſed Virgin this Salutation : ALL HAILE, &c. He pronounced her to be full of grace, he explicated the manner, how God ſhould be conceaued in her wombe : he foretolde the name and euerlaſting kingdome of her ſonne, who was to be borne; he vnfolded vnto her the fruitfulneſſe of her coſen Elizabeth. *Bleſſed are they who haue cleane harts: For they ſhall ſee God.*

Luc I.

CHA-

CHAPTER II.

THEY diuulge the birth of Chriſt.
There was neuer ſeene nor heard
a greater ioy amongſt the Angels in
this our world, then when their king
was borne in it; at other times one
alone or two at moſt, haue ſhewed
themſelues; but then a whole army
of them was both ſeene and heard
ſinging, this ſong of peace. *Glorie be* Lu: 2.
to God in the higheſt, and peace in earth to
men of good will. And they did alſo
call to their company and conuerſa-
tion poore ſhepheards. Neither were
they aſhamed of the meane cottage,
wherein their king lay, nor of the
rags, wherein he was wrapt. *Bleſſed*
are the poore in ſpirit; for theirs is the king-
dome of heauen.

CHAPTER III.

THEY prepare for the flight of
Chriſt into Egipt. You would
haue ſaid, that the Angels were too

solicitous and carefull of this diuine infant; for they did not only forbid the three kings, which came out of the East, to receaue, in their returne, king Herod's entertainemēt, but they did also defend this heauenly child, which Herod had already resolued to putt to the sword; and furthermore the Angel admonishing Ioseph to fly, said: *Take the childe and his mother, and fly into Egipt, and there stay, till I speake to thee againe.* This was as much as if the Angel had openly said: Indeede we are carefull of our king; O Ioseph; let it not be troublesome to thee, to change thy country-soile for banishment. For thou carriest the Treasure of both worlds with thee; but yet least thou shouldst thinke thy stay to be too long in Egipt, we will warne thee againe, when it shall be time. For this our king shall not wast his daies in Egipt. And so Herode being dead, the Angel returned, and brought newes, that the enemies of the child were dead; and opened to them the way to the land of Israël.

Mat 2.

O blessed are they, that suffer persecution for iustice sake; for their's is the kingdome of heauen.

CHAPTER IV.

THEY brought suftenance to Christ being hungrie. After our LORD's long fasting, and after so many daies past without meate in the desert, after the triple conflict of our Captaine with the diuel, and after the three victories gained, and the enemie's retreate, these cup-bearers, and as it were banket-makers of God came to couer a table before their Lord. O how much rather would I feede vpō the very crummes, which fall from this table, how spare soeuer they might be, then be partaker of the greatest and plentiefullest feasts of Herōd or Tiberius, with all their iollity and wealth. *O blessed are they, who hunger and thirst after Iustice; for they shall be satisfied.*

CHA-

CHAPTER V.

THEY comforted Chrilt, when he was fad, & praying in the gardin. For when our LORD at mount Oliuet, euen before his Croſſe and whippes, was all ouerbathed with a ſweat of bloud, ſad, and fearefull, and onely not quite dead, but was wreſtling betweene his prayers and the agonie of death; and, as it were; by a funerall in his life, caſt himſelf vpon the ground, ouerwhelmed with extreme griefes and anguiſhes, *an Angel from heauen*, ſaith S. Luke, *appeared to him and comforted him*, by whome he was made, and preſerued in Beatitude to all eternity. O what a ſpectacle it was to beholde the Lord of heauen caſt vpon the ground, and, as it were fainting, and his forces leauing him, pale, and ſweating out his owne bloud, oppreſſed with grief, & ready now to dye. *Bleſſed are they, who grieue; for they ſhall be comforted.*

CHAPTER VI.

THEY denounce the newes of Chrift's refurrection. Whilft the king of heauen was hanging vpon the Croffe yet aliue, the Angels abfent, as it were, through griefe, refufed to be feene amongft thofe impious murtherers, vpon the wicked earth. Neither was it a wonder; for the ftones themfelues fighed, the earth trembled, the heauens prepared his funeralls, the ftarres were darkened, lamenting his death; & the funne it felf, did, as it were, turne away his face, afhamed of fo great a wickednefse; and therefore as it were, couered it felf with a vaile; for which caufe, as was fitt, the Angels were alfo fad; but whē Chrift reuiued, laying afide their mourning garments, they take fuch as are white and fplendide. They tell, how Iefus of Nazareth being crucifyed, was returned to life; they fhew his fyndon, and the linnen, wherein he had bene wound; they

point at the place, in which he lay,
who was reuiued; they forbid all feare, they commaunde that this ioyfull
message be related to his disciples, and
that they go back into Galilie ; And
those Angels, who before were full
of sorrow, were now become full of
dutiefull ioy. *O blessed are the meeke; for*
they shall possesse the Land.

CHAPTER VII.

THEY accompany Christ ascending into heauen. This our
LORD's iourny into heauen, was
admirable. The Apostles were the
first, who saw that a man was able to
flie through the aire; and whilst they
most attentiuely beheld this wonderfull ascension into heauen, a
clowde coming downe like a Prince-
ly pauillion or throne, tooke vp their
Lord, and carried him from the eyes
of the beholders. *Beholde two men stood*
by them, all in white, and said: O you men
of Galilie; why stand you looking into hea-
uen? this IESVS, *who is taken from you*

A&t. 1.

will

will thus returne , as you now see him going into heauen. Behold, againe here are two Angels, and consider the rest are all busie at the arriuall of their king. These are present in their ioyfull and festiuall garments , ready to accompany the Triumph of their LORD , and withall , they foretell his returne to his Tribunal-seate of Iudgement. *Blessed are the peace-makers ; for they shall be called the Sonnes of God.*

CHAPTER VIII.

THEY will also follow Christ coming to his iudgement-seate. There is nothing more certain then the coming of this Iudge; for he himself foretells vs this : *when the sonne of man shall come in his Maiesty , and all the Angels with him, then will he sitt in the throne of his greatnesse.* There will therefore be none of the Angels absent. Who will not accompany Christ, *and all the Angels with him.* They will all be present ; and as it were

Mat. 25.

appeare

appeare like his Courtlie traine ; and
it is a very probable coniecture, that
the Angels will shew themselues to
the sight of all, in the forme of bodies, farre more excellent then humane, both for dignity and shape. For
seing that this sentence of Iudgement, is to be passed with all this pre-
paration, and with the greatest glory;
it is conuenient, that the Assistants
and ministers of this Iudge do shew
such splendour and brightnesse in
their habits, that it may seeme in the
eies of the beholders to encrease the
maiesty of the Iudgement ; especially
since it is certain, that the Angels are
to vse trumpetts, as Franc. Suares af-
firmeth;and that they are to carry the
standard of the Crosse before their
Lord it is very credible, that they will
performe these duties in assumed bodies. *Blessed are the mercifull ; for they
shall obtaine mercy.*

Tom.2.
disp.57
sect.8.

THE IX. HOVRE.

LEARNE TO DIE;
AND MEDITATE:

*How little in the houre of death, shall
I esteeme all the delights and pleasures of the world, which will then be
to me of no value? Why do I then
now, so much respect, and looke after
them?*

LEARNE TO LIVE.

Let thy life be a continuall dying.
Mortifie your members here vpon earth.
He is to be esteemed to leade an excellēt
life, who daily more and more dies to
his vices, and to himself.

Coloss.
8.

LEARNE TO PRAY,
AND CONSIDER.

Angels and men compared togeather.

1. DIFFERENCE.

AN Angel, heas a child in a Prin-celie palace, is borne and bred vp like a king to be the true inheri-tour of the kingdome. He neuer fin-ned, nor euer had a parent, that of-fended. A man, is the child of *wrath*; and alas of what an ignoble and vn-worthie originall doth he come? Nor can he obtaine the fauour of Almightie God, and kingdome of heauen, but by meanes of inceffant labours, paines, combats, and mife-ries; which if they be not alfo crow-ned by making a good end, all that hath bene done or fuffered before, will fall out to be in vaine. For which caufe, men are faid to obtaine and enioy the kingdome of heauen as

Al-

Almightie God's soldiers, but the
Angels, as his sonnes.

2. DIFFERENCE.

AN Angel doth with one onely
sight, penetrate and see all
things, we gather one thing from
another; neither do we discourse,
without wearinesse, and delayes; and
our minde and vnderstanding is of so
litle capacitie, that if there be anie
thing neuer so litle high & hard to
be vnderstood, it must be distilled into vs, drop by drop. The earth compared to the heauens, is but a point; &
a man paralelled with a Seraphin,
seemes but a litle ant. The most learned Diuines, in comparison of the
lowest Angel, are but like stamering
children, ignorant of their Alphabet.
Most truly saith the Wise-man: *All*   Eccl. 1.
things are found so difficult and hard, that
man cannot explicate them. By exteriour
meanes we seeke after, & diue into
many things; & yet our thoughts cannot penetrate into those, which euen

daily

daily occurre to our eies. Wretched men, that we are, we cannot comprehend the lowest things; and how shall we then be able to vnderstand the secrets of heauen? we deceaue our selues through a smooth and sweet kinde of blindenesse, and we often adore most vaine coniectures and ignorances, as though they were wonderfull sciences. But our knowledge is nothing, vnlesse we know, that we are ignorant of most things.

3. DIFFERENCE.

ALAS; how vnlike is the place, which men and Angels inhabite. They dwell in a high Tower, free from all enemies, and are on all sides secure: But we, being bannished out of Paradise, liue in a base obscure village, or in a poore smokie cottage; yet do we boast of our lineage and ancesters & of our territories and palaces. God hath so fastned the soule to the bodie, that she alwaies carrieth her prison with her; and is miserably

chai-

chained in it; but an Angel acts freely, and with great celeritie comes
downe from heauen to earth, returnes thither, and passes which way he
will. Angels were endued by God
their Creatour, with the Elder No-
bilitie, and were created six daies before man, whose half is meere durt, at
which we may blush. An Angel is
free from all corruption, payes no
tribut to death; but man being
corruption itself, doth by litle and
litle approach to it; and at length becomes a dead carcasse, and is cast out;
neither can anie one resist, but he
shall be made a feast for wormes.
Onely this hope comforteth vs, that
we shall be such as the Angels are now;
and this mortall creature shall put on im-
mortalitie.   1.Cor.
15.

4. DIFFERENCE.

THE will of an Angel is most efficacious, the memorie most re-
tentiue, the iudgement, and election
of things, immutable. But we are

more

more children then infants themselues; we iudge ill; and oftentimes
choose worse; we thinke it often gaine, to chãge golde for aples; & things
of price, for trifles. We preferre humane things before diuine; fading
things before eternall; and thinke it
an easie losse to be depriued of the
one, to enioy the other. Our WILL

Prou.
13.
is most inconstant. *The slothfull man
will, and will not.* Our memorie, we
may say, is nothing, and most slip-
perie in those things, which ought
to be retained. How often are we
scarcely parted out of the holie seate
of Confession, when we fall againe
into the sinnes, which euen now we
renounced; and in short time like
drunkards, we fall into the same offences, which we had bewailed before, when we were sober and were our
selues; and all this we do, by a most
damnable forgetfulnes. For this cau-

Homil
3. ad
pop.
se S. Chrisostome did not once, but
many times rebuke his Auditorie
with sharp words. There were often
earth-quakes at Antioch; and the in-

habitants

habitants feemed to be moued there-
with in their harts, and bent to penance. But how long did this amendment of their manners laft? no longer almoft then their earth-quakes.
For in few daies after, all things va-
nifhed, and were buried in obliuion,
and againe (as before) euerie one
haftened to that, which was forbidden. So do we liue here, and this is
the fault of our memorie; that now
we grieue for our finnes; but by and
by we returne with iolity to them a-
gaine, and fo doth a wicked obliuion
deftroy a WILL, which is dull and
flothfull of itfelf in doing good. To
accufe a man's feif, and notwithftan-
ding not to amende, is to incite God
to lay punifhment vpon vs.

5. DIFFERENCE.

ALTHOVGH we ourfelues do fo
much regarde our owne formes
and fhapes, and do not ftick to defire
to be honoured like men defcended

from

from heauen , or rather like Gods,
and Goddesses on earth, yet alas, how
flight a feuer makes our ruddie cheekes wanne and pale ? sicknesse and
death extinguishes the beautie of the
countenance , depriues the lips of
their purple , the cheekes of their
read ; so that they defile and staine the
comeliest countenance with duskie
and wanne coulours ; & that in such
sort, as not onely others , but euen
our verie selues looking in some
glasse, are forced to confesse our ignorance, and aske ourselues, who we
are. What, I pray you, is now become of that faire Adonis, or beautifull
Helene ? Humane beautie is not onely fraile and fading , but also of short
continuance ; and is farre from ap-
proaching to that of the Angels.
Summe vp all humane comelinesse
togeather , and let it all frame but
one, yet will not that be worthie to
be paralelled with the leaft of the
Angels. True it is that copper gli-
sters ; but of how litle a price and
worth is it in comparifon of golde ?

yet

yet is there a greater difparitie
betweene the beautie of Angels and
men, then betweene gold & copper.
Gulielmus Baldezanus reports, that
Francifca Romana, a woman of
wonderfull modeftie and fanctitie,
had two Angel-guardians, which fhe
often faw, and their garments were
white, and partly inclining to the
coulour of the heauens, their armes
were placed vpon their breaft in forme of a croffe, their eyes ftill lifted vp
towards heauen, their haire fhining
like gold; their countenance moft
bright and refplendent with a comely maiefty, fuch as befitteth Angels.
Yf anie fhape could draw neere to
that of Almighty God, it would be
that of Angels. Ezechiel fpeaking of
Lucifer faith : *Thou haft bene the feale*   *cap.28*
of the likeneffe of God, full of wifedome
and perfect beautie; and thou haft bene in
the delights of the Paradife of God. From
hence it will appeare, that all the
beautie and comelineffe of men is but
meere deformitie in refpect of that
of the Angels.

6. DIFFERENCE.

THeir force and ſtrength is ſuch, as that they are like giants, and we as weake dwarfes and pigmies. A wiſe man is ſaid to rule the ſtarres; but alas how weake and remote a dominion is this. Angels giue lawes to the ſtarres, and celeſtiall orbes, and are able, as S. Thomas of Aquin ſaith, to do wonders; as namely with great facilitie to produce windes, raines, tempeſts, darkneſſe, earth-quakes, and the like in a moment; to ſtay the courſe of riuers and fountains, to ouer-whelme mountains, to extinguiſh ſtarres, to illuminate hell, to caſt downe the firmament, yea and they are able (as we may ſay) with one litle fingar to tranſport great parts of elements, if not whole elements themſelues from one place to another, to cure or kill beaſts or men, to cauſe dearth or plentie; to quench fires without water, to teach lions to

be

be tame , to forme to themselues
in one moment most beautifull bo-
dilie shapes , and as suddenly to dis-
solue them into aire ; Angels haue
keyes to all lockes; all these things
aforesaid they can performe with
incredible celeritie. One onely Angel hath alreadie so manie thousand
yeares, and yet doth with ease rowle
the highest heauen about, with that
continuall and swift whirling, that
the sunne in one onely houre, runnes
260000. German miles; and this is
the course of the highest heauen,
which also with proportionable
swiftnesse doth turne and carrie the
rest of the planets and starres about
with it : and this incredible swiftnesse , one onely Angel giues vnto
it. How stronge must this arme
be , which thus turnes about this
immense bodie ? and what now _Esay.5_
is our force or power ? Esay saith:
Woe bee to you , whoe are powerfull
in drinking wine , and are stronge
men in making one another drunke.
This is humane strength and

power, to powre downe wine plen-
tifully out of the veſſell into the bellie; in all things elſe, we are ſo weake,
Iob 18 that Iob ſaith: *Thou ſheweſt thy power
againſt a leafe, which the winde hath ſha-
ken; and then pourſueſt a withered ſtraw.*

7. DIFFERENCE.

WHerefore do wee then being
but Pigmies, and of no force
& in reſpect of Angels like litle ants,
boaſt of our power, of our genealo-
gie and ſtock? it is a meere madneſſe
and vanitie. Let vs therefore, I pray
you, giue vp our foiles, and not pre-
ſume to arrogate to ourſelues ſo neere
affinitie with Angels; nor let vs ſhew
our ſelues ſuch as thoſe, of whome
Pſal 8 the Royall Prophet Dauid ſpeaketh;
who apply theſe words; *Thou haſt
diminiſhed him but a little leſſe then Angels;* to mankinde in generall. But
they are deceaued; that praiſe is nothing to vs; it is proper to Chriſt, as
Hebr. S. Paul doth well affirme ſaying: *He,*
2. *whome we ſee a little leſſe then Angels, is*

IESVS,

IESVS, *who for his death and bitter paf-*
fion is crowned with honour and glory.
But alas, we are far inferiour to Angels and yet notwithstanding they
serue vs with all fidelity, as if we
were their Lords and maisters. The
Angels white garments betoken
peace and ioy; but a sword, a hel-
mett, a buckler, and a coat of male
do rather befitt vs, according to holy
Iob : *The life of man is a warrefare*   Iob 2.
vpon earth. We are daily to stand in
battle array ; daily we receaue the
darts of temptation; and we are not
one moment free from combat.
The Angels continually enioy all
delights, which Poëtically haue bene attributed to Heathen Gods, and
are neuer to be depriued of their
ioyes. But of our dainty fare and
bankets holy Dauid sighing spea-
kes thus : *Thou haft fed vs with the*   Pfal.
bread of teares, and thou haft giuen vs   70.
to drinke in teares by meafure. And
Esaias faith : *Our Lord will giue you*   Efa.
a litle portion of bread and fcarcitie of   10.
water. Now we may fee, what an

extreme difproportion there is bet-
wixt Angels and vs. Here refts one
only comfort , that hereafter in
many things we fhall be like them.
It is the Oracle of Truth , which
faith it : *In the refurrection they nei-*

Mat.
12.

ther marry nor are married ; but are li-
ke the Angels of God in heauen.

THE X. HOVRE.

LEARNE TO DIE;
and meditate.

*Whome shall I haue moſt to be my frinds,
and whome to be mine enemies in the
houre of death? The Angels certainly,
and the diuels. Why therefore do not I
now giue eare, and yeilde my conſent
and obedience to thoſe my friends? and
with all my power reſiſt the diuels, who
are mine enemies?*

LEARNE TO LIVE.

*LET THY LIFE BE A DESIRE
TO ATTAINE TO THE HEA-
VENLY COVNTRY. O how delight-
ful are thy tabernacles, O Lord of vertue! my ſoule doth couet, and faint with
deſire, within the gate of our Lord.
Alas, how baſe ſeemes the earth to him,
who ſetts his minde vpon heauen? A
ſoule meditating ſtill vpon God & hea-*

Pſal. 83.

uen,

neu, esteemes all afflictions to be quiet-
nesse and rest.

LEARNE TO PRAY;
and consider.

What Angels do hate in man;
what they admire and
loue in him.

CHAPTER I.

WHATSOEVER hath the least
fauour of vice, that they hate;
but especially in vices, HEATE,
SMOKE and STENCH; the *heate of*
anger and *enuie* ; the *smoke of Pride;*
and the stench of Luxurie. The heate of
anger is sometimes so great, that as
Saint Chrisostome saith, *Anger strikes*
the soule like a thunderbolt, which, if she
once obey, is presently made mad. An angry man's speach is alwaies crimi-
nall, and he vtteres nothing but venime. An angry man, saith the same,

Golden-

Golden-mouth Chrisoſtome, is full
of the diuel ; and vttereth things as
well not to be ſpoken,as others ; and
oftentimes ſayth ſuch things, as af-
terwards may coſt him his life. An
angry perſon hath alwaies an iron in
the fire ; and if he be but toucht by a
word,he preſently breakes forth,and
ſtormes. Seneca ſpeaketh of Anger
with great affirmation, that no Plague coſts man ſo much as it doth,nor
is more peſtiferous to him. Of the ſame minde was holy Iob ſaying : *An-*
ger kills a foolish man ; and enuy killes a
litle or weake one. Anger is a furious
and a raging beaſt, whoſe clawes are
of iron, and his iawes full of firy venime. Wherefore Saint Auguſtin
doth earneſtly, wiſh his diſciples
thus : *O moſt louing Bretheren ; let vs not*
bring vpon ourſelues ſo great a miſchief ; it
is a diſeaſe to our ſoules, and an aliena-
tion of them from God, a beginning of
warres, a heape of calamities, and a
moſt wicked diuell. Saint Paul ſaith:
Let all bitterneſſe of anger, and indi-
gnation, be taken from you, and be you

Iob ;

Eph:
4.

benigne and peaceable one with another.

Prou.
26.
For as it is said in the Prouerbs : *Euen as wood and coales are apt to take fire, so is an angry man ready to stirre vp dissention.* After this ill heate comes a worse fire ; both which, Angels hate ; and this is E N V I E , which is like a hoate and deadly poison ; for it consumes both the eies and hart of an enuious person. Salomon saith:

Prou.
14.
Enuie consumes the very bones. And they, for the most parte, are the worst of all men , who are ioyfull at others aduersities, rich with others losses, pleased at others calamities , and thinke themselues immortall, by the funeralls of others. But why should we seeke to inflict punishment vpon one another ? and whome should we enuie ? Yf he be good, he is therefore worthy of good things. Yf he be euill, his owne malice is a sufficient thraldome and ruine to him ; and what neede is there then , that he should oftner perish ? Whosoeuer would be free from the plague of malice , let him loue that inheritance , which

the

the number of heires doth not diminifh; and which is one, and the fame
to all, and whole to euery one. The
loue of ETERNITIE is a fufficient
motiue, to ftrangle enuie. Wilt thou
afcend to heauen, thou muft not liue
after that manner. There, do infe-
riours reioice at the happineffe of
thofe, who are aboue them. Neither
do the Angels fuffer the diuels to lay
that plague vpon vs: For they thinke
it faid to them, which is in the Booke of Wifedome : *Neither will I keepe*
company or go a iourny with one, pining
away with enuie; for fuch a man fhall not
be partaker of wifedome. Lay then afide all enuie; for elfe thou haft loft the
Angels for thy friends, and heauen
for thy country.

Sap. 6.

CHAPTER II.

NEither do Angels brooke the
fmoke of PRIDE ; and let vs
not wonder at it, fince king Dauid

could

Pſal.
100.

could not beare with it, as himſelf
teſtified ſaying : *He ſhall not inhabite
my houſe, who behaues himſelf proudely.*
How can we then hope, that the
Angels will befriend our pride? they
hate it in kings; and they haue not
boᴡen with it in their equalls. A
proude beggar, is an vgly monſter.
True it is that Lucifer had that whereof he might eaſily be proude ; but
yet being proude, he cauſed his owne
ruine. But as for vs poore beggars,
that we are, whence ſhould we think
ourſelues great ? what cauſe haue
we to looke ſo big vpon the matter?
we abound in filth and miſeries, and
we conſiſt of durt, vpon which there
is ſett a litle gloſſe or coulour, which
preſently puffes vs vp. We are proude
beggars ; & conſequently vgly mon-
ſters. What can durt & clay boaſt of?
why then doth man grow proude?
whoſe life is but like a ſhip-wrack,
and whoſe being from the beginning
to the ende, is momentary. By pride
we are ſo farre from pleaſing the Angels, as that it makes vs hatefull to

them.

them. Most truly saith S. Augustin:
Euen a rich proud man can hardly be
endured ; and who then will beare
with one, who is poore and proude?
And no man will wonder, that Angels are such enemies to Pride, since
they yet tremble to thinke vpon the
ancient ruine, which came thereby to
their companiõs. Pride made an Angel become a diuel ; & it is the preg-
nant mother of all vice. It hath ouer-
whelmed towers, cõfounded toungs,
ruined Goliath, hangd proud Ha-
man, torne Nicanor in peeces, killed
Antiochus , drowned Pharao , cutt
Senacheribs throat, made lice consu-
me Herode. Pride hath alwaies hitherto cast downe headlong all her
children , and brought them to ruine
and perdition.

CHAPTER III.

ANGELS also cannot endure the
stench of LVXVRIE ; they dis-
daine & abhorre whatsoeuer we cõ-
mitt against Chastitie. they are full

of

of eies, and thofe moft pure. Afmo-
deus and Gabriel agree not well in
one chamber, much leffe in one
breaft. O men, become not like horfes and mules. Raphael difcouered
this fecret to Tobias: *Hearken to me,*
faith he, *and I will shew thee, who they
be, againft whom the diuel can preuaile:
they be thofe, who exclude God from themfelues in their minds, to the ende they may
attend the more to their owne lufts like
horfes and mules; ouer thefe the diuel hath
power.* Angels call thofe who are
men, not beafts, to their friendfhip
and familiarity. The diuine fpoufe of
heauen, is neuer better pleafed, then
when he is placed amongft the white
odoriferous flowers of Chaftity. He
onely admitts into his armes, thofe,
who haue bannifhed the fire of con-
cupifcence from themfelues; he only
loueth chaft and virgin mindes. For
he is the Sonne of a moft pure Virgin. Departe all you, who are impure;
departe hence; for you are hated both
by Angels, and the king of Angels.
Antoninus reports, how an Angel

4.Par.
fum.
Theol.
li.t.c.
6.§.1.

clothed

clothed in humane shape, accompanied an Anchoret vpon the way;they
by chance then passed by a dead carcasse; the Anchoret troubled with
the noisome smell, stopped his nose;
but so did not his companion. By and
by they mett a man richly adorned,
but one, who burned inwardly with
hidden lust , and for the rest most
complete, and he walked gracefully
with a comely pace. In such sort was
he perfumed with sumptuous and
costlie odours , that the winde carried from him such excellent sweet
sents, as would euen haue made a
man wish, (as Catullus did) to be all
nose, to haue enioyed the sweetnesse
thereof. But him did the Angel auoide like a stinking carrion, stopping
his nose , and turning his face from
him. And his companion asking him
the reason, he answeared, that a man
giuen to his lust is like a most corrupted and noisome carrion ; which as
soone as he had saide , he vanished.
ANGELS in fine cannot endure
the STENCH of LVXVRIE.

The

The fire of Concupiscence is farre from thofe, who by chaftity haue dedicated themfelues to Angels. They hate none more then thofe, whome they fee wallowing in the puddle of luft. O yong man, be not a friend to luft; for if thou be, thou fhalt haue all the Angels for thy enemies.

CHAPTER IV.

THERE is yet found fomewhat in vs, which the Angels do much admire. And an Angel expounding this to the Prieft Efdras faid : (although this booke of Efdras be not of fo great authority as the reft are) *The many paines, which we haue fuffered, are now paft ouer; and in the end is shewed the treafure of immortality. Be not thou therefore fo inquifitiue after the number of thofe, who perish. For they knowing that they muft die, did yet make vfe of their liberty, and defpife the Higheft.* This is the great admiration of Angels, that we know, we are not onely to die, but that we hourely die, & yet are we not fenfible of

the

Efdra 8.

the death of our foules:neither do we
abhorre the deftruction thereof, nor
amende our manners. It is no newes,
that a theefe fteale being alone, and
farre from the eye of an officer, efpe-
cially when he conceaues his oportunitie to be fafe; but it were wonderfull that a theefe prefently to be
imprifoned , and to haue fhackells
laide vpon him , fhould notwithftan-
ding, committ theft in the eye of the
Iudge ; this were ftrange and new;
yet fuch there be who at the verie
place of execution and vnder the
gallowes , do laugh and ieaft im-
pioufly : and euen fuch are we, who
haften to death ; and whilft we are
at the point of dying , we audaci-
oufly finne, either by admitting into
our mindes ftolen pleafures and luft,
or by malicious talking of others, or
doing them hurt. Alas we ftãd vpon
the fatall fteps of the ladder , and by
and by fhall be turned off, and yet we
leaue not our follies and wantonne-
neffe , *knowing that we dye* , and yet
conniue and winke at vices , which

liuç

liue in vs. This certainly is worthie
of the wonder and amazement of
Angels.

CHAPTER V.

THere is alſo (at the leaſt, in ſome
of vs) ſomething , which the
Angels extreamely loue; to wit, *well*
gouerned eies. It is an Oracle of Truth
left to vs by Chriſt our Lord, that the
health of the eyes redound to the
good of the whole bodie. *Yf the eye*
be ſimple, the whole bodie will be cleere
and free. The Angels , whereſoeuer
they be, do alwaies beholde God with
a watchfull eye, and that without in-
termiſſion; to which property there
be men , who ſtriue with emulation
to attaine ; & to them Almightie God
is alwaies preſent in the eies of their
mind. There was a certain Saint, who
admoniſhed vs of this property ſaying: that we ought to be like a baker,
who whē he mingleth his meale with
water, mixing the one with the other,
whilſt he endeauoureth to forme the
whole maſſe of dow , doth notwith-
ſtāding ſometimes caſt of his eyes , &

beholde

Luc 11

beholde him with whome he talketh;
So ought we not to giue ouer our labours, that we may looke vpon God;
but whilſt we are labouring & buſie,
we muſt lift vp our eies continually
towards his diuine Maieſty. This was
the document, which olde Tobias re-
cōmended to his ſonne: *In all the dayes
of thy life* (ſaid he) *haue God in thy minde.*
King Dauid reioiced that he had performed this ſaying : *I* ALWAIES
prouided to haue our Lord in my ſight.
Whence, it is euident, that Dauid had
moſt ſound eies. But bleare-eyed are
they, who on the way , at home, a-
broad, or in churches , can caſt their
eies , and pry into euerie corner ; and
yet with the eyes of their mindes, do
not ſeeke to finde out their God,
whome they haue loſt. Then are
our actions good, when our hand is
at worke , and our eye vpon God.
We do manie things idly and ſlouth-
fully. We pray, but where is our attention ? we giue almes, but where is
the affectiō ? we faſt, but where is our
deſire of pleaſing or appeaſing God?

Tob. 4.

Pſ. 15.

All

All which, betokens, that we neither haue God in our eies, nor do
we imagine, that God fees vs. So do
we manie things flothfully, inde-
cently, and by halues, becaufe we
behold not God as looking vpon vs.
O man, attend to thyfelf, and bend
thyne eies ftill, as thoug they were
faftened and attentiue vpon God.
*No thought is free from his knowledge, nor
is there anie fpeach hidden from him.*
Doft thou harbour lafciuious
thoughts, and not blush : *yet God
fees them.* Doft thou vtter impure and
vncleane words; and art thou not
afhamed ? *yet God heareth them.* Doft
thou ftretch thy theeuish and rob-
bing hand hither, and thy luftfull
hand thither, and art not afraide ? *yet
God is prefent.* Whatfoeuer thou doft,
whatfoeuer thou thinkeft, in whatfoeuer lurking places thou hideft thy
felf, remember ftill, that *thou lieft open
and difcouered to the Almightie G*
Clemens Alexandrinus faith; This
onely is attained by prayer, that one
may neuer finne, if he alwaies con-

ceaue

ceaue God to be prefent with him.
This precept of bleffed Dorotheus
made Dofitheus an excellēt Monke,
from a moft diffolute foldier : *Thinke
God to be alwaies prefent , and that
thou ftandeft alwaies before him. For certainly the eies of God do euerie where beholde the good and the euil. Our Lord is
the weigher of Spirits ; and all things lie
open and naked before his eies.* In the laft
day of Iudgement how manie hidden
finnes, how manie fecret wickednef-
fes, how manie monftrous offences
will come to light , and be publikely
knowen, which now lie couered vnder the cloake of hypocrifie and diffimulation ? The truft committed to
fecret walles, and that which lyes buried in filence and darkeneffe, God
feeth. He heareth all things; & who
can euer finde in his hart to finne,
who fees God alwaies prefent and
beholding him. O man, know that
whatfoeuer thou art doing , thou art
both feene & heard ; And remember,
that the eye of the Almightie doth in
all places difcouer thee.

*Prou
15.
Hebr.
4.*

THE

THE XI. HOVRE.

LEARNE TO DIE;
AND MEDITATE.

Would not I in my laſt ſickneſſe, forgiue all the world, and deſire to be forgiuen by all? why do I then now nourish ſo long and durable anger within me? why do I purpoſe ſo implacably to reuenge myſelf?

LEARNE TO LIVE.

Let thy life be a conſideration of the diuine preſence. Euerie deede done by fleſh and bloud is before him, and nothing is hidden from his eie. Nothing is ſhutt vp from God. And moſt true is the ſaying of S. Auguſtin: God is all eye, for he ſeeth all; all hand; for he doth all; and all foot, for he is euery where preſent.

Eccl.
39.

LEARNE

LEARNE TO PRAY,
AND CONSIDER.

The vertues of the Angels.

1.   VERTVE.

PVRITIE, chaftitie, and inno-
cencie, are honoured by the Angels in the firft ranke. Thefe heauenly
Spirits, and moft conftant friends
and feruants of God, neuer yet were
defiled with the leaft fpott; Of thofe
fpeakes God faying: *Come yee and let* | Gen.11
vs defcend, and confound their tongues.
S. Auguftin affirmes, that the Angels
are moft fweetly inuited to this def-
cending. *God loueth* (faith he) *thefe* | Aug.
his moft innocent children after the fall | li. 26.
of fo manie millions. An infant in the | de Ci-
cradle is faid to be an innocent An- | uit.
gel : yet notwithftanding he fin- | Dei.
ned in Paradife by the hands of | cap. 5.
another ; and his firft anceftour
tranfgreffed ; which cannot be
faid of anie of thefe holie Spirits,

whome

whome Chrift praifed and faid : *They
shall be like the Angels of God.* And if
we loue and efteeme our owne fimilitude and likeneſſe in others, certain
it is, that he will be dearer to Angels,
who is moſt chaſt ; for fo becomes he
moſt like vnto them. Therefore did
they defend the moſt chaſt Iudith
within the tents of the enemies. For
the fame reafon did they free the
chaſt Sufanna from the treacheries
and ambufches of the Elders. This
was the caufe , why they defended
Cecilia, Agnes , and Theodora from
the deuouring wolues. Where there
is a chaſt hart , there is the delight of
Angels.

2. VERTVE.

A Moſt readie obedience. *Are
they not all ferniceable Spirits ?*
which the kinglie Pfalmiſt alfo affir-
meth : *Who maketh his Angels fpirits,
and his minifters flames of fire.* When
they haue receaued anie commandement by word or deede, they at the

*He'r
to
Pfal.
103.*

leaſt

least intimation repaire swiftly like
to flying fire, whither they are sent.
Dost thou not send (said Iob) *lightnings,* Iob 38
and they go? and returning say vnto thee:
Loe, we are present? No number of
commaunds can wearie these heauenlie Spirits. For they are euer readie to go and come. *You shall see.*
(saith S. Iohn) *the heauens open, and* Iob. 1.
the Angels of God ascending and descen-
ding vpon the sonne of man. They go
and come like lightnings & offering
themselues for new employments,
say; we are present. This is the speach
of euerie obedient person: Beholde,
I am present, I am readie, I am prepared to go, to do whatsoeuer shall be
commaunded me. To be long in yeil-
ding ones consent, is the part of an
vnwilling seruant. It is the propertie
of a willing man to do a thing quick- Lib. 2.
benefic.
ly saith Seneca.

3. VERTVE.

Ngels do infinitly loue God; and
great is their loue to vs. An Angel preserued Isaac from the sword.

An

An Angel comforted a poore hand-
maide; and an Angel wreſtling with
Iacob vouchſafed to be ouercome by
him. It was an Angel; who freed
Loth from the fire. Who like a meſſenger lead Tobias forward & back-
ward. An Angel was ſewer to Elias
and Daniel. Before Elias he ſett bread
and water; and before Daniel, all
the delights, that harueſt could afforde. An Angel ſent Philip to the E-
thiopian Treſurer of Candaces. And
it was an Angel, who troubled the
waters of Hieruſalem for the good
of thoſe poore, who were infirme &
ſick. It was loue, which made the
Angels become the buriers of the
dead; and it was not one alone, but
manie, who carried poore Lazarus
into Abraham's boſome. They leade
vs in their hands, leaſt we fall; as elder children do their bretheren, who
are litle infants. There is no man
ſo impious, but if he repent the
Angels reioice at it. And S. Bernard
ſaith: The teares of the penitent are
the delicious wine of Angels. The

moſt Bleſſed Mother of God and S.
Iohn Baptiſt , receaued ſuſtenance
from Angels , as manie writers teſti-
fie. *The Angels refuſe not the baſeſt of-*
fices , through their loue to vs. O Charitie ! how great a Queene of Vertues
are thou ? and yet how art thou euery
where not only not eſteemed but
contemned ?

Suar
diſp.
24
ſ. ĉ. 3
part.
3. D.
Tho.

4. VERTVE.

A Wonderfull ſubmiſſion. Angels in the ancient law ſuffered
themſelues to be worſhipped. That
great Abraham caſt himſelf at their
feete, & almoſt quite a long vpon the
ground, and adored the three meſſen-
gers, who came from heauen ; & they
forbad it not, but receaued this honour. So did Lot adore two Angels
more, who did not forbid that honour & worſhip donn to them. Ioſue,
Tobias, Manue, adored the ſame,
and were not reprehended by them;
and many others did the ſame; and
they hindred it not yet did they not

herein

herein proceede against their submis-
sion in respect of Almightie God; they did onely accomodate thēselues to the decorū of that time. In the new law moued by the example of their king, they became more submisse af-ter their LORD had humbled himself so low, they forbad that anie should do that honour to them or adore them; for they had seene their great God not onely prostrate at the feete of men, but also washing their feete; at which new and vnvsuall spectacle to those heauenly Spirits, they did in a manner temper themselues, and descended below their nature and ordinarie custome. For an Angel

Apoc. c. 19.

tooke vp S. Iohn from the ground euen prostrated in an extasie & readie to adore him saying: *See that thou do it not; for I am thy fellow seruant, and one of thy bretheren, bearing testimonie of* IESVS; *adore thou God.* Behold these heauenly Princes do after a sort im-poure themselues; which S. Gregory admiring saith: that before the co-ming of our Redeemer the Angels

were

were adored , and they confented
therevnto , but now they refufe and
allow it not , fure it is that formerly
they defpifed humane nature ; but
after they faw it taken into heauen
aboue them , then they feared to fee
it proftrated in adoring them. Yea
the Angels do now euen beg of vs,
and haue often imitated that which
hath often bene done by kings and
Emperors, & do , in Pilgrim's habits,
vnknowne aske lodging, and hofpitality at our hands. There haue bene
many Saints, as the memory of their
Acts teftify , who haue often at their
table fed thefe rich beggars. To thefe
bleffed Minds adheres not one fpott
or blemifh of Pride; hence proceedes
their loue and reuerence to the poore , as it appeared , when they onely
brought the happy tidings of Chrift's
natiuitie to the poore fhepheards.
Neither were they euer feene in greater number vpon earth then at that
time , when their king was lodged in
great pouerty among beafts. Thefe
heauenly Powers blufhed not at the

poore rags of their Lord, nor at his cradle made of twigs or ſtraw, Chriſt forewarneth ſaying: *Whoſoeuer bluſheth or is aſhamed of me and my words, of him will the Sonne of man be aſhamed, when he ſhall come in his Maieſty with his Father and all the Angels in heauen.*

Luc 9.

5. VERTVE.

A Moſt conſtant Patience. Angels do receaue euen thoſe into their care, who they know are to be damned. Neither do they leſſe labour in inſtructing men, though they well vnderſtand they do it in vaine. *We haue endeauoured to cure Babylon, ſayd they; and yet it is not whole. Let vs forſake it.* They forſake no man, before the diuell haue him deliuered ouer to his power and carries him away *ad æternos carceres* to the perpetuall impriſonment of hell. What gardener in his garden, or what husbandman is ſo patient in dreſſing of his vinyeard, that when he knowes it will not anſwear his expectation & wiſhes, yet

Ierem 15.

defifts not from trimming and dreffing it? but Angels are of great patiéce, euen to thofe, who are moft defperate & wicked. And Antichrift himfelf fhall haue an Angel an admonifher. Iulian the Apoftata did certainly fee his Angel going frõ him, though he left this admonition, that he went from him(as a mother fayning to fly from her child;) to the end that he might ouercome his ftubborneffe. But yet Iulian euen fo warned, amended not, but breathed forth his laft gafpe, and loft his laft bloud, with blafphemy and execration. As for vs, if we admonifh any one of his dutie twice or thrice, wee thinke him fufficiétly warned, and fo giue him ouer: but the difpofition of Angels is farre differét from ours; For they admonifh vs hundreds & thoufands of times, praying vs to omitt this, and to do that; and the more obftinatly that one omitts things to be done, or doth things to be auoided, the more conftant is their patience; in which they haue alfo fome who imitate

M 2　　　　　them

them with an admirable conſtancy.
So did Ioannes Thebeus, who ſerued
Ammon being an old & ſicklie man

Vitæ
Pa-
trum
lib.7.
c.19.

twelue yeares ; during which time
this cruell froward old man neuer
vouchſafed him one milde word; But
being ready to die, taking him by the
hand , in preſence of others ſaide:
This youth is no man, but an Angel:
For I confeſſe ingenuouſly , that during all theſe yeares, I neuer ſpoke
kindely to him , and yet hath he ſerued me, being ſick, with a great deale
of care, induſtry, and patience. Moyſes by his patience was not only eſteemed by Pharao, & the Hebrewes
to be an Angel, but a God. Certain it
is , that the patience , which Angels
exerciſe, they loue and eſteeme in vs.

ib.7.
nu.31.

Pelagius the Deacon reports out of a
Greeke Authour , that which may
wonderfully confirme, and eſtabliſh
our patience in all things. There was
a holy old man, ſaith he ,.who dwelt
in a horride vaſte wilderneſſe , and
had already learned TO DO, AND
SVFFER much for God's ſake; his

can-

cannopy was the skie, his bed the
earth; watching serued him for sleepe, and fasting for meate; in steede of
speach he vsed silence; and in lieu of
a palace, a litle cottage; most things of
sustenance failed, but chiefely water:
which though it be an element of
common vse, yet cannot a man euery
where come by it, and therefore
whensoeuer he desired to quench his
thirst, he was forced to weary himself
in going to the fountaine, as it were,
to a markett-place, to buy a cup of
drinke; neither could he haue it, till
he had gone a long way, which made
his thirst to become euen hatefull to
him; desiring rather to be twice hungry then once thirsty: so farre dwelt
he from any water; neither could he
drinke fresh and coole water, vnlesse
he did drinke it at the fountain;
which oftentimes troubled this holy
old man, and excited him to anger. It
came to passe, on a day, that like a
thirsty stagg he went in his accustomed path, to his knowen fountain;
thirst and not feare added wings to

his feete, and made him double his
pace ; but hauing hardly ouercome
half the way, his iawes began to drie,
his tōgue to cleaue to the roofe of his
mouth, his voice to leaue him, his armes to fwagg, his legs to foulde vnder him, his breath to faile him, and
his whole bodie euen to fall vpon the
ground; for which caufe breaking his
wearied pace, he crept foftly on ; and
being more fitt for meditation then
he was before, he began to difpute
many things within himfelf, and to
caft his minde vpon this and that,
and at laft fpoke to himfelf thefe
words : Who (faid he) will now
bring thee drinke , when thy legs
are no longer able to carrie thee ? I
will not fpeake of the loffe of time,
which I might haue employed more
commodioufly in reading, meditating
and praying; whilft I fo often make
fuch long iournies ? Whome doth
moft precious wine coft more , then
water doth me ? how doth the heate
fcorch me in the fummer ? and in
winter how doth the colde weaken

and

and benumme me? whofe patience
could endure fo great and daily troubles? Pardon me, O God, I can no
longer abftaine from being angrie,
and vexed at my incommodious habitation. But is there no remedie or
inuention, that might be found
out, to haue fome litle brooke or
fpring neerer to me? Shall I al-
wayes go fo manie thoufand paces
to drinke? furely this wine-cellar is
too farre of from me; what if I fhould
goe neerer to it? for it cannot come
nearer to me, nor runne by anie new
channell? I will then do fo; I will
bring my feate neerer to it, and I
will place my litle houfe neare
the fountain, and fo will I fhor-
ten my immenfe labour. For why
fhould I be daily thus wearied? O
wretched and inconfiderate man
that I was! why did I not fooner
take this counfell? he had fcarce vttered thefe words, but he
might heare the noife of one following him; and as he was thus
going or rather creepi ng forwards,

he

he looked back, and faw a yong man
behind him, who was diligently
counting euery ſtep he made. The
old man preſently ſpoke to him:
Who art thou who thus ſilently doſt
reproach a wearied olde man? why
doſt thou number my ſteps vpon thy
fingars? we are not now of equall
ſpeede, as we were heretofore, when
my knees and legs were ſtronger; leaue of this mocking. Be not angry, ſaide the Angel (whon he thought to be
a yong man) for I am ſent from heauen to number all thy paces, which
thou makeſt to his fountaine, and I
ſhall ſee thee rewarded for euery pace
which thou haſt made, or doſt make;
but it will be in heauen; which ſaid,
he vaniſhed out of his ſight. Then
the good Heremit being amazed with
this heauenly ſpeach, proſtrats himſelf vpon the ground, and praying
cryed out: O my God, how great is
thy goodneſſe towards thy moſt vnworthy ſeruant? am not I that impa-
tient and angry wretch? am not I that
idle and lazy ſeruant, who did but

euen

euen now grudge and ſtorme at my
paines? and ſhall I ſell euery ſtep and
pace to thee, at ſo great, and deare a
rate? Pardon, I beſeech thee, o my
Creatour, pardon my anger and impatience; pardon my fooliſh reſolution; I recall what I thought, ſaid,
or determined My litle houſe ſhall be
hereafter further remoued from this
fountaine, that ſo my patience may
be encreaſed by the tediouſneſſe of
the way; and to ioyne hands with his
words, he preſently pulled downe his
houſe, and remoued it halfe a mile
further from the fountain. So the
Angel had more paces to number,
and God to rewarde. Whoſoeuer
then thou art, O man, thy Angel followes thee, he numbreth thy paces,
and not onely thy paces, but keepeth
reckoning of thy ſecret thoughts, of
all thy words and deedes. Behold how
faithful a Secretarie thou haſt; whatſoeuer thou doſt, he ſetteth downe
euery action. Doſt thou pray? he
numbreth the very words. Doſt thou
giue almes? he keepes account of eue-

ty farthing. Doft thou difcipline thyfelf? he numbreth the ftripes. Doft
thou chaftife thyfelf with fafting? he
keepes a iuft account of all thofe
things, from which thou abftaineft
or refraineft. Doft thou leffen thy
fleepe? he numbreth thy watchings.
Doft thou ouercome thy luft or paf-
fions? he keepes an Inuentory of thy
victories. Doft thou weare a haire-
cloth-fhirt? he numbreth the houres.
Doft thou apply thy minde to pious
meditatiõ? he keepes account of euery moment. Neither doth he euer
neglect his office in keeping this account, whilft thou praifeft God in
reading, writing, or whatfoeuer thou
doft. But know alfo, that thou haft
another attendant, one who is a thee-
uifh fpirit of hell, who layes not wai-
te to depriue thee of thy money, but
of thy foule. This is a banifhed citti-
zen from heauen, who iuft as thy Angel-guardian keepes accrount of thy
good deedes, fo doth he enter into his
table-bookes, what thou doft, in
fwearing or forfwearing; if thou

fpeake

speake lasciuiously he numbreth the
sillables; if thou thinke vpon wickednesse; he keepes a register of thy
thoughts ; if thou neglect anie diuine seruice ; he numbres the hourely
quarters; and last of all , if thou defile
thy self with any mortall sinne ; he
keepes reckoning of the very moments , vntill that moment come,
when he may haue the power to pre-
cipitate thee into hell with an vnre-
couerable fall , which will be at thy
last gaspe, if thou be found an enemy
to God , a disenherited heyre of heauen, and an oppugner of the celestiall
Spirits and Saints. O man , I exhort thee by tuine owne saluation,
to beginne to number (if thou be
wise) the yeares , which thou hast
consumed , the daies thou hast neglected, the houres thou hast lost.
Keepe also account , if thou canst,
of thy future dayes and houres,
seing thou art not certaine to be
secure from death this very houre, in
which I speake to thee. And lastly,
thinke vpon that ETERNITIE,

which

which thou canſt not number. A
learned man ſaide to this purpoſe,
that nuptials haue a short and pleaſant
ſong, but a long and ſorrowfull concluſion.
So may we truly ſay, that the pleaſure of euery ſinne is a ſhort and pleaſing ſong, but it hath a long and ſorrowfull end; to wit, ETERNALL
TORMENT. *O Eternitie , Eternitie!*
how often haue we wickedly ſinned,
becauſe we haue ſcarce once ſeriouſly
thought vpon thee. O *Eternitie,* which
art to be enioyed amidſt the delights
of Angels , or to be endured and neuer ended in perpetuall torments
amongſt the diuels. Conſult, ô man
with thyſelf and conſider , whether
thou deſireſt to haue ; the one or the
other to be thy friends. And laſtly
know that then thou wilt be a friend
to Angels , when thou art ſo to PA-
TIENCE and CHASTITIE.

THE XII. HOVRE.

LEARNE TO DIE;
AND MEDITATE:

Doth not Eternitie depende of the last moment of my life? certainly either euerlasting happinesse or eternall torment will receaue my last breath. Wherefore then do I not dispose myself to make a good end, by beginning now a good life? It is most secure and safe, that euerie man, whilst he is well and in health, do performe that, which in the last houre of his life he would wish he had done.

LEARNE TO LIVE.

Let thy life be a consideration of Eternitie.

I Haue thought vpon the ancient and past dayes, and I haue had the eter-

P*fal.*
76.

nall yeares in my minde, faith *the* Pfalmift. Whatfoeuer *is in this world, is*
vaine, short, and a meere nothing,
being compared with ETERNITIE.
And amongft men he is onely wife,
who prefixeth to himfelf, that nothing
is to be thought vpon in this life, nor to
be attayned vnto in the next, but oncly
the enioying of ETERNITIE *in*
heauen.

LEARNE TO PRAY.
AND CONSIDER.

The worshipping *and honouring*
of Saints.

I. CHAPTER.

TOBIAS the father hauing both
his fonne and eies, reftored to
him, calling his fonne fayd, to him:
What can we giue to that holie man,
which accompanied thee? To whome
Tobias the yonger anfwered: *O father,*
what rewarde shall we giue him, which
may paralell his benefits? And fo he beganne

ganne to repeate them, and laſt of all he ſayd : *What can we giue him, worthie of his acceptance ?* For whatſoeuer that be, it will ſtill be leſſe then he deſerueth. *And calling the yong man to them, they began to entreate him to accept of the half of all that, which they poſſeſſed.* And what ſhall we alſo beſtow vpon our Angel-guardian for ſo manie benefitts beſtowed vpon vs by the ſpace of ſo manie yeares ? Salomon ſaith : *If thou haue a faithfull ſeruant, let him be deare to thee, as thyne owne ſoule.* In what eſtimation then ſhall we haue our Angel-guardian, who preſerues vs with a more ſincere care and fidelitie, then anie guarde of the faithfulleſt ſouldiers can afforde their Prince and king.

Eccl. 33.

CHAPTER II.

THE Angels may be honoured in the ſame māner, as the reſt of the Saints are, to whome like the friends of God, we ſhew reuerēce by prayers, almes-deedes & faſtings. The Angels honour Almightie God with frequēt

praiſes;

praises; Let vs therefore vse oftener
to pray by their example. The Angels
are most pure and free from all fault,
and liue in a most chast integritie,
voide of all spott and blemish. To
imitate this pure vertue, frequent
fasts do much auaile vs. Angels are
most liberall in their benefitts towards vs, which in our almes-deedes
we must also striue to imitate. Con-
stantine the Emperour being truly
vertuous and pious, did at Constan-
tinople on both the shores of the Eu-
xine sea, erect two famous churches
to the honour of S. Michael the Archangel; and in honour of the same
S. Michael and other Angels, he
built from the ground six magnificēt
churches; perswading himself truly,
that if he had to friend, the Captaine
of those winged Legions, who had
ouercome so manie powerfull champions, then he should easily and for-
tunately wage warre with the Van-
dals. S. Francis that Seraphin a-
mongst men, besides that fast of
Fourtie daies, commaunded by the

Church

Church, vſed to chaſtiſe his bodie
with the faſt of other fourtie dayes,
in honour of S. Michell the Archangel. Otho the third, Emperour of the
Romans, in the yeare of our Lord
1000. did, as Petrus Damianus teſtifieth, in the life of S. Romualdus, go
from Rome to the mountaine Gar-
ganus in Apulia barefoote, to the
church of S. Michell the Archangel;
which was 50. long German miles;
and this he did, by the perſwaſion of
Romualdus, to expiate by this corporall affliction, a fault, which, a litle
before, he had committed.

CHAPTER III.

Since the Angels are moſt pure and
perfect Spirits, and free from all
fleſhlie dregs, it is a great honour and
ioy to them; when anie man putts
on the garment of intire Chaſtitie,
and by that meanes, makes himſelf
as like to them, as poſſibly his endeauours can obtaine, and becomes a
kinde of Angel by his Chaſtitie.

How

How manie times haue they teftified
the chaft & fingle life of many holie
men, to be heauenlie and celeftiall?
Neither is there more credit to be
giuen to a Grammarian in the ety-
mologie of words, then in this to
Angels. S. Hierome faith t'is a matter
of felicity to be an Angel, of vertue

to be a Virgin. Bafilius recounts, that
when Diocletian and Maximian ty-
ranized ouer Chriftians, Theophila
a virgin moft beautiefull in fhape,
and noble in parentage, being carried by force of fergeants and officers
to the ftewes, fhe prayed thus by
the way : My IESVS, my loue,
my fpoufe ; O fountain of chaftitie,
giue me timelie fuccour, and preferue
the chaftitie of thy fpoufe. Her hart,
her mouth, and her eyes full of teares, all feemed to fpeake, when fhe
entred into thofe vncleane houfes ;
and fhe drew forth from about her,
the holie Ghofpell ; and there were
fome, who tooke the boldnes to rush
in towards her, but none had the
prefumption to touch her. The Virgin

gin fate downe, and read, with a
chaft countenance compofed and
fetled to all modeftie. There was
prefent a yonge man from heauen,
who with incredible beauty did caft
forth moft pleafing fparkles of fire
from his eies, and that with fuch a
maieftie, that it terrifyed thofe, who
entred, from offering anie violence
to the Virgin. And this yonge man,
faith Bafilius, was a protectour of
the Virgin, as the chaft Daniel was
of Sufanna. No man loues the Angels, who hates chaftitie. For a
chaft life is the greateft honour that
can poffibly be performed towards
them.

CHAPTER IV.

WITH what honour do thefe
heauenly Spirits and God's
Embaffadours defire to be treated by
vs? They eafily teach vs this by their
owne exáple. In S. Paul's opinió they
are ▪ miniftering fpirits, full of good
offices & obfequioufneffe; and fuch

also

alfo they defire thofe might be, whome they inftruct. Ioannes Carrera a
moft chaft yong man was tranfpor-
ted with fuch an ardēt defire towards
his Angel-guardian, and arriued to fo
great a friendfhip and familiaritie
with him, that he did often confult
and receaue counfell from him; and
many times in doubts and difficulties
referred himfelf to his aduife, and finally became fo free with him, as that
he would daily awake him in the
morning before breake of day, and
ftirre him vp to his prayers; which
cuftome the Angel beganne to omitt,
becaufe the yong man ftirred vp by
him, did not prefently rife. But certainly if this were a fault, he fuffered
for it, during manie dayes, where in
the Angel hid himfelf from him. Yet
through the ardent defire of his Angel's prefence, making great fuppli-
cation to appeafe Almightie God,
and offering vp manie fafts, he at
length recouered what he had loft;
and being receaued into the former
familiaritie, the Angel admonifhed

and

and tolde him : I therefore hid my felf
from thee , becaufe thou didft not
prefently correfpond ; when I ftirred
thee vp to pray : and God did therefore punifh thee , that fo hereafter
thou maift learne not to vfe delayes
in thy rifing. As the morning is a
friend to the Mufes, fo is it to Angels;
their defire is , that in the morning
we fpeake to God , and all the day after of God , and not forgett our offices towards others. They fufficiëtly
fhew vs , what honour they expect,
by the obfequioufnefle they afforde
to others. They rightly vrge vs, that
whatfoeuer we do to others , we
fhould do it *fpeedily* and *freely*. An vnwilling and flow courtefie is litle
better then a neglect. A good office
cannot pleafe, which comes not with
alacritie and *readineffe*. He affordes a
double help , who giues it fpeedily.

CHAPTER V.

THere are fome , who honour
their churches with diuerfe

guifts , fome prefente wax , others oile , fome tapers, others altars and precious veftements ; fome giue artificiall and rare pictures , others goulden chalices, and the like. S. Auguftin faith: We are iuftly admonifhed by the kinglie Pfalmift, TO VOW and TO PAY OVR VOWES, in two manners ; there be fome, which giue wax , oile , veftements, perfumes, golde, and the like, but thefe are not exfpected but from the rich; but we haue yet more noble guifts , then thefe , which may be brought out of poore men's chefts , and if they be offered to Angels, they cannot but be acceptable to them, and in this order doth S. Auguftin number them as figured by gold, cedar &c.

Serm.
3. de
nas.
Domi.
ni.

1.   Firft, whofoeuer bridles and reftraines the anger which he hath conceaued againft another, and for the loue of God doth blott out the receaued iniurie, offereth a prefent like moft pure oile.

2.   Secōdly, whofoeuer hath vfed to wallow in the puddle of Luxurie, &

at

at length repents and washes himself
cleane from those impure desires, and
secretly calls thus vpon Almightie
God. O most mercifull Lord, most
mercifull God, let it suffice that I
haue hitherto dallied with thee, and
that hitherto I haue cõtemned thee;
I haue sett thy lawes at naught, in
satisfying my vnrulie and carnall
concupiscence; but now, O my God,
I returne to thee, and I make thee a
vow to forsake all my wickednesse.
And thus he offereth most white and
pure virgin-wax, aud a present most
deare to Angels.

3. Yf anie one be troubled with
enuie, if he reioice at others losses,
and repine at others felicitie, which
S. Augustin saith, is a most deadlie
sinne, yet let him promise and purpose rather to meditate and lodge in
his minde, acts of Loue then of malice or enuie; and he offereth a vow,
and bestowes vpon the Angels a golden chalice.

4. Yf anie one hath inferred an
iniurie to another, and hath euen

mur-

murthered him after a fort ; let him
purge his owne minde fo full of ve-
nome with forrow and fasting , and
not touch the holie bread of Angels ,
till he haue intirely reconciled himfelf to God, and the iniuried partie,
to him ; and fo by this he offereth this
prefent : He restores an altar to the
Angels, which by him had bene made
vnworthie of them.

5.   Yf anie be accustomed to carpe
at others words and actions, and not
to regarde their owne, but to detract
from the honour of euerie man, ex-
cepting none from the poifon of his
mifchieuous and malicious tongue;
Let him vowe thus to God and his
Angels : Hitherto haue I fpoken of
others, and not looked to myfelf. I
was more wretched then they , yet
did I efteeme others miferable.   O
tongue of mine : thou haft fufficiétly
vndone both myfelf and others ; I
will hereafter keepe thee tyed with
clofer bonds ; I will ferioufly amend
thy   lafciuioufneffe , and lauifh-
neffe. This man offered a prefent,

and

and letts vp, as it were, a brazen Ita-
tue in honour of the Angels.

6.   Yf anie one obſerue himſelf to
be ſparing in almes-deedes , ſharp
towards the poore, miſerable towards
his domeſtiks; Let this man vow to
God and the Angels a milde and pleaſing liberalitie; and he ſhall alſo offer
a munificent preſent; and beſtowes,
as it were, a golden veſtement vpon
the Angels.

7.   Yf anie one finde himſelf verie
deſirous of humane praiſe, or that he
be inſolēt & boaſting; Let him vow
to vſe meekeneſſe and modeſtie : and
he offereth vp a Tapiſtrie worthie the
eſtimation of Angels.

8.   Yf anie one delight and giue himſelf more then is fitt to wine; Let him
vow a ſparing diett and temperance,
and he ſo offereth a rich preſent to the
Angels equiualent to the value of
much golde and pretious wine.

9.   Yf anie one finde himſelf Languiſhing and diſmaide and that he be
ſlow and faint in pious exerciſes; Let
him vow alacritie and feruour to di-

                 N   uine

uine things; This man offers a precious vow, & doth, as it were, hang vp in honour of the Angels, a siluer lamp burning, and casting forth most odoriferous smells.

These pious guifts and presents to Angels, I assigne according to S. Augustin's words, who saith: Most deare Christians, when you haue done all this, you offer to God a most pleasing vow; and you do as it were repay Christ, for his bitter passion; and after this a bountiefull blessing will light vpon you; and your presents will be layd before the Tribunall of Christ. Let vs imagine, how sweet & pleasing it will be, when the Angels shall offer vp from vs, in sight of the Diuine Maiesty, such vowes and presents, as are here described.

CHAPTER VI.

IT is a speciall honour to the holie Angels and such as both is most befitting them, & profitable to their clients, to beare great reuerence to

their presence. And to this purpose
S. Bernard saith excellently well : In
whatsoeuer Oratorie or whatsoeuer
corner thou art in, haue still a reuerent respect to thy Angel. Darest
thou do in his presence, that which in
my sight thou darest not doe? Certain
it is that thy Angel-guardian's most
chast eies & eares (to vse a humane
phrase) are verie watchfull, and alwaies bent towards our actions, our
words, and euerie thought of ours.
Seneca being a heathen could say,
that nothing was a more efficacious
meanes to roote out vice, then continually to imagine, some graue & wise
man to be present. I now incite thee
by the same words, which Seneca
vsed to his Lucilius : Receaue, said
he a most wholesome and profitable
counsell ; which my desire is, should
neuer parte from thy minde: Choose
some good and graue personage (and
who can be fitter then thy Angel-
guardian?) and imagine him euer
present before thine eyes, to the end
that thou maist liue, as it were, al-

Serm. 13. in Psal. 90.

N 2   waies

waies in his prefence; and that thou
maift do nothing but as it were ftill
in his fight. For a great parte and occafion of finne is taken away, if to
them, who would finne, there be a
witneffe by. Let thy minde haue euer
prefent fome one, whome it may re-
uerĕce; to the ende that by his autho-
ritie euen the moft fecret things may
be performed with the more pietie.
O happie he who reformes not onely
his actions, but euen his verie cogita-

Lib. 12
Epiſt.
84.

tions. Wifely faid the fame Seneca
in another Epiftle, that we fhould alwaies liue fo, as though it were to be
in open view, that we fhould fo ma-
nage our thoughts, as though fome
bodie were able to pry into our verie
harts; which certainly there is one
can do. For what auailes it a man to
do anie thing in fecrett, when all
things lie open to God? he is prefent
to our mindes, & to our moft inward
cogitations. He is euer prefent, and
not as one, who fometime departs.
Nothing could be fpoken more wifely by one who was no Chriftian,

then

then what he recommends to vs. And it is moſt true, we alwaies haue God and his Embaſſadours the holie Angels, witneſſes of our thoughs and deedes. Of what can the Angels be ignorant, who know and beholde with a moſt perſpicuous, euerlaſting ſight: Almightie God, who knowes and ſees all things?

CHAPTER VII.

PErhaps ſome good bodie will deſire to know by an eaſie and ſhort methode, what may be daily done to the honour of the holie Angels.

1. Firſt he may daily ſay attentiuely, nine times ouer, our Lord's prayer, & the Angelicall Salutation.

2. He may daily vſe the Letanies, the litle office, or other Prayers intituled to the holie Angels.

3. He may daily offer them ſome pious worke, or ſome victorie gained ouer himſelf.

4. Since by Holie Scripture it appeares, that there are 9. Quires of holie

An-

Angels , he may attentiuely obserue
in anie good and pious exercises the
number of 9.

5. Let him chiefly attend to Chastitie; it being a vertue most recommended by the Angels.

6. Let him endeauour to propagate
and encrease their honour and veneration amongst others.

7. Let him frequente the churches
dedicated to them , and obserue their
feasts; chiefly that of the 8. of May,
of the 29. of September , & the Sun-
day, which is most sacred to them.

8. Let him , in honour of the Angels, Lay aside and suppresse whatsoeuer hatred, enuie, or strangenesse , he
hath conceaued or harboured against
anie whosoeuer. For the diuels are
full of hatred and enuie; but the Angels abound in loue and goodnesse.

9. Let him continually , or at least
often in the day, imagine his Angel
present , and in all aduersities or dangers , let him call to his help and succour,the holie Angels, & the Queene
of Angels the Mother of God.

THE
ANGEL-GVARDIAN'S
Epilogue to his Charge.

I Haue taught thee, O my charge, what rules thou shouldst follow of WELL DYING, WELL-LIVING, and PRAYING WELL. But if now thou know them, and follow them not, thou art in a double fault. Hearken to our Lord's words, who saith: *A ser-* *uant , who knowes his maister's* *will , and doth it not , shall be* *beaten with many stripes.* It is not the part of a Christian to busie himself after the seeking of many lawes ; he hath but few; nay, one only. Let him lo-

ue

ue God , and he keepes all his
lawes. Whatſoeuer other
lawes containe, it is all found
in this one. To the Hebrew na-
tion there was impoſed a burthenſome number of Precepts.
The Hebrew Doctours affirme, that in Moyſes his fiue-fold
Volume , there were compre-
hended nine hundred and thirteene Precepts, ſo diuided, that
thoſe , which commaunded
anie thing to be done , were as
manie in number as the Chirurgeons do attribute parts to
the body, to witt, two hundred
fourty eight ; & thoſe amongſt
them , which prohibited the
doing of any thing, from being
done, equaled the number of
the dayes of the yeare , which
are accounted to be 365. And
thus were the lawes appointed

to the Iewes , in number six
hundred and thirteene. Of all
which , Chrift our Lord compofed One : LOVE THOV
GOD , and thou obeyeft all
the lawes. Who loueth , fulfil-
leth the law. Wherefore then,
O my Charge, fince thou haft
but one only law , and that fo
pleafing & delightfull in condition; why doft thou contrary
to God's will , runne thyfelf
headlong and voluntarily into
the bottomeleffe precipice
which difobediéce leades thee
to. *Take pittie vpon thy foule , by*
pleafing God Containe, and gather
thy hart and fpirit togeather in the
holy obferuance of his lawes. Take
pitty, I fay, vpon thy foule; and
whereas thou feekeft after many things , and thy ambition
carrieth thee into many more,

Rom.
13.

Eccl.
30.

N 5   feeke

seeke but one, & aspire onely
to that, which ought to be no
other, but onely TO PLEASE
GOD. I pray thee, tell me; thy
other delights , which thou
dost so often thirst after, and so
ardently desire, how vile and
base, yea how short are they?
art thou in despaire of heauen?
This life is but a moment; and
eternall delights will follow
it. Reserue thyself for those;
and restraine thy hart from
wicked, impure, filthy, bitter,
or malicious cogitations. And
certaine it is, thou canst neuer
sufficiētly keepe thy hart cleane , vnlesse thou maintaine a
guarde ouer thy eares , thy
tongue, thy hands & thy eyes.
Belieue me, a chaste minde and
an vnchast eye neuer dwell togeather; & a wanton tongue,

and

not ignorant , what kept the
foolish Virgins from entring
into heauen, and shutt the gate
againſt them. They differred,
till they fell a ſleepe; they pro-
tracted it from houre to houre,
their counſell was not euill,
but it was too late. So doſt thou
& ſo manie periſh, who thinke
to amende their manners , but
too late: they intend to ſerue
God , but they giue the firſt
fruits to the world and the diuel; and by that meanes they
come into a great wood, where they wander , till ſudden
death ouertake them , and at
vnawares cutt the long ſpunne
thread of their delayes. Reade
but prophane hiſtories, & they
will teach thee the ſame. O
Alexander of Macedon, where
are thou ? in whome this was

eſne-

eſpecially obſerued, that thou
becameſt victorious ouer the
whole world, becauſe thou
didſt neuer vſe delayes. *There-*
fore, O my Charge, take pittie vpon
thy ſoule, and be aſſured, that ſo
much the more piouſly thou
wilt die, by how much the
ſooner thou doſt compoſe thy
ſelf fitt for death. Since life is
ſo contracted and short, and
death ſo vncertain, it is a moſt
rash and foolish thing to putt
of, differre, and delay a buſi-
neſſe ſo perilous, and dãgerous
to thy ſaluation. I haue alreadie
often beaten theſe words into,
thyne eares. *Remember to die,*
Remember to die, O too too
forgetfull creature, though a
thouſand houres may ſpare thy
life, yet one will take it from
thee; & perhaps it will be that,

which

which thou leaſt ſuſpecteſt.
And wilt thou now, that I reduce into three or foure words
all thoſe things, wherein I haue
inſtructed thee, tending either
to a better death or a more holy
life, or to more pure & deuout
Prayers ? LEARNE therefore
TO DIE, and be prepared, becauſe thou knoweſt not the day
nor the houre. Ishboſeth while
he tooke a nappe in the after
noone, hauing a maide ſleeping
at the doore, was ſlaine. So
will ſinne & death conſpire to
cutt thy throat, if the memorie
of death ſleepe in thee. Death
is moſt bolde, yet it aſſailes none but vnawares, & as it were
behind their backes. Samſon
while he ſlept in Dalilae's lappe, loſt all his ſtrength. Now
giue thyſelf ouer to thy plea-

Matt. 24.

Reg. 2. c. 4.

ſures,

fures, and meafure thy owne
fortune by that which befel.
to him. Death was wont heretofore to fight againft men
with its owne force, as olde
age, plague and other difeafes;
but now it, vfeth other weapôs,
as meate and drinke, gluttonie
and luft. It drownes manie in
water, but more in wine, euery
where it lies hid in ambush.

Ef. 38. *Do thou therefore difpofe of thy.*
houfe ; for thou shalt die, faith
Efay: And thus shalt thou be
feparated from humane things
for euer after. Oh how often
Luc. doth Chrift admonish vs: *Let*
10. *your loines be guirt, and burning*
lampes in your hands, and be you
like men expecting their maifter,
when he returnes from the wed-
ding. Thou shalt be prepared
to meete death, if thou obferue

thefe

thefe three things recommended to vs by God's owne com-
maundement, and doft make
vfe of a gyrdle, a torch, and a
bell. Doft thou remember,
what I haue admonifhed thee
in diuerfe Houres aforegoing,
concerning the gyrdle of Chaftitie? and S. Hierom's admonitions may be a thoufand times repeated : *If thou want the
gyrdle of Chaftitie , all goes to
naught, and to the ground.* Gyrd
thy loines ; for they die wickedly and ill, whome Luxurie
hath dis-ioynted. Thou carrieft
a torch in thy hand , yf thou
knowe the Ten Commaunde-
ments and followe them. Thy
Confcience is to thee a bell,
which is often and daily ftrict-
ly to be examined. Defcend
into thyfelf, and looke into thy

life; & do not only heede what
thou intendeſt to do , but conſider often, what thou haſt done; vſe in this manner to ſound
that bell, and daily ſearch into
thy conſcience ; and finde out,
what haue bene thy thoughts,
thy words and thy deedes during that whole day; Thus make vſe of the reſpit of time,
which at the inſtant of death,
thou wouldſt perhaps in vaine
ſeeke for , and now is granted
thee. LEARNE TO DIE; or
I shall be forced to ſay that to
thee, which an Angel obiected
to a Biſhop of Carthage , who
lay grieuouſly ſick: *Thou feareſt*
to ſuffer; thou wouldſt not departe
out of thy bodie ; what ſhall I doe to
thee? Take pittie therefore vpon thy
ſoule ; and by how much the
more treacherouſly Death is

Cypriã
ſerm. 4
de
mort.
Baron.
to. 2.

to

to approach , by ſo much do
thou, the more often meditate
ſeriouſly vpõ it.LEARNE alſo
TO LIVE,by liuing chaſtly &
carefully. Yf thou be not carefull,thou cãſt not be chaſt.Iob
the mirrour of Patiẽce did not
only honour Chaſtitie, making
a couenant with his eyes , that
they ſhould not induce him to
thinke of a woman; but he alſo
liued moſt carefully.There ſhi-
ned in him a great ſanctity;yet
he feared,he trembled,and he
was full of care. *I feared*, ſaid
he , *and was carefull of all my*
workes , knowing that thou wouldſt
not ſpare a delinquent. He alwaies ſuſpected whatſoeuer
he did , leaſt he ſhould do that,
which might be diſpleaſing to
God. This ſincere and ho-
lie man knew , that the ſen-

Iob.9.

tence of Almightie God was other then the iudgements of men; and for this cause he feared all his actions, being truly carefull and chast. Learne here and imitate him, to the ende thou maist liue so much the more chast, by how much thou art in all things the more circumspect and carefull. *Haue pittie vpon thy owne soule by pleasing Almightie God.* But LEARNE ALSO TO PRAY. Christ our king requires not onely at thy hands frequent, but continuall prayer: *Because we must alwaies pray.* And how faithfully doth he often exhort vs saying: *Watch yee and pray; because you know not, when the time will be* &c. *Pray yee without intermission. Therefore be thou not interrupted from praying alwaies.*

Luc. 18.

Mar. 13.

Thess. 5.

Eccl. 18.

This

This moſt excellent art of *praying* thou canſt neuer learne, vnleſſe thou pray often , and that feruently. Manie pray faintly and coldly , becauſe they vſe it ſeldome. Vſe makes expert : and by frequent praying one becomes a ſincere and feruent ſuppliant to the Diuine Power. And it is more beneficial , to vſe short and feruēt prayers , then thoſe, which are long and languiſhing. A prayer is ſcarce of anie force which hath not fire of deuotion in it. A faint and lukewarme prayer is much like a quenshed fire. S.Paul praying, breathed forth hote fire,for the more ſtirring vp whereof he ſaide : *I will pray in Spirit and minde.* What doth the ſtirring of the lippes profitt , when the

1. Cor. 14.

hart

hart is mute. That prayer is
rightly to be esteemed feruent
and fierie, which ardent and
frequent sighes accompanie &
eleuate towards God. But on
the contrarie side, prayer is friuolous and colde, when being
of that consequence, it is onely
committed to the lippes and
tongue. And therefore if thou
wilt rightly know, how to
L I V E, P R A Y feruently.
Neither of these is difficult to
a willing minde. And that I
may leade thee by the shortest
way of all tending to heauen,
keepe still in minde this the
Summarie of my words, and
let no obliuion euer reach to
these 2. admonitions.

1. Continually consider, that
thou daily and hourely appro-
chest neerer and neerer to that

ETER-

ETERNITIE, in which thou art euer to endure either torments amongst the damned, or to enioy euerlasting happinesse in companie of all the Saints ; and thus shalt thou LEARNE TO DIE well.

2. Neuer faile to see and imagine Almightie God present at all thy actions ; and so shalt thou euer LIVE WEL.

To the greater honour and glorie of God, of the blessed Virgin, and of all the holie Angels.

FINIS.

RALPH BUCKLAND

An Embassage from Heaven

[*1611*]

A N
EMBASSAGE
FROM HEAVEN.

Wherein
Our Lord and Saviour Christ Iesus giueth to vn-
derstand, his iust indignation against al such,
as being Catholikely minded, dare
yeelde their presence to the
rites and publike praier,
of the malignant
Church.

By Raphe Buckland Priest.

Posuit in nobis Deus verbum reconciliationis pro Christo,
itaque Legatione fungimur, tanquam Deo exhortante
per nos, obsecramus pro Christo reconciliamini Deo.

2. *Cor.* 5. *verf.* 19.

God hath placed in vs the word of reconciliation, we be
therefore Embassadours from Christ ; God as it were
exhorting by vs : we beseech you for Christes sake, be
reconciled to God.

Printed with Licence.

AN
EPISTLE TO AL
Schismatikes.

TO you, oh you miserable, who straying from the pathes of peace, runne as confidently forwards in darke and slippery waies, as if ye traced the steppes of truth and righteousnesse, neither wandred one jot from the high way to saluation.

The Preface to the Reader.

WHo hath eares to heare, let him heare, a courteous and a friendly admonition (gentle reader) of that most mighty, and most humble Prince, who sendeth this Embassage to prepare the harts of his disloyal subiects, to more perfect obseruance of his lawes: which many inconsiderately, (because they feare to heare them) doe violate; and feare to heare truly expounded, least they should vnderstand them, and vnderstanding them a-right, should powerfully be moued to obey them, with losse of their reputation, life, and goodes. Which inconueniences (for so they esteeme them) least they might incurre: they stoppe their eares and wil not listen to the voice of the wise enchaunter, telling them, that the Kingdome of heauen, is without comparison of more value, then al their worldly pelfe: and that the troubles of these times,

※ 2.   are

are not to be waighed in regard of the future glory, which shal be reueiled in them; euen in this life, through the testimony of a good conscience, but chiefly in the next, and euerlasting life, by the perfect enioying of almighty God, and seing him there face to face as he is: to which beautifying vision, by seruing God with a pure hart (for such only shal see him) thou art earnestly intreated by this booke (Godly reader) what euer thou art that hast a soule to saue, rich, or poore, learned, or vnlearned, luke-warme Schismatike, or cold Catholike, for this worke concerneth you both, though with indifferency: in the perusing whereof the more attention and heede thou doest bestow, the better thou wilt accept of the authours pious, and charitable indeanours; and reape vnto thy selfe great fruit to saluation, which whiles it is ripining in thee; shew thy selfe I pray thee, no lesse gratefull to the religious authour hereof, by praying for his soule, then to his yet suruiuing friend, at whose earnest suite, this so necessary and profitable a message is deliuered vnto thee, not without approbation and counsaile; after a careful view and examination of the same.

Fare-wel.

AN

AN

EMBASSAGE FROM
HEAVEN.

 Earken ye erring foules, who wil not enter the Arke, or-dained for the fafety of my Elect? yet hope to efcape the vniuerfal floode of my wrath; who refufe to leaue Sodome ? yet feare not fire and brimftone; who forfake not the Tabernacles of Chore ? yet dread not to be fwallowed of the earth; neglect to flie from Babylon , yet expect nothing leffe then to be oppreffed with the ruines thereof. Oh ye loft fheepe, who hauing receiued my marke, enter another fold; yet wil needes be tearmed of my flocke, runne with the Theefe, and wil be holden innocent; partake in iniquity, yet wil be accompted righteous; Ye broken branches ignorant of your owne decay; Ye that rent my vnfeamed coate , not acknow-

The margin: 1. The dangerous e-ftate of Schifma-tikes.

A   ledging

ledging a fault; teare my body without
fence of sinne; breake the vnity of my
Church vvithout scruple of Schisme.
Come forth before me and iustifie your
selues if ye can, cal together your wits,
search the depth of your harts, ponder
the reasons of your frailty, and the cir-
cumstances of your defence, in equity I
wil argue your offence, and contending
by iust iudgement. I stand against you
to your face : my Maiesty shal not pre-
iudice, to alleage what you can, I wil
neither oppresse you with authority, nor
ouer-rule without reason, but your owne
guiltinesse shal appale you, & the cleare-
nes of your crime, shal make you dumbe.
Laying a-side the person of a Iudge, I
the Creatour of al, referre the cause to
the censure of al my creatures. To al
both Angels and Men, I appeale to Catholikes and Heretikes; to Christians and
not Christians, to your owne consciences
if ye haue any.

2.   I haue tried you and found you faith-
Schisma- lesse, I haue giuen occasion of manife-
tikes no sting your fidelity, and found you a dis-
true seruāts
of God.   loyal

loyal generation ; I haue prouided for you a plentiful harueſt of glorious and eternal merits, I proffer the purchaſe of the Kingdome of heaueu ; but I perceiue you ſet at naught my wiſdome and bounty, contemning the treaſures of my Kingdome, as not worthy the vile price of temporal detriment. I haue proued you at the touch-ſtone , and diſcerned you to be baſe : I haue weighed you, and found you to light. Oh ſeede of Samaria, and not of Iuda , I hate your diſſimulation , I deteſt your cowardize, and abhorre your blindneſſe ; my ſoule loatheth your halting harts. Great is my indignation againſt you , and digeſt your frowardneſſe I cannot.

If any man with-hold your right , an action is ready , he is ſerued with proceſſe and exclaimed againſt , for vnconſcionable dealing. How long ſhal I demaunde the intereſt vvhich I haue in your ſoules , and you giue no eare to my claime. You diſdaine to be contemned at your ſeruants handes , you brooke not diſobedience in your children ;

3.
Vngratitude of Schiſmatikes and their injurious dealing towards God.

A 2

dren; In caſe the fieldes and orchyeardes
yeeld not their fruits, ye ſtorme and rage:
But where is your owne duty? the honour of your Maker, the loue of your
Redeemer, the awe of your God? where
are the fruits which my care haue deſerued? Long haue I trauailed in manuring
your barraine ſoules: I haue ſent my labourers, who imploy their diligence, I
haue by many occaſions ſollicited your
harts, and with ſweet inſpirations, I haue
at al times endeauoured to mollifie your
obſtinate mindes. VVhat is that I ſhould
doe to you and haue not done it? yet
reape I nought but contempt, nor finde
you other then ſtiffe and vntractable, vnprofitable, and voide of al towardneſſe;
VVhatſoeuer you haue is of my beneuo-
lence: your very life and being is of my
bounty: neither dependeth your continual preſeruation vpon any other aſſu-
rance, then the protection of my right
hand. If al this be too little, I am ready
to doe more, and greater matters I wil in
your behoofe performe, then your ſelues
would either haue expected, or deſired:

and

and the good that I purpofe toward you, in cafe you make your felues vvorthy thereof, cannot by mortal hart be conceiued. For which then of al my benefits doe you thus injury my patience? wherein hath my gratious goodneffe deferued the contumely and reproch, vvherewith your iniquity doth daily vexe me? Wicked and peruerfe people, yeeld you this thankes to my kindneffe, this recompenfe to my deferts? Why doe ye thus forfake me and deny me, difpife and difobey me, oppugne and affault me?

Ye forfake me, and deny me, and fay with a bold countenance, wherein haue we forfaken and denied thee? Haue ye not renounced my feruice, caft off my liuery, departed from my family, paffed from my campe and coulers, to the aduerfaries tentes, and yeelded to the profeffion of a Proteftant? Ye difpife and difobey me, yet blufh not to fay, wherein (oh Lord) doe we difpife or difobey thee? Haue I not commanded you to loue me aboue al, and to confeffe my name, my beleefe and Church, and to contend euen

4. Schifmatiks deny, difpife, & impugne God.

A 3. vnto

vnto death for my truth fake ? Where is
your loialty ? Haue not I ordained Sacraments for your fpecial comfort, a Sacrifice celeſtial for memory of my exceeding munificence, and as an homage of
Chriſtian fubjection ? haue I not in my
Church determinate ceremonies and obferuances, for the greater dignity of my
feruice, and abfoluter vnity of my family ? Al which fithence you frequent not,
where is your loue of me ? or the regard of my honour ? you oppugne me
alfo and affault me, and diffemblingly
fay, wherein doe we oppugne and affault thee. Oh Sauiour ? your example difcomforteth others, vvhich would
elfe doe wel, diffolueth the courage, de-
creafeth the number of my part, weake-
neth the caufe of faith, and fortifieth
the enimy.

5.
Schifma-
tikes wil-
fully de-
ceiue them
felues.

You flatter your felues notwithftan-
ding al thefe injuries, foothing your confciences with a vaine pretence, that you
loue and honour me ftil, and with a falfe
gloze that you would not for a thoufand
worldes forfake my feruice, nor deny my
sacred

facred name. How iniquity wil lie vnto
it felfe, and beare the port of innocency?
you lift not found the depth of your owne
hartes, for feare of touching the quicke,
and efpying the default, which you would
not fee, becaufe feing you would not a-
mend, and not amending muft needes
feele the continual fretting of a difquie-
ted confcience, and thinke your foules
to hang ouer the Dragons mouth. But
I wil fearch the ground of your hollow
hartes; reueale your deepe diffimulation,
vnmaske your vaine pretences, and
launce your feftered foares to the very
bottome.

Doe ye not as *Peter* deny your felues,
to be of my company? doe ye not appa-
rantly renounce, yea and fometime abjure
the fellowfhip of my followers? Doe ye
not pretend to haue nothing to doe with
their conuerfation, dreading to be prefu-
med, as one of their number? what is this
but to difclaime from my Religion, to
depart from the corps of my vniuerfal
Church, and to feperate your felues
from the Congregation, vvhich among

6.
By Peters
denial is
proued
that Schi-
fmatikes
deny
Chrift.

A 4. al

al the people of this land, is al only left
for my inheritance, and among whom
only I am ſerued and honoured? To deny the communion of my flocke, is to
deny me to be the true Sheep-heard, to
renounce the fellowſhip of the houſe-
hold of faith, is to renounce me for your
Lord, and to diſauow my ſeruice. In not
partaking with my children, you caſt me
off as none of your Father, and in diſioy-
ning your ſelues from the reſt of my members, you giue ſufficient argument, that I
am not your head. Thus you renounce
me for your God, denying vtterly my holy name and Majeſty. If you be not vr-
ged to deny my God-head, no more was
Peter : If you be not willed to reuolt in
hart from your Redeemer, no more was
he : If you be not expreſly commanded,
to appoſtate from your faith and conſcience, no more was he : If you deny with
mouth no one article of beleefe, no more
did he. In ſound beleefe of hart he paſſed you farre (or if compariſon ſhould
paſſe betweene you) I ſuppoſe you wil
vaunt no prerogatiue. His zeale had in
                              other

other respects beene often proued, as yours daily vpon smal trial, deserueth reproofe. Your vvickednesse may almost justifie his weakenesse, at leastwise the enormity of your crime may extenuate the guilt of his frailty. Though he denied me his Master, by denying himselfe to be a Disciple, yet waded he not so farre, as by any other external signe, to beare shew of an enimy. Though he wickedly spake, and rashly perjured as ouer-carelesse what he replied, to a Girles question; Yet before the Magistrate at publike trial of his faith, he shewed more constancy, accomplishing by losse of life, the period of this penance, then which neither could he offer vp, nor I require any greater satisfaction. After thrise offending, he conceiued harty and profound contrition, neither euer relapsed into like sacrilege, but presently bewailed vvith bitter teares, the grieuousnesse of his sinne; and lamented the longest day of his life. The crowing of the Cocke was a peale to his penance, a memorial infallible to showres of remorse, and what

one

one day had committed of finne, al
daies following omitted not to fobbe.
How different are your deferts from his?
how contrary a courfe doe ye take? mul-
tiplying your finnes without al modefty,
if not without meafure; not priuatly and
fodainly fpeaking a word of Apoftacy,
but publikely in the face of the vvorld,
committing actes of Herefie, vvithful
deliberation, with a hart refolued to hazard fhipwracke, and giue aduenture vpon the fhelfes of finne. Not conten-
ted vvith efchewing the exercife of the
Catholike faith, and participation with
the faithful, in profeffion of confcience;
ye make no fcruple to frequent the rites
of a falfe beleefe, and partake vvith my
vtter enimies, in the facrilegious impiety
of their profeffion. Yet whereas in him
you acknowledge a damnable, and mortal denial of me, the Lord of Hoftes;
your owne more apparant and odious,
you wil not vnderftand. But you re-
ply (a crafty generation, as you are,
crafty to deceiue your felues, and as ingenious in iniquity, as flow to piety)
                                    you

you wil returne vpon me the reproofe of an vnjuſt complaint : ſaying , that you be Catholikes , and remaine firmely vnited to the Church my Spouſe.

Dare ye then ſay that Catholike Reſantes , are not my proper flocke ? Or can ye maintaine , that your ſelues are of their band , members of their Church and Fraternity ? or vvil ye a-uouch that any company can be mine, vvhich imbraceth not wholy their faith ? For vpon one of theſe three , of force ye muſt rely, if ye vvil juſtifie your ſelues, to be Children of my Church , or for-tifie your errour vvith hope of ſalua-tion .

Recuſants to ſtand vpon an aſſured ground , none can juſtly deny, or vvith reaſon cal their ſaluation in queſtion ; vvho cleaue ſtedfaſtly to their fore-fa-thers faith , departing neither on the right hand , nor on the left hand, from the rule of religion , but agonizing e-uen vnto death in that Confeſſion , vvhere-unto their firſt chriſtined Aun-ceſtours vvere conuerted , and vvherein

al

7.
Schiſma-
tikes are
not of the
Catholike
Church.

8.
The aſſu-
red groũd
where vp-
on Recu-
ſants ſtãd.

al their Godly Predeceſſours, both ver-
tuouſly liued and happily died. Ye your
ſelues, though ſlacke imitaters of their
piety, cannot but admire it, and praiſe in
them that perfect reſolution and heroy-
cal courage, which bold affection though
ye feele not, though in fits of remorſe, ye
ſome time wiſh it. The very view, and
regard whereof, might make you bluſh
before men, and ſhal confound you at
the ſupreame judgement.

9.
*Recuſants
highly to
be cōmen-
ded for
their zeale*

Theſe are they vvhich nouriſh the
ſparkes of that fire, which I came downe
to kindle on earth : theſe only maintaine
in this Realme my heauenly lampe, that
it be not extinguiſhed, ſupport my law
that it be not ruinated, glorifie my name
that it be not vtterly defaced. Theſe remaine like ſtarres in the darke night, like
greene bayes in the midſt of hoary winter, like liuely freſh fountaines in the ſan-
dy deſert. Theſe are they who liue vnſpotted, a-midſt a peruerſe generation,
whoſe vertue ſtaieth my fury, and with-
holdeth my ſword from the reſt of the
people. They walke in light, and know
what

what they doe, ye confesse them to doe best, and their vowed enimies acknowledge them to be in state of saluation.

With these you may wish to consort in conscience, to partake in profession of faith : ye may in bare tearmes auouch as much, but shal neuer with reason be able to make it good. To become joynt-heires with them in the heauenly inheritance, ye may foolishly hope vpon rash presumption, but shal neuer attaine it for want of merit. Wil ye with them raigne, with whom ye doe not sustaine? Wil ye deuide in the labourers hire, nor partaking in his trauaile? Wil ye reape of their joyes, with whom ye sow not in teares? Thinke ye to feast with them, in the eternal Holy-day of the resurrection, with whom ye fast not the lent? Or beare a part in their Musical *Alleluia,* which hold no voice in their tragical *vah?* in the Psalmes not in the Threnes? Shal deniers be joyned with Confessors? disclaimers with Disciples, fugitiues with followers, faithful Souldiers with false cowards. Assoone shal shamelesse Aposta-

taes

10.
Schisma-
tikes haue
no part
with Re-
cusants,
neither are
of the
same
Church.

taes be enthronized with my holy Apoꝰ
ſtles, as peruerted Runnegates with my
ſtedfaſt Recuſants; you deny your ſelues
to be of their congregation before men;
and ſhal I acknowledge you for one of
them before my Angels ? At the time of
battaile you wil be none of them, and ſhal
ye be found vncaſſered at the time of pay?
Nay, nay, they which beare not my badge
ſhal not be cladde with my liueries; they
which be not of my retinew, ſhal not be
fedde of my diſpenſe. What then ? you
are and wil be of my ſuite and ſeruice, as
the beſt Catholikes are.

II.
Schiſma-
tikes are
not Ca-
tholikes.
And are you indeede? aske the Recu-
ſant, and he rejecteth you : aske the Per-
ſecutor, and he imbraceth you not : aske
the Saints and Angels, and they abhorre
you? I neuer yet tooke you for ſeruants of
mine, ſince you caſt away my cogni-
zance, neither did I thinke that you durſt
be ſo bold, as to aſcribe your ſelues to
my family, who are retainers to another
traine, and ſet your feete vnder my foes
table. Are ye to be deemed of the true
Church, making your reſort to the malignant?

lignant? may they be numbred in the fociety of the faithful, vvho are affociate
with Infidels? How are ye of my flocke,
who affemble in another fold, and approch not to mine; feede of other pa-
ftures and forfake mine; heare the voice
of other fheepe-heardes, and difobey
mine? Haue no confidence in vaine lying
wordes; fay not in your hartes we be Catholikes: ye are none, you haue gone
forth from among them, you haue feperated and diuided your felues, for feare
of the world, refufing to be partakers of
their punifhments and calamities, and
to beare the yoke vnder vvhich they
groane. Cal not your felues children of
my Church, vaunt not to fit in the lappe
of my beautiful Spoufe. Ye are become like blacke a-moores Brats, and
like Ægiptian Elues.

Out of my fight, whom to behold is
my griefe, the view of your vgly defor-
mity I cannot abide. As I did to *Chore*
and his cōpany, fo did I to al thofe which
negligently ftaied among his Tabernacles; as I did to *Samaria* who had quite

12.
Schifma-
tikes fhal
receiue
judgemēt
with He-
retikes.

caſt

cast off my beleefe and law, and to her
Idols, so did I to Hierusalem and her
Idols, although shee pretended no reuolt from my seruice. And as in the day
of vengeance, I wil plague Heretikes and
Infidels, who manifestly rebelled against
me, and impugned my faith, so wil I
with the same Scorpions, scourge al those
who for feare of friendship (or what respect soeuer) adhere to their faction, and
yeeld to their fury, al copartners in iniquity shal together haue their portion, in the
lake burning with brimstone, I am a jealous God, which wil not beare any com-
petitor in interest of my inheritance, any
riual in the loue of mans soule, nor indure
that the reuerence due to my diuine seruice, be exhibited to any vngodly sect,
and the personal obseruance, which my
espoused Queene challengeth, be performed to an Adulterous Synagogue.

12.
Indifferé-
cy in reli-
gion in ef-
fect Apo-
stacy.

No man can serue two Masters, without displeasing the one, no man can
warre vnder two aduersary Princes, without being a Traitour to the one. Mine
you are by generation, by regeneration
more

more mine then before, by dependance of conseruation, ye are more mine then your owne, yet wil you both in hart haue recourse to me, and in act to *Belzebub.* You say you loue my Temple, but you enter into *Bethel* and *Galgala* : like the Schismatical Israelites ; you commend my Sacrifice, but frequent the Calues of *Hieroboam.* Ye pretend to the Hil of Syon, but ye ascend to adore in the prophane Hil of Garazim as Samaritans, becomming thereby companions of Diuels, and wounding the consciences of the weake, together with the true God, ye adore the false. As those libertines among the Corinthians, relying vpon your inward beleefe, ye freely eate of Idolatrous Sacrifices, as those of Laodicea, ye are neither hotte nor cold, and therefore loathsome to my stomacke. Ye resemble those which sweare by God and by *Melchom,* vvhom therefore I threatned with vengeance, with wicked *Achab* ye worship God and Baal, nay your exteriour open worship, is whole to Baal, and not to me ; you remaine with

Amos c.5. vers. 5.

4.Reg.17.

1. Cor. 8. & 10.

Apoc. 3.

Aba.1.v.5.

me

me in fayned falſhood , and not in al
your hart : nay rather you remaine with
them , and on their ſide ; if not in al your
hart , yet in outward profeſſion ; if not
wilfully yet willingly ; if not diſpitefully,
yet diſobediently. Loue not me in word,
but in worke ; not with lips, but in hart ;
not in pretence, but in truth and ſincerity.
The peruerſe, for faſhion ſake demanded
Luke 18. *what they ſhould doe to accompliſh my wil,*
and when it was told them, neglected to
fulfil it .

If you be children of my **Church** ,
doe the workes of children ; if you be my
ſeruants , doe the vvorkes of ſeruants.
Haue acceſſe to my **Prieſts** , frequent my
Sacraments, cleanſe your ſoules by humble confeſſion and penance , haue in due
reuerence my rights and ceremonies, honour my ſeruice with your preſence, pro-
ſtrate your ſelues before my holy Altar,
liſting vp pure hartes and handes. Adore
with zealous indeauour , at the houre of
my dreadful Sacrifice ; when propitiation
for the liuing and dead , when memory
of your Redeemer is celebrated. This
ſeeke

feeke through fire and vvater, through fwordes and fnares. Let neither diftance of miles, nor friuoulous danger of places, nor furmifed peril of your owne perfons impeach Godly indeauours, what fhould I fay more, declare by your deuotion, that you hunger and thirft faluation, and that you fet by nothing fo much, as by the exercifes of your religion, and the prefence of me your Sauiour. Aboue al flie the Synagogues of Sathan ; flie al prophane praiers, al heretical couenticles, al vngodly rites, al participation with any thing, that belongeth to the table and cuppe of Deuils. This doe, and then cal me *Father of heauen, and the Church Mother of earth*, I wil bleffe you in life, and fhee fhal prefent you to me at your death.

Here you ftraine courtefie, here flefh and bloud reclaimeth, the fpirit taking the foile, and the old man triumphing ; fome of you difcharge themfelues of their crimes, by my ftewards ouer rigorous aufterity ; and by cóplaint of injury in being fecluded from my facred mifteries ? vnderftand ye what ye aske, oh ye hypocrites?

14. Schifmatikes juftly repelled from the Sacraments.

B 2.   in

in this one thing only happy, that your
ſuite is ſuſpended, and prudently rejected
by thoſe which know, that they are ordained for diſpenſers, not for ſpenders and
vvaſters of my celeſtial prouiſion, and
that the childrens foode, is not to be giuen to dogges, nor pearles to be caſt before ſwine, why demaunde ye that which
would augment your damnation, which
though moſt diuine, yet would no more
ſanctifie you then it did *Iudas*, nor more
preuaile you, then the Arke did profit the
Philiſtian. The ſweeteſt conſerues in
vndiſpoſed ſtomackes, turne to gal and
choller; the moſt nouriſhing meates,
breede moſt annoy in infected bodies,
and nothing is wholſome, where wanteth digeſtion. What flower or herbe
the Spider feedeth on, turneth to venom,
be it neuer ſo pleaſant; and vvhat Ser-
pents deuour, turneth to poiſon, be it neuer ſo wholſome.

How dare you proffer to approch to
my Altar, where ſo great a Majeſty is re-
ſident, vvithout ſufficient examination
and proofe of your worthineſſe? how can
ye

ye be proued, vnlesse ye be purged? how
purged, but by penance? how admitted,
to penance and pardon, either not acknowledging your guilt, or not in purpose of amendment?

Wel then, among my Catholikes
since you are not, where shal I finde you?
where are your raunges; being that you
cleaue to Sectaries in actes of their Schismatical profession, I pronounce you
Proteſtants, whose proceedings in departure from the faith, though in priuate
opinion (or poſsibly in talke) ye reproue,
yet by preſence at their houſes of Idolatry
you in appearance honour, by obeying
you allow, by example you further, by
deedes you confirme, by diſſembling you
eſtabliſh. You goe thither as one of them,
you ſit there as one of them, you behaue
your ſelfe reuerently as one of them.
The Caluiniſt taketh you for Proſelites,
and as either conuerted or conformed;
not altogether abhorring their pretended
religion, not ouer reſolute in the old faith,
and finally as perſons, not farre from their
Kingdome. The poore Catholike ſcan-

dalized

1 5.
Schiſma-
tiks are to
be preſu-
med for
Heretikes
and why.

dahzed at your impiety, frameth no other conceipt, then that either you are quite peruerted to herefie, or at leaftwife that your faith is in the wane; that your Sunne is fet, your deuotion done, the light of your foule extinguifhed, that you are loft fheepe, diffemblers, Schifmatikes, and at the brinke of bottomeleffe herefie. And haue not thinke you the one and the other, juft reafon of their cenfure. You giue your hand, though you vvith-hold your hart; you weare the Deuils coate, though you cal him not Lord; you honour him, though you hate him; though you abhorre him, yet you obey him.

16.

Thofe which goe to the conuenticles of Heretical rites, are juftly and properly called Schifmatikes.

Abhominable is Schifme, and horrible is the name of a Schifmatike, but why fhould this be a word of offence, to whom the fubject thereof, and the facrilege of fo great a finne, is neither fhame nor remorfe. Men are men, not priuy to the fecrets of harts: the vnderftanding cenfureth, as by the fenfes is deliuered. The Church therefore judgeth, by that which fhee feeth, not by that which fhee

feeth

feeth not. The deede (as reafon wil)
doth prejudice the contrary word, and
vpon the fact rifeth fentence of faith?

When my Church in her firft prime,
vvas nipped vvith fharpe perfecution,
fo that diuers bloffomes fel from her
branches, thofe which through paffio-
nate feare condefcended to Idolatry,
vvere by the Bretheren condemned as
fallen from their faith, rejected as A-
poftataes, and denounced excommuni-
cated, neither receiued againe vvithout publike fatisfaction, and many yeares
penance.

He that fhould keepe the Saterday holy, and pray with Iewes in their congregation, were to be fuppofed a Iew : Euery man would exclaime againft the fact,
vvithout caring for the caufe. He that
entreth any of *Mahomets* mefchits, prayeth in his Temples, or kiffeth the bookes
of his law, is of euery Chriftian man de-
fied for a Runnegate, and of the Turkes
priuileged for a Boferman ; no man in-
quiring whether loue of their Mahome-
try, or dread of extremity, whether carnal

B 4 fen-

ſenſuality and liberty of their law, or
worldly proſperity, did moue him : fix-
ing their eies vpon his outward action,
men let the intention repoſe it ſelfe in the
profound abiſme of the hart, what then
ſhould hinder, why you alſo aſſociating
Heretikes in their actions, yea principal
and proper actions of their profeſſion,
ſhould not be blazoned for adherents to
Infidelity, bearing the blot of departers
from my Church Catholike, and conſequently of Schiſmatical perſons.

17.
Proteſtāts
cannot be
of the Ca-
tholike
Church,
neither in
their faith
can be
ſaluation.

I know, I know, what it is that lieth
at your hart, a miſchiefe ſo corrupting
your appetite, that it deſireth not good,
and your taſt that it diſcerneth not euil;
a priuy poiſon, but ſo peſtiferous, ſo be-
numming (not the ſenſes, but the ſoule)
that if it be not exhauſted, an incureable
letargy, a mortal and euerlaſting ſleepe
enſueth, ye are not perſwaded forſooth,
that the Proteſtants religion is ſo abhominable; they are to preciſe, which either
make them Heretikes, or thinke that
Heretikes muſt needes miſcarry. What?
we be al Chriſtians, beleeue in one Sauiour,

uiour, expect one heauen, and enjoy one
redemption. Haue not al men foules to
faue : little differences make no great
fquare, in the foundation we agree. At
leaftwife, whatfoeuer their liues be wicked, and doctrine falfe, their praiers and
Churches muft needs be of God, becaufe
they be good, and needes be good, becaufe they honour God.

Ah ingenious impiety, how thou tur-
neft and toffeft to winde from thy accufer ? nay rather, ah foolifh ftubborne
blindneffe, which wil not fee that, which
is as cleare as noone day, which taketh
for one (or as not much different) thofe
thinges which are as wide diftant as the
two poles of heauen. To take your felues
for a particular Church, is vnpoffible for
a heedleffe multitude, who haue neither
Temple, Altar, Prieft, nor Sacrifice, neither diftinct members, nor any band of
vnion. Afwel you may thinke of going
at the latter day, neither to heauen nor to
hel, as to thinke in this life of a Neutrali-
ty ? Blinde you are, if you perceiue not
your felues to be feperated from my
Church ;

Church; but if you imagine that thoſe whom you cleaue vnto, may be my congregation, and that in their praiers, holyneſſe; or in their faith, ſaluation may be found; then are ye both blinde and impious.

Pro. 17. Take heede what you ſay, to juſtifie the wicked is as deteſtable, as to condemne the juſt. Wil you diuide my Church, whoſe eſpecial marke and property is vnity? or wil you giue me two Bodies miſtical, two Spouſes vnſpotted, two chaſt Turtles, two Citties on hilles, two Kingdomes, two Families, two Pillars of truth; Am I an adulterer, or am I deuorſed from my loue. To ſay that Proteſtants may by their profeſſion be ſaued, is either to make an other God beſide me, or to make me none; to make an other *ſummum bonum*, or to make me euil, to league me with *Lucifer*, or to make *Iehouah Sathan*, to conclude me as authour of diſſention, or patron of impiety, a double diſſembler, or a flat Heretike.

If I can haue two Churches ſo different

rent in rites, so contrary in doctrine, so
naturally and necessarily tending the one
to the vtter extirpation of the other,
then giue me two heauens for them, and
contrary glories for their opposite deserts. Diuide my God-head vvith furious *Manes*, and defend one God good,
and an other euil; or say that I am mu-
table good, and badde by enter-change
of places, and enter-course of times.
If there bee two Churches, prouide
them of two Christes; if there be two
Moones, finde them two Sunnes: An
other Sunne to lighten this other Moone;
an other Christ to illuminate this other
Church; an other Redeemer to wash
her in his bloud; an other Holy Ghost
to Sanctifie her: for I dyed but for
one, my diuine Spirit sanctifieth but
one.

If on the other side, you joyne Calui-
nists with Catholikes in one Church, then
set togither the Woolfe with the Lambe;
couple the Lyon vvith the Hart; the
Gos-hawke vvith the Partridge, and
they shal wel agree. No, no, heauen and
hel

18.
The per-
fect oppo-
sition and
contrarie-
ty of Ca-
tholikes
and Pro-
testants.

hel haue as much affinity, as haue thefe
two religions , and fhal affoone fhake
handes, the one being fure, the other furmifed; the one infallible, the other vnpoffible ; the one founded by my felfe
from the beginning , and vpon a Rocke;
the other newly reared by mans imaginations, cherifhed for pollicy, hauing no
other ground then flitting and foundring
fand , the one intituled by prefcription,
the other fetled in poffeffion, the one e-
rected by diuine prouidence, the other
feazed by intrufion, (and to be briefe) the
one mine , the other *Belzebubs* , the one
diuine , the other Deuilifh. Where are
my indifferent mates, that can beare two
faces in one hood, carry fire in one hand,
and water in the other, that can breathe
both hotte and cold , that can hold with
the Hare and runne with the Hound :
Weather-cocks vvhich turne with the
winde : Camelions transforming their
hew , according to the prefent object
which they fee. Let them vnfould the
whole fardle of their fancies, and bring
me forth the golden meane, which they

so much commend.

Combine me fire and vvater in one bundle ; make me vnderstand (oh ye Neuters) how these two faiths can be reconciled together , or constitute one faithful company , being so opposite , that of necessity the one must be plaine blasphemy , or the other Idolatry : For as much as my dreadful Eucharist is irrefragably beleeued by the one, to be my true body ; not in figure, but in verity ; not in conceipt, but in *re* ; not in shadow, but in substance ; not in faith only , but by my personal presence , and consequently is adored with due veneration, whereas by Hugonots and other Heretikes it is injuriously reuiled , vpbraided as an Idol , torne , spit at , and troden vnder foote (beastly Monsters as they are.) Of other maine differences , consider vvith your selues the particularities ; in number of Sacraments, in vse of Images , in inuocation of Saints , in forgiuenesse of Sinnes, in heauenly Glory, in Infernal paines , in Iustification of the liuing , in praying for the Dead , in Faith , Hope, and Charity,

in

in Faftings and Praiers, in Sinne and
Merit, in Predeftination and Free-wil,
in Scriptures, in Traditions, and almoft
in the whole fumme of Faith. Shal
Arius, Neftorius, and *Eutiches* with o-
ther old Heretikes be juftly credited, by
vniuerfal confent of al ages, and by your
owne verdicts to roare in the bottomeleffe pit for one or two points (for further
they went not) and ftagger ye vvhat to
thinke of them, who haue toffed ouer
euery ftone, reuerfed the whole frame of
faith, and turned al vpfide-downe? Or is
not rather their departure, and diuifion
from my Church, a fufficient vvarrant of
their judgement, though but in one point
only, they varied from the faith.

19.   Caluinifme then being doctrine fo dia-
How ab- bolical; what are the fruits thereof? what
hominable are al thinges which depend vpon it, or
the Scrip-
tures, prai- are annexed thereunto? Haue this for cer-
ers, and taine, vvhatfoeuer concurreth with my
Churches faith, concurreth with me; and whatfoe-
of Here-
tikes are. uer hath affinity with herefie, confpireth
with Sathan, who is the father of lying,
and fofterer of falfhood. You miftake
much

much, if you take their Scriptures to be my word: Fie, none of mine, they are the word of the Deuil, false adulterated, poisoned, peruerted, ful of corruptions, which belie me in euery leafe, and make my spirit to speake thinges, which I neuer thought, oppugning my faith and church, for whose maintenance and comfort they were inspired, I disclaime from them as from a counterfaite copy, and renounce them as no deede of mine.

You erre if you thinke their praiers to be praiers, whatsoeuer they say, whatsoeuer they sing, it is in my eares the howling of Wolues, the bellowing of Bulles, the screetching of Owles, the mutual answering of night Rauens in the deserts. Oh how illusion bewitcheth you: if you deeme Ministers to succeede in the authority of my chaire, and participate in my keies, they are of heresie heresies, pensioners, officers of Antichrist, his Heralds, his Prolocutors, his Scribes, his Preachers, his fore-runners, his Apostles, and the Angels of his Kingdome. Lesse danger to the body is to sucke Adders egges, then

Hierom.in c.4.Osee.

then to the soule miniſtration of their
prophane bread ; and better it were to
ſwil the dregges of a fatal boule, then to
ſippe the cup of their communion. Their
rites and ceremonies, though few and
fantaſtical, yet not a little noiſome and
infectious. They are not holy, but prophane; not religious, but ſacriligious ;
yea, euen thoſe which they retaine of the
auncient cuſtome, as Faſtes and Holy-
daies, which ſithence they haue tranſlated to vnder-propping of their ſuperfi-
cial and ruinous edifice, and to diſguiſing
of their falſe ware and fradulent traſh,
doe pleaſe me euen as much as a man de-
lighteth to be wounded with his owne
blade, and diſpighted with his owne in-
uentions. Yea their Churches and Temples (be not carried away with the accu-
ſtomed phraſe) are no more holy , no
more my houſe, no more the place of my
Sanctification.

They were, they were mine ; but then
mine, when none of theirs ; for becomming theirs, they ceaſed to be mine.
Why cal you that mine which is con-
                                    quered,

quered, poſſeſſed, and polluted by my e-
nimies? My aduerſary, yea your aduerſary, and the aduerſary of al mankinde,
boaſteth in the ſeate which was holy, and
hath placed his chaire of peſtiléce, where
the ſacred Altar my earthly Throne ſtood.
In ſteade of Quyres of Angels, which   Chryſ.
earſt frequented about it, deſcending and
aſcending (though mortal eies were vnworthy of the ſight) as the dignity of my
preſence required, legions of infernal
ſpirits there now daunce, (though for a-
uerting your mindes, they bewray not
themſelues) triumphing not only as in
their moſt proper reſidence and Pallace,
but more, as in a ſubdued fort, victo-
riouſly obtained againſt me. Woe to the
betraiers, that of faint courage, firſt gaue
ouer my hold, and rendred my ſigniory;
and woe to al thoſe which ſhal thither
now goe, to yeeld their homage and alleageance. The honour which there is
exhibited, keepeth courſe of ſpeech by
pretence of my name, but in verity touch-
eth not me, but is appropriate to *Lucifer*,
who alwaies affecting to paragonize the
C higheſt,

highest, his hatred is so strong; his enuy
so cankred, his insolency so haughty, that
he reckoneth as nothing al other honours, which Heathens and Pagans vnto
him exhibite, except he may draw to
himselfe, whatsoeuer is wont to be mine,
and magnifie himselfe with the brauery
of my plume.

Genes.12. Bethel vvas my house, where *Iacob*
& 31.   and the Patriarkes both adored and Sa-
1.Reg.10. crificed, but after King *Hieroboam* had
3.Reg.12. cut off Israel from Hierusalem, and had
& 13.   there erected a Religion, Priests, and
Sacrifices, of his owne inuention? vvas
Deutr. 11. Bethel any more my house? Garazim
& 17.   I ordained for a hil of benediction; but
Ioh. 4.   when the Samaritans vsurped it for a place
of their adoration, was it any longer a hil
Genes. 12. of benediction? Sichem where I appeared to *Abraham*, was a place sanctified
* 3.Reg.12 and adorned by him, in memory thereof
Iohn. 4. with an Altar, but when the Schismatical
Where Si- people had made it the * Metropolitane
char is af- See of their seperation, was Sichem from
firmed by thence-forth sacred? Or are the Turkish
S,Hierom mesquits houses of diuine praier, becaufe
to be al
one with
Sichem.
they-

they were in times paſt Chriſtian Churches? No more then *Iudas* was the Temple of the holy Ghoſt, after the tempter
had inuaded his hart, when the place is
ſo prophane, becauſe of the ſeruice therein exerciſed, what can the ſeruice it ſelfe
be but meere abhomination?

Oh thinke not it can be to my worſhip
which is ſo wicked. Remember, that Altar is raiſed vp againſt Altar, Prieſts ſet
vp againſt Prieſts, Sacraments againſt
Sacraments, Seruice againſt Seruice,
Faith againſt Faith, betweene vvhich
there is not, (neither poſſible can be)
any vnity concord or conformity; Or
to ſpeake more properly, and not by
the common peoples tearmes, vvho i-
gnorantly confound the names of thinges
cal to minde, that againſt my venerable
Altar, there is erected a plaine communion Table, in defiance of the pretious
and veritable Hoſt (my owne quickning
and ſanctifying Body) is exalted, the
Idol of their contemptible Supper, a
baſe and vnprofitable peece of bread,
in liew of my anointed Prieſtes, are

20.
The Pro-
teſtants
publike
praier,
how vn-
lawful &
deteſtable

C 2, ob-

obtruded the Miniſters of darkeneſſe, for
a reuerent, worthy, ſound, and vndoub-
ted faith, is crept in baſtard, counterfaite, vncertaine, and fained miſcreance.

If Maſſe and Mattins, were fully and
wholy vſed in their aſſemblies, and that
publike praier had nothing of their owne
corruption, yet were it abhominable in
my ſight, proceeding from their Mini-
ſtery, who haue runne away from my
Church, and ſtolen away with them her
ornaments; and to couer the ragges where
with they are rigde; jet vp and downe,
cladde in her robes. Can the veile of a
Virgin, make a ſtrumpet honeſt, or ſtolen attire beautifie hereſie? Is this any o-
ther, then with Iewes to bow the knee,
and ſpit in my face, to crowne vvith
thornes, and then ſalute as King.

If the ſeruice (I ſay) were perfectly
Catholike, yet wil I giue no licence and
leaue to Sacrifice in Ægypt, but wil be
ſerued among a chaſt generation, and
rather in the deſert, then among the Æ-
gyptians. How then ſhal I brooke a
forme of praier, a ſhadow of diuine ſeruice,

nice, wholy tending to maintenance of heresie, not only abrogating, disanulling, suppressing, my auncient and approued rites, but directly substituted in defiance of me and my misteries, and of the faith Catholike, which is put into English, to insinuate that my Church erreth in not vsing the vulgar; blotteth out inuocation of Saints, as open Idolatry; and praier for the dead, as plaine superstition; cancelleth Confecration, as vanity and falshood; abhorreth Eleuation, as detestable impiety; praieth expresly for propagation of their Sect, and in imprecation, joyneth *Peters* Successour (the Rocke of faith) with the Mahumetan Potentate, and his confederates.

See here the seruice, which they who mocke me, cal mine, and they who delude themselues, name the old seruice translated: where are the memories and representations of my Saints? (lessons of instruction to the ignorant, and examples of piety to the simple) are they not dispitefully broken and brent as Idols? where is my standert, the eternal monu-

C 3. ment

ment of my triumph, at the sight whereof the furies quake, and whose sight is to euery good Christian as a sentence, heard or read out of my passion? where are my Tapers, which warne people, to see that their life be light, and their soules free from darkenesse? where are the Vestments and Vessels of sanctification, doth not the face of al thinges in their Temples, import a perfect and absolute alteration in faith? doe not the very walles & pillers cry out, that Catholikes should not come there? Ah ye poore Schismatical soules, how long vvil ye erre and runne forward without remorse, if reason stay you not, regard the examples of constancy, which stand before your eies; and how faithful beleeuers behaue themselues.

21.
Schisma-
tikes vain-
ly build
vpon per-
nitious
examples.

You can say that Priests did in many Parishes follow the new course, and many of them yet liuing, continue in the same. And why rather leane ye not vnto the example of the Bishops, vvhom no lesse learning and sanctity then their Superiours function, more commend vnto

you;

you; vvho vniuersaly died in long and lingring imprisonment, no one yeelding to vnconscionable conformity, but rather choosing to loose both liuings and liberty and to see their aduersaries possesse their chaires. Oh but great Presidents moue you, and many wise fellowes haue assaied this Ice before you. Ye pry vpon the corruptest soules, as Kites when they seeke a carkasse; and like the Rauen, vvhich *Noe* let flie, ye rather wil stay your selues vpon a carrion, then returne to the Arke. Why rather returne ye not vvith the Doue, although ye should haue found greene boughes, whereon to recline? you propose to your weary and tired spirit, to your fainting harts, the examples of certaine which seeme to you wise, but are in very deede fooles; seeme learned, are ignorant; seeme religious, are meere worldlings.

Aswel you might build, that theft, extortion, murder, or adultery, vvere no wickednesse, because they sometimes fal into these sinnes, whom a false shew of wisdome or vertue had before cõmended.

C 4. Euery

Euery man that sinneth, doth not straight thinke it lawful, wil you direct your life by his rule, who perhaps condemneth his owne, yet if any wil stifly defend their Schisme, to cleare themselues from sinne, is this sufficient security, to follow such mens fantasies? where haue these Pastors the key of knowledge; vvhence fetcht these Doctors their profound learning? where waded they, through the depthes of diuinity? No man in his waighty cause trusteth the warrant of a puny student, contrary to the opinion of Counfailors, no man crediteth his life to a raw practisioner, against the aduise of the experiensed Philition. And wil ye hazard your soules vpon a presumptuous smatterers conjecture, neglecting what they teach, whose only labour is to guide to heauen; whose life and study is the daily meditation of my law.

22.
Examples fit to be regarded by Schismarikes for their instruction.

Why rather fixe ye not before your eies, so many both of the spiritualty and laity, who haue in your owne memory, but yesterday, yea daily, sustained bloudy and ignominious death, rather then runne

runne your race and incurre damnation?
Walke to the prifons, fee if they be not
ful of my Confeffors? there haue you examples juftly to be imbraced, not one
but many, not many but multitudes.

If thinges prefent pleafe you not, caft
your regard vpon ages paft, confider
what the faithful in al antiquity hath beene
wont to doe in like cafe, as yours is now.
Weigh what *Tobias* would haue done Tob. 1.
in thefe times, who when al Ifrael frequented the Calues of *Hieroboam*, though
he were of their Tribes, yet would neuer
beare them company, but contrary to the
Kinges ordinance, and the peoples practife, went yearely to adore at Hierufalem, what thofe religious hartes would
haue performed, who being Ifraelites for-
fooke their natiue Country, becaufe of
the Schifme, and went to dwel in Iuda 1. Paral.1 %
vnder a right belecuing Prince.

What conftancy the feauen Brethe-
ren would haue fhewed, who were facri- Mac. 7.
ficed by vnfpeakeable torments, for refufing to eate fwines flefh, at King *Antiochus* commandement, becaufe it was
an

an act abhorring from the profeſſion of their law.

Mach. 6.

How would *Eleazarus* haue behaued himſelfe, who gladly ſuffered death, rather then to giue ſcandal by ſeeming conformable to the ſame wicked decrees, refuſing moſt conſtantly ſo to diſſemble, as publikely to eate meates, not forbidden indeede by *Mayſes*, yet proffered vnto him, and pretended to the beholders as ſwines fleſh, thereby outwardly condeſcending to the Infidels proceedings.

How reſolute would *Machabeus* haue beene, how couragious his Sonnes? What a firery and zealous anſwere gaue the Father to the Kinges Commiſſioners, exacting his obedience to the late edicts, concerning alteration in religion. *If al men obey the Kinges commandements, yet I and my Sonnes wil neuer doe it*. If to theſe Preſidents ye pleade that *Moyſes* was greater then I, my ſeruant then my ſelfe, that more perfection and zeale was to be required of Iewes, then of Chriſtians, that my old Teſtament, was more holy and more preciſely to be ſtood vpon
then

then my new, bethinke your selues of my
Apostles and Disciples, whose heires and
imitatours as ye pretend to be in faith, so
ye ought to be in profession.

Would *Peter* thinke you haue broo-
ked *Luther*, founder and grand-father of
so many falshoods, who for one article of
misbeleefe, bidde *Simon Magus* auaunt
as ful of bitter gal, and the child of perdition? Would *Paul* haue spared Ministers
the seducers of many soules, who stoutly
called *Elymas* the Deuils Sonne, and eni- Act. 13.
my of righteousnesse, for diswading one
man from the faith, & by his word stroke
him with blindnesse? Would my diuine
Euangelist *S. Iohn* haue endured *Iohn Cal-*
uin that Arch-heretike, the corrupter of
whole Prouinces, who at the sight of pet-
ty *Cerinthus*, subuerter not of the thou- Iren. lib.
sands person, in comparison of the other, 3. cap. 3.
cried out to the people, that they should Euseb. hist
flie from his company, least the place cap. 22.
where they were, together should for *Ce-*
rinthus sake fal vpon their head. Perhaps these pillers of my church, would to
saue their goods or liues, haue reuerently
heard

heard the common praiers of *Simon*, *Elymas*, and *Cerinthus*, honoured their abhominations, and receiued communion bread at their handes. What apprehended ye of al my auncient Martirs? thousands of whom each day throughout the yeare, hath regiftred in the booke of life, and crowned with an immortal Garland, becaufe they would not partake with Idolaters, in any act of their vngodlineffe.

23.
Participation in workes of Herefie worfe then in actes of Idolatry.

If now you be fo fimple, as to thinke that Herefie is not worfe then Idolatry; that to forfake me, is not worfe then neuer to haue followed me; to deny me, then not to confeffe me; to abjure me, then not to know me; to blafpheme, then not to honour me; that Infidels for their ignorance, fhal be beaten vvith many ftripes, and Herefie for her peruerfneffe; malice and apoftacy fhal be beaten, with few; that to caft two or three graines of Francumcenfe vpon a Heathen Altar; or to lay a bunch of Grapes before *Bacchus*, to crowne *Ceres* with eares of corne; to moue a little the bonnet before *Iupiter* be

Syndas
Nicephorus.

be greater sacrilege, then the courtesie
of cappe and knee, and reuerential presence, at their thrise Idolatrous communion; or then the seruice to maintenance
thereof erected; euery jot of whose ri-
tual customes, and publike praiers vvas
inuented, commanded, practised, and is
stil continued, only in detestation, defiance, extirpation, and denial of my faith
Catholike.

Then, oh then how are ye deceiued?
seing euery falshood, the more it hath of
truth, is the more apt to beguile; the
more apt to beguile, the more pernitious
to the distruction of soules, and more
abhominable. False Prophets which cry
the Lord, the Lord, when I the Lord haue
not spoken vnto them, are worse ten-fold
then the Prophets of *Baal*, sooner shal
the Publican be justified, then the hypo-
critical Pharasie, viler and more hatefull
before me and men is the Adultresse,
which by Matronlike demeanure would
seeme a Saint, then the open Strumpet
which carrieth lightnesse on her backe,
and vanity in her face. A plaine fable is
laughed

24.
Heresie
worse
then Infi-
delity and
Idolatry.

laughed at, but not hated, becaufe it is not made to deceiue, neither is apt to deceipt if the authour would, but a lie forged, and obtruded for truth is intollerable; Yet if fo be that wilfulneffe hath amazed reafon, that whereas you are refolued to die, rather then yeeld to Idolatry(for fo now and then you would make your felues beleeue) yet you would yeeld to herefie, rather then fuftaine any damage.

Reflect then once at my requeft, vpon my good Chriftians, whom (Idolatry being ouer-come)I exercifed by Arianifme; fome-what alwaies, being neceffary to try my elect. Reflect (I fay) your vnderftanding vpon their excellent zeale : (except perhaps ye refufe with foare eies, to behold the Sunne, for feare of greater annoy) marke wel how they fortified their faith againft the Arrian Heretikes.

Socrat.l.2. c.12.22.23. 24. Theod. l.4.cap.14. Niceph. l. 9. cap. 24. Regard how in Greece, they withftood the Proclamations of *Valens* the Emperor, choofing rather to be fcorched, brent, flaine, at their affemblies without
                                the

the Church walles, then they would be present at publike praier of their heretical Superintendent, though their seruice which he said were nothing altered from their owne ; set before your eies the horrible calamities, and intollerable vexations, vvhich Catholikes in Africa endured, vnder their Vandal Princes, for refusing to partake with them in their Arrian rites, and for priuately frequenting Masse, vvhen it was forbidden.

Victot Vtic. de persecuti-one Vandalorum.

Finally, muster before your selues the Martirs and Confessors of al ages, from the beginning of the vvorld, to this present time, from *Abel* to the last which you haue seene (or might haue seene) with your owne eies. Let the very names of *Martir* and *Confessor* exhort you : the first whereof admonisheth you, that I require your testimony : refuse not therefore to beare witnesse of my truth ; the other that I challenge your suite and seruice at my Court, your duty and attendance at my feasts, your vassalage and alleageance confesse therefore and deny me not.

Martit signifieth witnesse.

Oh

Oh ye ſtubborne bowes, which wil rather breake then come to the juſt bent,
which the true meaſure of Chriſtianity
requireth? Oh peruerſe generation, how
much ye want of the perfection of auncient beleeuers? Nay, how much want ye
of the true zeale, which a number of good
ſoules declare, on whom yet I haue beſtowed leſſe gifts, either of nature or of
worldly proſperity? In caſe you ſay to
your ſelues, that you ſee not the actions of
auncient times, yet the example and conſtancy of theſe, doth euery day in euery
place hitte you on the eies, and might
wound your hartes, if they were fleſh, and
not of flint: nay, if they were not too
fleſhy, and voide of al ſpirit. How juſt
cauſe haue I then to exclaime againſt you
(oh diſloyal wreatches) how long wil ye
reject my authority, and kicke againſt
my Commandements? who am I that
charge you? am not I the Omnipotent?
who am I that cal you? am I not your
Creatour? You put your hand in your
boſome, and draw forth an empty excuſe
from your hollow hartes, you can remember

25.
By what
cōmande-
ments of
God going
to the He-
retiks prai-
ers is for-
bidden.

member no law of mine, that you brake
by going to heretical feruice, nor can
finde any precept to the contrary. I perceiue that you are deeplier feene in the
ftatutes of men, then in mine ordinances,
in the common law, then in the Canons,
more minde the managing of fecular affaires, then of your foules, and better
know how many yeares purchafe a peece
of land is worth, or how much a loade of
corne commeth to at fuch a rate, then
what price heauen is to be valued at, or
what fumme of felicity merits added to
merits, wil at length amount vnto, which
is that great and maine commandement,
not the principal point only, but the a-
bridgement of the whole law?

Is it not, that man loue me with al his
hart, vvith al his ftrength, with al his
foule? you anfwere, this ferueth your
turne, and that you loue me afmuch as I
require: But defcend to the particulars,
and you fhal be taken with the lie.

Did I no where wil, that befides be-
leeuing in hart, you fhould alfo profeffe
your beleefe before men. Or vvil you

D   vio-

violently make me to meane before Iews
and Heathen, but not before Heretikes;
in time of religion flourishing, but not in
time of persecution, to the obtaining of
credit or commodity, but not to detriment? Did I not adde, that he which denieth me before men, shal be denied of
me, in the presence of Angels. He which
shal be ashamed of my religion, I wil put
him to open confusion, and which shal
saue his life temporally, by yeelding to
the persecutour, shal loose it eternally
being condemned at a more dreadful tribunal, when vniuersal Sizes are held o-
uer al the world.

Isay 42.　　　Haue I not said, that I am a jealous
God, and wil not giue my honour to ano-
Deuter.7.　ther? Did I not seuerely forbidde my people, to entermedle in Heathenisse rites?
Exod. 23.　did I not for peril thereof interdict them
al society, and conuersation with Infidels?
did I not denounce by my Apostles pen,
that as in hart men are to beleeue, that
Rom. 10.　they may be justified, so with mouth they
are to confesse their faith, that they may
be saued? If by mouth, how much more
by

by deedes, and the whole course of their life? Or wil I (thinke you) contrary my owne decrees, approue him which confesseth me in wordes, and denieth me in profession?

And what if I had not in such expresse wise prescribed your duty? doth not the light of reason, the law of nature, the office of a Christian man, suggest, teach, command, that ye cleaue firmely to your faith, and that for no cause possible to be imagined, ye commit any thing, in word or deed, or omit any thing by negligence or slouth, which may import a departure from your religion, or be so interpreted and accepted; or that may seeme in any one point a conformity; to a strange and false faith, a yeelding or agremēt to irreligious proceedings? If he which breaketh one commandement be guilty of al, as a violater of charity; shal not he likewise, vvhich faileth or falleth in one point of faith, be fully guilty of Infidelity? To beare truly the title of a faithful soule, it is not enough to beleeue a-right in one or two articles, but my whole law, that

26.
Schisma-
tikes vio-
late the
law of
nature, by
going to
the Pro-
testants
Churches.

is the entire word *of faith*, must stedfastly
be imbraced. If then I shal say ; *goe ye
curfed* , for not doing good, for omitting
only hofpitality , and workes of mercy,
shal wickednesse goe scot-free, shal partaking with Heretikes in their abhominations , passe as innocent ? Shal departure from my Church , my Faith, and Sacraments , deserue to heare : *Come ye
blessed* ? Is there nothing for me to exa-
mine , but whether you be murtherers,
theeues, or adulterers? doe I much respect
that you should not offend your neigh-
bour, and contemne my owne injuries.

27.   I foretold, while I conuersed on earth,

Herefie & that heresies of necessity must be for the
perfecutiō
purpofely trial , and manifeftation of mens hartes,
permitted that it might be apparant, who would of
of God for a proude and contemptuous spirit em-
trial of
més harts. brace herefie , who would of faint hart
and pufilanimity obey it , who contrary-
wife vvould meekely trace his reuerent
Fathers fteps , and preferre the authority
of the vniuerfal Church , before his owne
imaginations , and not to be shaken as a
reede , with any tempeftes of bluftering
                                                    per-

perfecution. I fore-warned that I came Luke 12.
not to fend peace but feperation , betweene Parents and Children, Subject
and Prince, Mafter and Seruant , betweene Wife and Husband , Bretheren,
Kinsfolke, and Friendes, that perfecuti-
ons fhould be raifed on al fides , and that
he which loueth parents or children , or
what elfe more then me , and wil not
take vp his Croffe and follow me , is not Math. 10.
my Difciple , nor worthy to haue part in
my Kingdome.

Are you Chriftians, and thinke your 25.
felues excufed from the precept , which I Diffembling
gaue to the Synagogue, that if any man is abho-
would draw you to a ftraunge faith , he minable.
fhould not be obeyed, for that by fuch I
make proofe of my feruants , I difcouer
the fecrets of the hart ; and fift the branne
from the fine flowre, try the wheate from
chaffe ..

Are you Chriftians, and know not that
to follow a falfe faith , is to ferue a falfe
God , and to beginne new and ftraunge
doctrine of faith , is to erect a new and
ftraunge Idol. If you doubt thereof, I

D 3.   affure

affure you it is fo. And now is your time of trial: now are you called vpon, follicited, yea commanded to follow new doctrine, to ferue *Caluins* Idol, now are you caft into the furnace, now fhal you proue your felues, either gold or droffe, and the calamities of this prefent time, I haue purpofely fent that the fecrets of al hartes fhal be reuealed.

Reuealed you are to your owne fhame and to my griefe. What fhal I doe to your ftony hartes, to whom my ferious commandement, of profeffing fincerely your faith by your conuerfation, is but as a puffe of winde againft a mountaine? Shal I charge your confciences vvith *Moyfes* ceremonies, and caufe you as I did the Iewes, to beare the remembrance of this commandement vpon your bodies, feing it is fo flune from your hartes. Shal I forbidde you to vveare linfeywoolfey in your raiment, to joyne in the plough the Affe with the Oxe, and to fow with two kinde of feedes. Though thefe obferuances were appendant to the

old

old law, doubt ye not but the significa-
tion of them, taketh place in the new.
He which walketh simply and plainely, Pro. 10.
walkes confidently; Dissimulation and
double-dealing, I in euery thing hate;
but in factes of religion, I vtterly abhorre.

Admit that neither reason nor rule of 29.
conscience suggested vnto you, nor that Schisma-
I expresly exacted of you such firme con- temne the
fession of faith, yet ought not the autho- authority
rity of my Church, to weigh so light in of the
your conceipts, as neither to hearken Church.
vnto my Priests, who to reduce you
from Heretical conuenticles, set nought
by their liues, and haue by their bloud
confirmed the thing to be vnlawful, refusing to accept pardon of life, vpon so
damnable a condition; nor to my Vicar
in earth, who sollicitous for soules, spa-
reth neither care nor cost for your saluation, nor to the declaration of my
General Councel at Trent, which resolued (when this case came first in question) that not without grieuous sacrilege,
D 4. you

you could yeeld your presence, at the
Heretikes Churches, or Ecclesiastical af-
semblies ; or by any other manner of
signe, giue external consent to their detestable rites. A thing indeede, which
by men of vnderstanding could neuer
haue beene doubted off, if worldly feare
had not blinded peoples harts, and made
them hard to beleeue, that which pleased not their humour. What can they
therefore accompt themselues, who wil
not hearken to my Spoufes voice, nor o-
bey her admonition ; but to be vvorse
then Heathens and Infidels. Let them
know, that not to obey her, is as sacrile-
gious as idolatry, and al that contemne
her are accursed.

Besides that principal precept, of louing your God aboue al ; and that other
absolute statute of constant profession of
my faith Catholike, which suffereth no
exception. If you wil but a little looke
about you, ye shal finde that I haue yet
left you another commandement, as a
continual helpe against mans frailty, a so-
ueraigne preseruation against al infection
of

Math. 17.

2. Reg.

Tob. 13.

30.
Heretikes
how pre-
cisely to be
shunned.

of peſtilent doctrine. It is more auaileable againſt the ſpiritual enimy, then any armour of proofe, or a ten-fold ſhield: and might in theſe darkeſome daies be a torch vnto your ſteps. Wil you beare to heare it? wil you indeauour to follow it, that my preſent admonition, may not turne to your greater damnation? you wil, if you may heare it from my owne mouth, it ſhal be joyfully receiued, as comming from heauen, your wordes are reaſonable.

Wel then, whoſe ſpirit but mine inſpired, and eſtabliſhed as a perpetual obſeruation, to the worldes end, that Heretikes ſhould be vtterly auoided, as *men* ſubuerted and already damned by their owne judgemēt; as *ſowers* of ſchiſme and authors of diuiſion, by teaching contrary faith, to that which was firſt receiued; as *whoſe* ſpeech creepeth like a canker; as *louers* of pleaſures, rather then of God, making a ſhew of piety, but denying in effect the vertue thereof; as *Wolues* in ſheepes attire; as *authours* of blaſphemous Sects, bold, ſelfe conceipted, walking

Tit. 3.
Rom. 16.

2. Tim. 2.
2. Tim. 3.

Math. 7.
2. Pet. 2.

king after the flesh ; as *those* who following their owne fancies and desires , *haue*
issued out from among the faithful , and
fallen from the truth , * *turning* the grace
of God to vncleanenesse, and are therefore already appointed to iudgement ;
as *false* Apostles , deceitful labourers ,
Ministers of Sathan , whose end shal be
according to their workes , and (to conclude al iniquity , imaginable vnder one
title) as *Antichrist* , I wil not therefore,
that ye eate or drinke , or haue familiarity
with them , I wil not that ye friendly *sa-
lute* them , for in so doing you partake in
their wicked workes , and bolster them in
their proceedinges , and by iust conse-
quent must be partners of their damnation .

How long shal the light of reason and
conscience sleepe ? how often must ye be
admonished , that right beleeuers must
not participate with Infidels ; that I can
haue no society with *Belial* : nor my cup
vvith the cup of Deuils . If light and
darkenesse can loue ? If I ioyne in any
respect with *Lucifer* , if euer any mercy,
loue,

Marginal notes:

a. Pet. 3.
1. Ioh. 2.

2. Tim. 2.
* Iudæ 4.

2. Cor. 11.

1. Ioh. 2.

Ioh. ep. 2.

loue, or amity, any league or confent,
be betweene him and me, then let Catholikes adhere to Heretikes. If no fuch
thing can poffibly be, but that eternal
enmity bee fworne betweene vs, why
then fhould children of Hierufalem,
come to the folemnities of Babylon?
they which looke to be heires of heauen,
make pact with hel? expecters of life e-
uerlafting, marchandife for their temporal with accurfed death? He that runneth with the theefe, fornicateth with
the adulterer, murthereth with the Tyrant, is in no cafe to be excufed, no not
although they doe it for feare, more
then for affection to the finne.

Shal they then vvhich profeffe herefie, with Heretikes bee found cleare?
Of like I had no reafon to forbidde
you their company, for you are proui-
dent and difcreet, firmely grounded in
the Catholike faith, ftronge Rockes,
vvhome no vvaues nor tempeftes can
moue, vveake vvreatches, and fo
much the vveaker, by how much you
prefume more of your felues, and rely

31.
Schifma-
tikes are
infected
with he-
refie and
not with
pure
Schifme
only.

more

more vpon your owne indeauours, then vpon my grace : how feeble ye are, your actions giue better teſtimony, then your imaginations.

Are ye they, which can liue in the fire, and not be ſcorched in the flame, and not be ſmothered; wade vp to the lippe in the ſurges of the Sea, and not be ouer-whelmed; handle pitch and not be defi-led, eate and drinke, conuerſe, contract, (not only bargaines, but marriages) di-ſport, diſcourſe, play, pray, liue and die vvith Heretikes; and yet found at my terrible examen, neither attached with their infection, nor touched with conta-gion ? I fore-warned my auncient and firſt people, that if they vſed the conuer-ſation of Infidels, among whom they Ioſ. 23. dwelt, they ſhould finde them ſtumbling blockes of ſcandal, by giuing occaſion of ruine, and prickes to their eies, in put-ting out the inward light of faith, what by example, what by cuſtome and per-ſwaſion. Experience proueth this true in them, and the euent argueth it more true in your ſelues.

Are

Are not moſt of you infected, ſome with one hereſie, ſome with another ? I haue to charge you withal, beſides go-ing to Church, how ſoeuer you thinke your ſelues, to be ſome-what vertuous, and Godly; Rarer then a white Crow is he to be found among you, who either cancelleth not faſting-daies by his owne authority, or diſpenſeth not with meates prohibited, as often as he liſt, or doub-teth not of ſome article of faith, if not of al ? One improueth Confeſſion, another Purgatory, this man inuocation of Saints or vſe of Images, that man praiers for the Dead, or the office in Latin. There are that ſuppoſe Antichriſt ſhal not be one ſingular perſon, but includeth a company or a ſucceſſion. Many doubt nothing of this, yet acknowledge no vnion of the Church, vnder one head viſible; or de-tract from the authority of Councels, and decrees Eccleſiaſtical: Moſt of you feare leaſt the gates of hel haue preuailed againſt my Rocke; leaſt the ſpirit which I gaue her, haue not fulfilled my pro-miſe, neither taught her al truth, but
that

that shee may diuersly erre.

The stench of the damnable memory , and the fume of their brimstone ,
ascendeth from the bottomelesse lake ,
who of Schismatikes haue at last become
flat Heretikes , yea Persecutours , yea
and of an il beginning , made a vvorse
ending ? vvhence al this ? not becaufe
the longer ye liue , the skilfuller ye waxe
in Diuinity, the carefuller of your soules,
more desirous of heauen , or are oftner
visited with inspirations celestial, but becaufe ye vvaxe weary of expecting my
pleafure , in that I come not at your ap-
pointment , but let my secret and eternal
prouidence haue the determinate courfe,
ye thinke I haue either forgotten my
Church , or cast her off ; supposing quite
contrary to Christian doctrine , that ad-
uersity is an absolute signe of my indignation, and of a reprobate religion. Wax-
ing more and more in loue vvith the
world , ye haue lesse sence and feeling of
remorse ? by neuer talking with Priests,
nor conferring of matters touching the
spirit ; by being loden with secret sinnes ,
which

32.
By what
meanes
Schisma-
tikes grovv
to be He-
retikes.

which either you wil not acknowledge, or minde not to forsake, or cannot be indured to reforme by restitution and satisfaction ; it commeth to passe, partly through the nature of such negligence, partly through my just permission, for your vngratitude toward me, that you beginne to loath the religion, vvhich checketh your humour, and assureth not heauen to sinne and iniquity.

Amidst these your sensual, carnal, and worldly affections, heresie buszeth about your eares, plausibly inuiting you to her cuppe of pleasure. Thus lying open to the enimy, and destitute of my grace and protection, you are made a pray to the roring Lyon ; vvhile with conuersing among Heretikes, ye become like them in life. Becomming like them in conditions, you quickly delight in their sutable doctrine. Poyson, poyson, lurketh in their company, as in domestical Adders, and in the familiarity as in Cocatrice eies. VVhat though at the first ye be not Conquered ? He which loueth peril, shal perish therein:

what

vvhat though their arguments be but weake and foolifh ? Drops of raine in continuance pearce the hardeft ftone, a fmal worme in time decaieth the roote of the faireft Vine, and contemptible Yuie being let alone, ouer-creepeth and ouer-maftereth in time the taleft tree. Flee therefore fociety of Heretikes (afmuch as you may) euen in temporal bufineffe, becaufe of your peril, and becaufe my counfaile is fo to doe. Flee it abfolute in fact of religion, not for peril only, but for finne, not becaufe of my aduife only, but for my commandement fake. Flee Babilon, flee Chore, flee Sodome, flee from the aduerfary campe in time, as ye wil at the day of my victory, at the day of your death, at the great day of judgement, not be taken for enimies.

33.
The obfti-
nacy of
Schifma-
tikes and
ingratitude
towardes
God.
Perceiue ye not, for al that I can fay or doe, the horror of your offence, (oh ye my traitours and rebels) how long fhal I cry out to a people, which haue ftopped their eares, and alleage reafon to them, which fay they wil not vnderftand? how long fhal I preach repentance to them, which

which repel knowledge, and catch hold vpon euery simple shift, as vpon a staffe to sustaine their halting and trembling consciences. The eare discerneth wordes, and the eies coulours, the mouth tastes: This rude wilful people hath reason, and yet discerneth not iniquity. They repel al outward admonicions, for feare they should be conuicted; secret inspiration of contrition, they reject as melancholly; remorse of conscience, they hate as a hart sore.

Shal I for this hold my peace, and leaue to lay open their faultes? If it be little that I haue yet alleaged against you, heare more if it be not too little, but enough to condemne you, and too too much for you to finde any euasion, yet wil I adde more, to see if any thing can moue you; yea though nothing wil moue you, yet wil I adde it to justifie your condemnation, and my complaint, woe, woe, to you who wil not know the time of your visitation.

Behold, I haue stoode at the dore, desirous to be let into your hartes, and you
E   haue

haue not opened vnto me , when therefore ye fhal defire to enter into my Kingdome , and reft I wil anfwere you , that
which the foolifh Virgins heard , with
forrow enough : *Ye come to late , the gate
is fhut , and it fhal neuer more be opened.*
I haue fought reft in your foules, to make
there my manfion , and I finde as at my
natiuity, that *there is no place in the Inne ;*
I muft feeke fome-where elfe. I come
to your boundes and territories, to caft
out your Deuils, and heale your infirmi-
ties : you like fecond *Gerafens*, becaufe
of temporal loffe of your Swine, requeft
me to depart your confines.

Luke 1.

Math. 8.

    I wil depart, and when in neceffity you
cal me backe , I wil not returne. I inuite
my felfe to your dinner, as I did to *Za-
cheus*, to worke in your houfe faluation ;
ye contrary to him refufe my courtefie,
and wil no faluation to your houfe. I wil
feeke more worthy Hoftes , and I wil
fhake off the duft of my feete againft you.
I cal you as *Lazarus* foure daies dead,
(foure yeares dead , if not fourty) out of
your ftinking graues ; I cry **come forth,**
come

some forth, and ye wil not arife. Poffibly you imagine, that as I in raifing *Lazarus*, brake the common courfe of nature, to fhew my glory, fo I wil in you
fwarue from the ftature of your creation,
and violating your free wvil, make you
Catholikes by force fo to faue you, wel
lie ftil in your putrifaction, whom my
voice could not raife to faluation, my
Angels fhal raife them to judgement. I
haue fo long ftoode and cryed: *Yewhich
trauaile and are loden come vnto me,and I
wilrefrefh you.* I haue openly proclaimed
that vvhofoeuer thirfteth, fhould come
vnto me, and I wil giue him drinke of the
water of life. Which importunate indeauours of mine, and vehement prouocati-
ons fince they nothing auaile, feing ye
contemne my loue, and fet not by the riches of my mercy. I am forced to an out
cry againft you: *O al ye which paffe by
the way, behold and fee if there be any
griefe like vnto mine?* See if any man
were euer fo handled by his enimies, as I
their God by my creatures. See if euer fo
great kindneffe hath beene recompenfed

with

with so monstrous vngratitude : if Superiours were euer so dispighted by their
Subjects, Lordes by their Vassals. See if
at any time beggarly necessity despised
so bountiful munificence ; or apparant
peril of ruine and vtter destruction, were
so securely neglected. See if any memory can record so high a Majesty, to haue
loued so affectionally as base a bond-
maide, and to haue beene so ignomini-
ously repulsed in his suite.

What fettered caitiues were euer called to such glorious liberty, and would
not come out of their dungeons ? What
languishing in such loathsome malladies
were proffered health, and loued better
their noisome calamity ? Consider and
see how the Courtly cates, the Royal
cheare, which I haue prepared for my
feast, hath beene frustrate and disgraced
by vnworthy companions : one excuseth
himselfe by cares, an other by couetous-
nesse, an other by carnality, one hath
businesse, an other is bargaining, the
third hath married and cannot come.
Nay ye shal not come : but the time shal
come

Luke 14.

come when like dogges, ye ſhal hunger
and runne about ſearching, and ſhal not
finde for your famine. Ye ſhal craue and
wiſh, cry and cal for the crummes, which
ſhal fal from my childrens table, and from
the trenchers of my houſe-hold, but ſhal
not obtaine them, ye ſhal roare after one
draught of water to allay your thirſt, neither ſhal it be reached : yet vvhen you
haue done your worſt, by not comming
when ye were called ; my banquet ſhal
not be blemiſhed. I wil oppoſe to your
ſoules of better talent, you fruſtrate my
feaſt, but it ſhal not be fruſtrate, I wil fil it
with better gueſtes; you diſgrace it, but
I vvil grace it with more honourable
roomes; ye ſhal be eternally barred from
the table of the Lambe, Heretikes ſhal
enter before you into my Kingdome,
Heretikes ſhal be conuerted, to ſupply
your place; and Infidels wil I fetch from
Eaſt and Weſt India, to ſit in my glory,
and ye ſhal be throwne into vtter darkeneſſe. They ſhal poſſeſſe the Thrones
ordained for you ; they ſhal enjoy the
Crowne, which hong ouer your heades,

in

in expectation of your deſerts. Faith ſhal
be giuen to them , to them ſhal the grace
be tranſlated which ye refuſe , and they
ſhal fulfil the righteouſneſſe belonging
to their beleefe.

34.
Schiſma-
tikes by
their euil
example
impugne
the Catho-
like faith.
But oh that only ye loſt your owne
Crownes , and that ye were not occaſion
of perdition to thouſands more. Oh that
though ye honour me not your ſelues, yet
that ye would not worke me that contumely and reproch, which I may not beare
at your handes. Euery where am I bla-
ſphemed through your example, my religion growing in contempt, becauſe ye
ſet ſo little by it , who are thought to beleeue it. The edifice which I ſo carefully
founded , ye like mouldring ſtones decay
by your faltring and relenting, that which
my Saints haue built by their bloud (or
rather I by mine owne) ye ruinate by the
world and fleſh, as faſt as zeale laboureth
to kindle holly flame , ſo faſt doth your
coldneſſe extinguiſh it. Marke how de-
ſolate my houſe is , and how many haue
forſaken my Church, one through an-
others example. It is your diſſimulation
that

that betraieth my caufe, without which perfecution could little preuaile. For introduction and confirmation to your errour, ye fet the examples of others before your eies, as pillers of your actions, others fhal make you the ground of their vngodlineffe.

The contagion runneth among you from one to an other: as Chored fheepe and blafted fruit, ye daily are deftroied and deftroy by mutual infection, you fay you hurt not me or my caufe, but the joy of the aduerfary, and the dole of the Catholikes conuinceth it. If you could now fee the triumph, vvhich you adorne for the Deuil, and the forrow of the Angels and Saints, as you fhal one day know it, you vvould confeffe no leffe, then I now charge you vvithal, in the meane fpace that which you fee in the Children of light, and in the Children of darkeneffe, how the one is grieued, the other encouraged, and how each fide laboureth, the one to vvinne you, the other to hold you faft, is fufficient to informe you and

E 4. con-

condemne you, becauſe *Moyſes* and *Aaron* did once by their example not ſanctifie me, I would neuer let them enter the land of promiſe, and ſhal you enter into my reſt, who diſhonour me before people euery day? He which is the ruine of one poore ſoule, were better be drowned with a milſtone, and thinke ye it a ſleight matter to deſtroy, ye knowe not your ſelues how many? The children of Iſrael repining againſt the difficulties which they found, when I ledde them through the laborious deſert, (as I now conduct my Church in England, through the vncouth dreadful and paineful waies of affliction and tribulation) I cauſed them euery one to die in the wilderneſſe, except only *Ioſua* and *Caleb*, becauſe they two aſmuch as in them lay, encouraged forward the reſt. Shal then your murmuring and rebelling againſt the croſſes, laid vpon my flocke eſcape my judgements? Wherein chiefly lay the ſinne of *Ophin* and *Phines*, for which I plagued both their father, their children, and al their poſterity? was it not the alienating

and

and difcouraging of people from my facrifice by prejudicial behauiour? wil any King going to warre-fare endure him, which fhal by faint wordes or cowardly examples, detract the journey and diffolue the Souldiers hartes from battaile? I fuppofe not : for one fuch perfon hurteth more then feauen enimies, if he vvould; fhould he not build with one hand, and pul downe with the other? How then can ye be excufed from being both impediments and impugners, of my religion? feing as in skirmifh, fo in contention about religion, the apprehenfion of man and his frailty is fuch, that if one fhrinke ten faint, and if ten yeeld a hundred flie; and diuers not ftanding to their tackling, the ouerthrow of al followeth, and flaughter of the reft.

Oh ye fugitiues from my pauilions and campe, ye cal me King, but where is your fubjection, you cal me Captaine, but where is your courage? you cal me Lord, but where is your feruice? ye cal me father, but where is your fillial loue? ye cal me Sauiour, but where is your care

35.
Schifmatikes grieuoufly abufe God,

of

of saluation ? ye cal me Redeemer, but
where is your thankefulnesse ? ye cal me
Creatour, but where is your obedience
and loue ? ye cal me Omnipotent, yet
ye feare not my power; ye cal me iust,
yet feare not my rodde; ye cal me wise,
yet thinke not that I pearce your dissimulation ; ye cal me merciful, yet accept
not my pardon, which I here offer you
yet againe, if ye wil presently repent.
Ye cal me good, yet vse it not, but abuse
my goodnesse : ye cal me righteous, yet
doe me wrong : ye cal me God, yet haue
more respect of man. Ye say ye are not
wicked, but what greater impiety, then
to associate your selues to my aduersaries, to betray my cause, to deny my religion, and forsake the participation of my
Sacraments. To haue more care of your
substance, then of your soules, to poise
the world and me in ballance, and preferre it before me; not to deale with my
Priests, not to assemble at my praiers,
to liue like Heathens, acknowledging
the seruice which ye haunt to be folly
and sacrilege, yet otherwise wanting al
exercise

exercife of Religion ? Curfed is hee that doth my worke negligently and fraudulently, and curfed is he which doth it not al.

Why doe I thus reprehend a fort of innocents, who wifh wel to me and my faith, and with al their hartes, defire the returne of their fore-fathers daies, helping my diftreffed members to their vttermoft power. It is not they which haue denied my faith, and abolifhed my lawes; or which perfecute with fuch extremity. What they doe, is againft their wil vpon meere compulfion, not fo much for regard of their owne particular, as of children and family, neither from the hart, but for fafhion fake and obedience, and only for a time. They purpofe not to die otherwife, then graffed into my body Myftical, and true members of my Church, and in the meane fpace redeeme the time of their finne, vvith workes of mercy.

Can iniquity thus teach your mouthes an vntrought ? Pyned confciences, howe greedily they pray vpon the
foode

36.
Excufes of Schifmatikes refelled.

foode of falfhood. The bread of lying rellifheth wel in your taft, but the grauel thereof fhal grate your mouthes, and fret your mawes : Againft your owne foules ye pleade.

37.
Schifma-
tikes are
not excu-
fed by pre-
tence of
helping
the Ca-
tholike.

Others indeede made the breach in *Peters* Net, but why haue ye with them fallen head-long forth? others ouer-fow-ed the cockle, but why are ye choaked there-with? others raifed the fmoke, but how hapneth it that your eies are blin-ded? others purfue and affault my Ca-tholikes, but why haue ye through your departure vveakened them, and made them a pray, to whom if ye had manfully ftoode, neither they fhould haue beene fo oppreffed, nor you liue in fuch flauery of confcience, nor I haue beene fo difho-noured in this Realme, and almoft quite exiled. What tel ye me of your fimple affiftance, which is the leaft that ye ought to doe, but farre from the moft that ye might. Is your continuance in Schifme to further the conuerfion of England? What? Shal my Church be reared in iniquity, and Syon founded vpon dam-ned

ned foules ? Can not I maintaine my
power without your finnes ? or (though I
vfe you as I finde you) wil I euil that
good may redounde thereof ? I feeke
not your goods, but your good ; not your
fubftance, but your fanctification ; you
and not yours. Build not your finnes vpon my backe, for I wil caft you headlong ; I neede not your diffimulation,
you are not neceffary to me at al. If I
feede you without other mens aide, fo
can I feede others without you. Perhaps
I am beholding vnto you, that ye are not
fuch flat Heretikes as fome are ; I had as
liefe ye were. Oh we are luke warme ;
I would ye were cold : oh vye doe not
wholy follow *Baal*. If *Baal* be God follow him wholy ; if I be God, follow
him not at al, but me : halt no longer
betweene both. And what is it that ye
dreame off, your good vvorkes ? and
frame imaginations of I know not what
manner to redeeme your finnes.

    Pretend ye to be Chriftians, to be of
vnderftanding, to know wel what ye doe,
and are ignorant that al workes done in

38.
Schifma-
tikes me-
rit not
glory nor
remiffion
by their
good
ftate workes.

state of sinne, and out of grace, how much soeuer they tend to piety, or intend my honour, are aboundantly rewarded, if in consideration thereof I temporally blesse you, with health, wealth, or other prosperity : seing they neither satisfie my iustice, nor merit remission of offences. Hauing dismembred the vnity of my Church, by your departure, and violated the sacred bond of her peace and charity, whatsoeuer ye doe, though ye gaue al to the poore, and your bodies to the fire for my sake, ye are nothing, ye doe nothing, ye shal reape nothing. I spit at your workes, if you thinke that done out of grace, they serue to saluation.

Nothing saueth but by liuely vertue, and force of my Passion, with which none can haue affinity, who haue by sinne made themselues dead, detestable are such in my sight, vntil by profound and perfect repentance, they be reconciled to my fauour. No workes are holy, where the soule is not sanctified, no branch can beare fruit, except it bide in the

the ſtocke, cleanſe your veſſels, then put in your wine , and your floore before you heape corne. Ere vp a freſh your ground & caſt not away your ſeede vpon thornes. My Church is a Vine, whereof I am the roote ; become branches of this Vine , and then may ye beare fruit to ſaluation, keepe perfectly my Commandements , 1. Ioh. 3; and then haue confidence.

Out of my ſight vvith polluted and blinde Sacrifices : away with the workes which ſmel of the contaminated caske. Abhominable are the offrings of the wicked ; neither wil I be greſed with the oile Pro, 15; of ſinners, ſuch as the die is, ſuch is the coulour : ſuch as the pipe is, ſuch is the liquor. Ye holy ? your very juſtice and righteouſeſt actions are as ragges of office ; the choiſeſt of you is but as chaffe, the ſmootheſt a Thiſtel , the beſt is a Bryer , and the holieſt among you an Hypocrite. Ye rich in merits ? ye are vvretched , poore , miſerable , vvhen your heape (ſuch as it is) ſhal come to the Mil, ye ſhal finde that your graines were hollow and worme-eaten , fuller

of

of filth then pure flowre. Wel voide,
to the voide , and ful to the ful , they
which haue, fhal haue more and abound,
and from you fhal bee taken that little
which ye haue. I wil fuffer you to haue
your courfe : ye are cold , but ye fhal
waxe colder : ye are runne farre from me,
but ye fhal runne further, I wil puffe away
your almeffe as afhes, your giftes I wil reject as from diffembling friends. I weene
ye meafure me by your felues, and thinke
to bribe me before the day of judgement,
your expectation fhal be deceiued, and
your finnes argued before al the world.
What fhal I doe vvith a multitude of
your praiers , the lip-labour of defiled
mouthes, and flattery of faithleffe harts?
Let not the confidence of them ouer-

Ecclef. 15. whelme you, my praife is not fitting in the
mouthes of finners , and execrable is his

Pro. 28. praier, which wil not heare my law. Sa-
lute not me, Lord, Lord, except ye fulfil
my wil. If blafphemous tongues can
magnifie me a-right , then fhal your
mouthes perhaps praife me worthily ,
whofe deedes blafpheme me, I heare not
finners.

finners.

What magnifie you your faftes external , neglecting the folemne and great
faft internal , from finne and wickednes ?
Your faftes are infected with felfe wil ,
(in following your owne defires and not
mine) with worldly feare , with hatred of
correction , and reprehenfion vvith froward auerfion from the truth , with deadly finne, what of your feaftes, holy-daies,
and other auncient obferuances , wherein you choofe what ye lift , and what ye
lift ye contemne ? ye faft the Eues and
keepe Holy-daies, poffibly more then
ordinary , in difcerning of meates, many
of you are more precife then you neede.
But to communicate through feare with
Heretikes in their facrilege ; to abftaine
altogether from my Sacraments through
feare, to deny me before men , is no matter of fcruple. Oh Pharafees which very precifely tith-mint and rue , condem-
ning whofoeuer fwarueth one jot from
his duty , or doth not more then he is
bound in thefe fmaller matters, and breaking freely the maine precepts and principal

F

*Ioh. 9.
39.
Schifma-
tikes pre-
cife in
fmaller
matters
neglect
the grea-
teft.*

cipal points of my commandement : Hypocrites. Thefe greater thinges ought by any meanes ſtrictly to be obſerued ; and then are the other not to be omitted. Firſt obſerue the ſubſtantial part, then haue care of ſecondary reſpects : Firſt, hold faſt ſurely the poſſeſſion and profeſſion of your faith : then neglect not the ceremonies thereto belonging. Why ſtraine ye a Gnat, and ſwallow a Camel, feare a Mote and dread not a Beame, ſtoppe at a Straw, and ſtagger not at a Streame? To whom, but to ſuch as you did. I cry by my Prophet, that when they faſt and pray, I wil not heare them, and when they lift vp their handes, I wil turne away my face.

Ieremm.14.

Let not the bare name of obedience blind-fold you. I forbidde you not to giue vnto Cæſar, that which is Cæſars, but deny me not mine. No, not though Cæſar would arrogate to himſelfe, that vvhich appertaineth to me. Yeeld to Cæſar goodes, life, al temporal ſeruitude, as farre as behoueth to the Countries commodity and regiment. Render

40.
The objection of obedience is felled.

to

to me a pure hart , and sincere obseruance vvithout al exception , this I
challenge as my right . Honour the
Prince for my sake, but honour me for
my selfe. So I say , Honour me , Feare
me, Loue me, Reuerence me, Obey me,
Serue me ; which of you wil indure, that
his Sonne shal disobey him , and for his
excuse , that he did it by your seruants
commandement ? ye must not obey my
seruant against me the Master , neither
my Magistrate against me the Soue-
raigne Lord of al.

Be ye your owne judges in this case,
whether ye ought most to obey man or
me : Goe ye to heretical conuenticles for
obedience to the law ? More tollerable
shal it be at my great day to them , which
yeeld of frailty and feare, not aggrauating
their offence , by acknowledging prerogatiue ouer soules , besides that alone
which I haue appropriated to my Church
and keies; neither joyning their exteriour
schisme with inward schisme and heresie.
If obedience be a pretious thing performe
it to me, to whom al subjection is due, and

to whom al powers bow, I command o-
bedience to ſuperiour preeminence, but
not in derogation of my owne prerogatiue, neither am I contrary to my ſelſe.
Neither muſt the law of the ſupreame
Court, giue place to a meaner ſeate, neither my celeſtial Throne, to a terrene Tribunal. What obedience is that, wherein is
the greateſt diſobedience poſſible ? what
dutiful ſubjection, where in is moſt noto-
rious and perfidious rebellion ? If the
name of obedience be holy, whatſoeuer
it pretendeth, and that againſt the ſilla-
bles thereof, no reaſon can be heard,
then obey the body commanding againſt
the ſpirit, the world againſt heauen, the
Deuil againſt me.

41.
The excuſe
of feare
rejected.
What now, if ye be not ſo madde as
to allege that you ſinne againſt my law,
by way of obedience, to the lawes of the
Realme; but that what you doe of any
goodneſſe, ye doe for loue of me, and that
which ye omit, ye omit for feare of the
world. Nay, what if al the good ye doe,
be done for feare of my wrath, or for
vaine-glory, and not for my loue ? and
that

that which ye doe not, ye omit for loue of
the world, preferring the same before my
feare? for how can ye feare the world,
but that ye loue too much the world, and
feare least it should not loue you? Why
stand ye in awe of her frowne, but because
ye would allure her fawne? you would
not dread her bended browes, if her smile
pleased you not too wel, and tickled not
your hartes with delight. If you loathed
the world, and could brooke either the
absence of her company, or the eie of her
displeasure, ye would not feare what shee
could doe vnto you, which to speake the
most, is but to vse you frowardly, or to
banish you her sight. This if shee did, am
not I presently ready with armes displai-
ed, to receiue you into my bosome, into
my Pallace, into my eternal and incom-
parable Tabernacles? If ye loued me, ye
would not so loue the world, ye would
not so feare her : Seing ye violate my
commandement, because of her coun-
termande, how is it not manifest, that
wherein you obey me, ye obey me for
feare of my reuenging rodde, which also

ye would soone treade vnder foote, if the world should thither in like fort extend her prohibition.

Oh faithlesse cowardes, and not faithful champions : oh Hares and not Men : oh patternes of pusillanimity, what auaileth it you for excufe, feare indeede (as you fay) driue you from your duty ? I euidently denounced that ye should not feare them, which kil the body, and cannot deftroy the foule; but me, who can caft both body and foule into euerlafting flames. Haue I no way deferued, that you should fuffer for me ; Number the pricks of my fharpe pearfing thornes, number the bloudy and renting ftripes, receiued ouer al my body, from the rage where of no part from the crowne, to the plate was free, if ye cannot number thefe being innumerable, confider my fiue deepeft woundes, confider my defpightful death, and what I fuffered for the redemption of al mankinde, for yours in particular amongft the reft. Or I pray you, if you fuffer any thing for my fake, is my future glory an vnworthy recom-

recompenſe. Am I a ſlow pay-maſter, or a poore Lord, notable to make you a-mends, or are ye richer then I, and can expect no juſt retribution? If now while ye are my enimies, I haue prouided you, and furniſht you vvith many neceſſary thinges, and ſuffer you to enjoy the fruites of my excellent vvorke-man-ſhip, the Earth and Skie; haue I re-ſerued nothing in ſtore, to gratifie my friendes.

Giue credit to my wordes, I tel you that bleſſed and a thouſand times happy are they, which ſuffer perſecution and croſſes for my name ſake, and for their conſcience, for great is their reward in heauen. If perfect wiſdome were to be talked to vnperfect hartes, I vvould tel you how to endure for religion, is a thing which in ſo ample vviſe ſatisfieth, for humane negligences and former offences, combineth ſo ſingular a Gar-land for the ſufferers; ſo exquiſitely conformeth to the type of my Paſſion, and maketh men ſo like to mee their Sauiour, that Saints in al ages haue

F 4. with

with teares of harty affection desired it;
with joy imbraced it, drawing neare and
feruently sought it, when it was farre off:
why feare ye and tremble (oh ye of little
faith) why dispaire ye, & cast your selues
away, O ye of no faith? The shippe-man
calleth to me from the bottome of the
Sea, in expectation to be swallowed, and
I heare him. The trauailer passing through
the midst of the eues craueth my aide, and
I conduct him safe. *Daniel* was secure
in the Lyons den. *Ionas* in the Whales
belly, the three children in the furnace,
becaufe I assisted them. I forsooke not
my Disciples and shippe, though some-
time I seeme to sleepe, and to forget
them. If your eies were worthy to be o-
pened, you should see as my seruant *Elizeus* did, millions of Angels in readinesse
for preseruation of my Church and company. Feare not therefore, that from
which both I can deliuer you if I wil, and
wil as I see it best.

Deny ye my omnipotency and ability
to deliuer you; or if I cal you to suffer
some-what for me, who are ye that dare
detract

detract and say, ye wil not, if ye be so bold, can ye aliue or dead escape my handes, but that I wil make you suffer euen in this life, much more for your sinnes, and that without al consolation, thankes, or recompence?

That which ye feare shal come furiously vpon you, and oppresse you like an armed Giant. Though ye feare to serue me, yet wil not I be afraide to repay your dastardy, with a dreadful hire. The slouthful person feareth to be stoned with a peece of turfe, pretendeth for his lazines : *A Lyon is without the dore : in the midst of the streete I shal be denoured.* What ailest thou Prophet of slouth, if thou take courage I am with thee. Feare me and my law, he which feareth man, shal soone perish; but he which trusteth in me shal be assured. What fearest thou persecution as a Lyon : Feare sinne and flie from it, for it is a Serpent, and a two edged sword. You heare not, you are not perswaded : Goe your waies ye vnkinde wreatches; ye shal not suffer for me, for ye are not worthy.

Ecclef. 22.

Pro. 29.

Necessity

Neceſſity you ſay hath no law ; but deſerueth pardon. Oh how you vexe me with wilful blindneſſe. What neceſſity is there, why ye ſhould deny your faith by going to the malignant congregation ? Neceſſity forceth you to ſaue your ſoules, for if ye doe not, in vaine ye haue receiued them, nay curſed is the houre vvherein ye were borne, vvho haue fruſtrated the end of your creation, vvhich was that glorifying me in this life, ye might be glorified by me in the life to come, and cauſed my bloud to be ſhedde for you in vaine, and ſhal be damned for euer-more, without al redemption.

But no neceſſity compelleth you to ſaue your life, much leſſe your goodes. What if ye become poore, yea moſt poore ? What if ye die ? is not the cauſe mine ? Is it not your faith that ye ſuffer for ? I repeate it againe. No neceſſity conſtraineth you to ſaue your life, much leſſe your goodes ; neither care of your ſelues ; neither care of your family.

Can

Can not I prouide for you and yours, without your sinne ? Aske the Birdes, Fishes, and Beastes, who feedeth them, vvhereas they neither sow nor reape. Say not with the murmurers : *Can God prouide vs foode in the desert*, feare their example, I gaue them sustainance, and when they were not content with such as I sent, I condescended to them their hartes desire, but while the meate was in their mouthes, my wrath fel vpon them. The expectation of the careful shal perish, and the lesse ye trust in me, the lesse regard I wil haue of you. Seing you discard me from your accompts, I discharge my selfe of your care. Wilt thou needes prouide for thy family ? thou doest wel ? doth natural loue instigate thee to seeke their maintainance ? So doe I also, yea I tel thee, if thou feele not this instinct, thou art vvorse then an Infidel . But how behoueth it thee to prouide ? by hooke and by crooke, by sinne, Schisme, Infidelity, Perjury, Theft, Murther? must al things be lawful to thee for maintainance of thy family, according to thy calling ?

43.
Care of family is no excuse of schisme.

Rom, 11.

calling ? Or muſt thou prouide for them
only by induſtry, labour, or any other
honeſt and juſt meanes ; and touching
the reſt, commit them to me ? My commandements doe not one impugne the
other, neither haue I willed any man to
offend.

Eccleſ. 15.   When I commanded to loue me a-
boue al, did I except wife and children?
did I not peremptorily auouch, that he is
vnworthy of me, whoſoeuer preferreth
them in any thing before me ? Curſed
ſhal the child be, which ſhal be reſpected
aboue me and my commandements; be
he innocent, yet ſhal he ſuſtaine the recoile of his fathers iniquity. And he
which taketh hold vpon the natural loue
engraffed by me in your hartes, why doe
ye not inferre with your ſelues, that if he
who prouideth not for his family temporal neceſſaries, is worſe then an Infidel,
he which neglecteth prouiſion for their
ſoules, is a very Deuil : Vnleſſe ye thinke
that the body is more pretious then the
ſoule. But I aſſure you that al is loſt if the
ſoule be loſt; ye ſhew wel therefore, that
                 you

you loue your children for your owne
fakes and delight, and not for me or my
wil, thus turning the law of nature, a-
gainft me the authour of nature. Goe
forwardes ye vvho are fo follicitous for
your houfe-hold and pofterity, proceede
in your cares ; vvhen ye haue al done,
both hazarded and loft your foules, and
daily offended me for their fakes; who
is it that foftered and preferued them ?
you or I ? who filled their Mothers brefts
with milke ? who gaue to you that affection of loue, which maketh you to affift
them ?

Tel me whofoeuer thou be, which
trufteft more in thine owne follicitude,or
(to fpeake plainely) more diftrufteft me,
then that thou dareft commit them to my
handes, canft thou feede thy felfe without my prouidence ? I, who but I ? che-
rifh the younge Rauens, cloath the Lillies and Flowres, open my handes and fil
al the earth with bleffings, I number not
the ftarres only, but the very haires of
your head, why then dare ye not rely vpon my refuge.

I haue

44.
The true cauſe why Schiſmatikes going to Church are ripped.

I haue laide before you the excuſes, which the beſt of you with vnſacred lips, and vncircumciſed hart doe forge. Wicked and vnſearchable is mans minde, but I vvho am the ſearcher of hartes, wil finde out euery corner. The reede on vvhich you leane, ſhal runne through your handes and breake. Are theſe your cauſes and pretexts? Pretexts they are, but not cauſes. He eaſily findeth occaſion, which wil needes breake friendſhip. If you wil not vtter the very cauſe, but are aſhamed thereof; then heare it at leaſt, and confeſſe a truth. Charity is waxen cold in your hartes, the world or the fleſh haue ouer-whelmed you, ye want faith; of the Catholike beleefe, you haue no certainty, as infallible; but opinion only, that is probable.

Your ſoules are ouer-growne vvith ſinnes and ſenſualites, as a barren field with buſhes and brambles; your corrupt affection tieth you more ſtrongly to the world, then if you were chained by one foote to a ſtake, you can not ſoare aloft, nor lift vp your hartes to congitation of celeſtial

celeftial and fpiritual thinges. If fometimes ye caft vp as it were one eie to
heauen, ye cannot but fixe the other on
earth ; if ye proffer vp one foote , the
other is faft clogde ; ye cannot moue, if
ye offer to vfe the triple winges of grace,
reafon , and free-wil : the maffy poife of
flefh and bloud abafeth you prefently ,
before ye can make winge . Ye vvil
fuffer nothing, ye wil loofe nothing , ye
wil beare no paine , fuftaine no detriment , incurre no difgrace , indure no
calamity , ye wil diminifh no diet , impeach no fleepe , abate no part of your
port , impaire no credit , abridge no liberty, caft off no fuperfluity.

Ye little thinke, that to ferue me is per-
fe&t liberty, to loofe for me is great gaines:
it commeth not to your minde , that a fecure confcience is a continual banquet,
and that the fruit of a religious hart, is joy
and peace. What fhal I doe to fuch a
nice, delicate, and vnmortified generation ? If the times were good, could ye eafily goe to heauen : not fo foone as ye
fuppofe . Ye vvil neuer take vp my

Croffe

Ecclef. 1

Crosse and follow me, who when I lay it
vpon you, and help you to beare it, thruſt
it from you with violence, and hurle it a-
way with a miſchiefe. Let your fainting
hartes meditate defence of their conſtancy : but they ſhal not be innocent. Build
pretence while you wil, but ye ſhal not be
guarded from the tempeſt of my wrath.
Waſh your ſelues with ſope, as long as
ye liſt, ye ſhal neuer be cleane : Why
being inuited to my heauenly banquet,
deſire ye to be holden excuſed ? Why ſay
ye that ye cannot come : what neede
theſe complements ? Speake plainely, ſay
as the truth is ; ſay, *we wil not come.*

Oh fie, ſuch wordes to our Lord God ?
ſuch a flat denial to our maker ? *Nay,
Spare vs a while O Father of heauen, we
wil but ſet things in order, and waight a
conuenient time, at leaſt once before we
die, we wil approch to thy ſanctified Table.*
Craue you then daies and deliberation ?
Is it for my behoofe or your commodity,
I inuite you ? Need I your ſaluation, more
then of ſo many other ſoules, Iewes, Infidels, and others, which I hourely ſuffer

45.
Againſt ſuch as or defer their côuerſion.

to

to perish, and inuite them not to life?
whom if I inuited, I should finde multitudes of them, answerable to my inspirations, and if I had giuen them some few
of those opportunities & motiues, which
I afforded to you, they would long since
haue done penance in sack-cloath and
ashes, and beene conuerted perfectly
from their wicked waies. Or if besides
my Quyres of Angels and Saints, I yet
would be glorified of more, can I not
create more children to *Abraham*? or
when ye haue done your best, haue ye not
beene vnanswerable to your talents as
vnprofitable seruants? Did I choose you
first, or did you choose me? I chose you
and loued you, before ye were in nature,
before ye were any thing, and now ye be
some-thing ye forsake me. And yet
though ye haue forsaken me, I haue not
so forsaken you, but that I inuite you once
more to returne. Turne vnto me, and I
wil turne vnto you. Nay, behold I turne
vnto you; turne therefore vnto me, I
humble my selfe to seeke first the attone-
ment; I inuite you gratis to my super-
G   eminent

eminent glory. Aske any man if he wil
intreate you, or hire you to partake of his
bleſſings: yet behold I inuite you.

Come, come, my children, come
poore ſoules, take your fil for thankes,
not Wine and Milke or Honny, but of
ſupernal, immortal, and Angelical foode,
vvhich who ſo eateth, liueth for euer,
and who ſo eateth not, can haue no life
in him. Come, and ye ſhal not only be
wel-come, but I wil giue you preſent
grace, as pledge of future glory, I wil
giue you remiſſion of ſinne, I wil make
you one with me, I wil endew you with
ſome eſpecial fauour. For I am not he
that enter any where and am wel enter-
tained, but I there bountifully leaue my
remembrance. If euer I deſerued wel
at your handes, if euer ye expect any further pleaſure, if ye loue me, if ye honour me, if ye feare me; come, delay
I may not beare. My fatlings and fowle
are killed, al thinges are in readineſſe,
and I wil not ſtay. If ye wil not come
for my ſake, come for your owne.

Come while you are in health : Forſake

fake the world before it forfake you.
This is merit and thankes. Come while
your fenfes ferue, vvhile your wits are
your owne, while as reafonable you may
vfe reafon, before ye be drowfie and
fpeachleffe as beafts, or rauing as damned fpirits.

Come quickly, leaft ye be taken in
a trappe, at an houre vnlookt for, and
neuer come; or at leaft vvhen you
vvould, no meanes occurre; vvhere-
by ye cannot come. Bring forth the
vvriting, vvherein I haue indented
with you, not to cal you til ye be ready; if you haue any deede or leafe
of life or yeares, fhew me my feale,
and then build vpon my affurance:
If you haue no fuch, fhew me at leaft
fome parrol vvarrant; if ye hold only at vvil; why dally you, vvhy delay
you? Why preuent ye not my fodaine
fummons, hauing no Charter of e-
ftate?

Oh miferable foules, vvhofe chiefeft hope is, that vvhich of al o-
ther thinges is next to damnation, the

G 2. moft

moſt horrible ? that is to be conuerted at
the end of your life ; then which, what is
more perilous or vncertaine ?

There are among you, which are not
yet ſo forward , as to purpoſe to turne to
me at their laſt houre ; but can finely
ſhift themſelues from the ſeuerity of my
judgement, although they acknowledge
their actions to be il. They can ſhunne
the blame thereof vpon the Prince and
the law-makers, who are the cauſes of
their ſinne. Your ſoules indeede I vvil
require at their handes, but what is that
to you , who periſh in your iniquities.
What may the puniſhment of the acceſ-
ſary auaile the principal felon ? of juſt
actions, the motiue is not reproueable,
nor the cauſe il , if your act be not damnable, what is their offence. Are ye Infants ? or wil ye pleade ſimplicity ? or are
ye men who becauſe their free-wil cannot
be forced further , then they liſt themſelues , are at their owne peril to looke to
their doings. The theefe alleageth his
neceſſity, the fornicatour the violence of
his paſſion ; you the terrour of the lawes ?
Aſwel

46.
Againſt
thoſe
which ſay
the Prince
ſhal an-
ſwere.

Afwel you might al thinke your felues excufed, by cafting the fault vpon the Deuil, who tempreth you.

Loe here the weakeneffe of your fortifications? Either you goe for obedience, or compelled for feare, or for loue of your family : either you lay the fault vpon others, or you deferre your conuerfion. Scar-bugs and vifards to terrifie children, not to amaze men ; excufes to mocke fooles, not to fatisfie him which requireth reafon.

Are thefe the bulwarkes that muft fuftaine the day of my wrath ? are thefe your trenches for time of battaile ? If Spiders webs can with-hold the Eagles flight ; if a thinne boorde can recoile the roring Canon, then fhal thefe allegations ferue for a good plea. Souldiers truft not in gilded armour, nor the marrmer in painted fhippes. Dare ye venture your foules on fuch friuoulous illufions ? you may deceiue others, you may deceiue your felues, but me ye cannot deceiue ; no not though you thinke to ouer-reach me, and perfwade me to be content ;

47.
Excufe of Schifmatikes how vaine and weake.

G 3. I fee

I fee not as man feeth, for man ouer-
feeth, but nothing efcapeth my knowledge, yet if as man I fee; what man is
fo blinde that feeth not your diffimulation and offence ? I wil waigh al your
actions euen to a graine, and keepe tale
of al your finnes euen to one; I wil rippe
vp your hartes, difcouer the center of
your cogitations, and lay open your barren rootes, your adulterate loue I reject;
your fained obedience I renounce; your
pretended deferts I caft out off my memorial.

Pro. 11. There is a vvay which feemeth to a
man not to be vnrighteous, and the end
thereof leadeth to death : Such is the
courfe which you enfue. There is a generation which feemeth pure to it felfe,
Pro. 30. and is not cleanfed from her filth : fuch
a generation are ye. But (as I told
you before) the reafon hereof is, becaufe vanity bewitcheth you, obfcu-
ring that which is beft, and peruerting
Ecclef. 8. your vnderftanding. Becaufe judgement is not out of hand pronounced a-
gainft you, therefore ye fecurely wallow

low in finne : ye loue your felues and not me. Selfe-loue I fay you haue, for indeede ye loue not rightly your felues, if ye did, ye vvould loue me more then your felues. Hee that loueth finne, is the Enimy of his owne foule.

Tob. 12.

What fhal I fay to you ? though al excufes faile you, yet wil you not faile to excufe, when nothing ferueth your turne, then appeale you to my mercy. Appeale to my mercy when ye harty-ly repent, not while ye purpofe to continue in finne; vvhile ye liue, not when ye be dead ; while ye be yet at li-berty, not vvhen ye be apprehended, and caft iato prifon for my debt, I am merciful. Now come to mee, and I wil take you to mercy. Wil ye not come ? Then in calling mee merciful ye mocke me. To fay *the Lord is righteous, and we are wicked,* fhal no more auaile you, then it did *Pharao*, except ye forfake your iniquity. Shal a Man for-giue his Wife, if fhee perfift ftil in her

48. Againſt thofe which appeale to Gods mercy.

Exod. 9.

G 4 adulte-

adulterous minde, or his Sonne if he continue his contempt? if such may be found yet wil not I be so fond. Oh desperate boldnesse: Because my word extolleth my mercy, and examples of my clemency are maruailous, in confidence thereof to waxe malepart and bold, and to tel me before hand, that presuming there-vpon, you wil neither care what you doe to me, nor what I say to you.

Shal then the Arbiter of the heauens be vnjust, and the Iudge of Iudges be corrupted? Shal I so abuse my selfe, as to absolue whom the final verdict shal finde guilty? Then vvere my iniquity greater then yours. If ye hope to finde mercy, without conuersion to the fountaine of mercy, and auersion from your wickednesse, ye gape to feede vpon winde, and follow birdes flying in the aire, your hope is as thistle-downe, which euery breath scattereth. In this consisteth my aboundant mercy, that I haue not al this while taken you away in the midst of your sinne, but patiently a long time put vp al abuses, and expected you

to

to repentance ; that I haue louingly giuen you diuers motiues of remorse, that
I haue by secret meanes remoued from
you diuers occasions of further sinne,that
I haue not suffered the enimy,to execute
his malice against you, in such sort as he
would haue done, and as ye deserued ;
that yet also I am prest to receiue you
once more, euen now inuite you againe
to saluation.

As for the rest, you haue heard (I am
sure) and by authority authentical, that I
am a hard Lord, reaping where I sowed
not ; a seuere creditour, that wil exact of
vngrateful debtours the vttermost farthing ; a precise Iudge, which wil exa-
mine and cal to accompt euery idle word.
A straight Prince, which wil damne to   Math. 25.
vtter darkenesse an vnprofitable seruant,
a terrible God, vvhich for negligences
and omissions of smaller matters, then
exercise of religion and profession of faith
wil denounce : *Goe ye cursed into euerla-*
sting fire. Haue I not flatly proclaimed
that the way to heauen is straight, the
gate narrow, and few shal enter ; that
                                    scars

scant the just shal be saued. If it shal goe
so hard vvith good Catholikes, vvhat
shal become of you ? if the flourishing
and fruitful tree shal scant escape fire,
what shal the dry and vvithered stocke?
This if ye wil not now vnderstand to
saluation, the tempter shal beate it into your heades, at your final houre to
desperation.

49.
Schisma-
tikes rely
vpon hu-
mane wif-
dome.
     My wordes I wast, not able to per-
swade this wise and circumspect company, vvho cast beyonde the Moone, and
thinke vvith their farre reach to sur-
passe my prouidence, vvho deeme it a
feate of the greatest folly that may be,
to venture goodes for grace, their liuings for my loue ; to hazard terrene
honour, for hope of Celestial glory,
and a little temporal prosperity, for
eternal felicity. This is the summe of
your reckoning. First and principally,
before the care of God and conscience,
I wil quietly enjoy my wealth, and liue
in estimation among al men to my power : Shal I be in danger of want, or seeke
a straungers table, vvho am now able
                                        to

to entertaine others ? Shal my enimies
haue aduantage ouer me, and treade me
vnder feete ? Shal varlets and ribauldes
possesse themselues of my substance,
which I haue so painefully gotten together, and so carefully kept ? Shal I liue
in prison, and be vsed I know not how,
who now may goe where I list, and sport
at my pleasure ?

Vnderstand what is true pollicy (oh
ye babes) learne perfect prudence (oh
ye fooles) that which you say is vanity ;
and the practise thereof is meere madde-
nesse. The beginning of wisdome (if Pro.1.&.9.
your vvisdomes wil consider it) is my
feare, and the accomplishment of wis- Ecclef.12.
dome is the awe of me. This is the beginning and the end, this is al in al. The 1.Cor. 3.
wisdome of the flesh is foolishnesse before me, and the waies of the wicked shal Pro.12.
finally deceiue them, ye say ye are not
blinde; your owne wordes condemne ye, Ioh.9.
and of them I take witnesse, that ye erre
not of simplicity and ignorance. Beguile
not your selues, I am not to be jested
vvith al. Measure your fore-sight, Pro.23.
                                           trust

truſt not ouer-much to your deuiſes,
which I wil bring to confuſion, but haue
confidence in me with al your hart. Be
no longer wiſe in wickedneſſe, and ſimple in goodneſſe : Seeke firſt the Kingdome of heauen, and the righteouſneſſe
thereof, and al thinges elſe ſhal be ſup-
plied by me. The wiſdome of the fleſh
is death, but wiſdome of the ſpirit is life
eternal. If ye abhorre to be a triumph
to your enimies; Let not the Deuil the
chiefeſt foe of al, braue me by the ſpoiles
of your ſoules.

Pro. 3.

Rom. 8.

Now you are captiue, now may your
backe friendes ſcorne you, now doe they
treade vpon you, when they haue made
you yeeld vnto them, and for feare of
them, to doe that which is both a ſhame-
ful ſhift, and which they know vexeth
you to the hart : For he is neuer ouercome vvhich maketh reſiſtance, but he
whoſe courage failing, recanteth as re-
creant. Neither is your eſtimation to be
ſtoode vpon, as a matter of worth, for
honeſty may be wel thought crackt,
where Chriſtian duty to God hath taken
her

her flight. It cannot be expected, that he wil be loyal to man, who hath violated fidelity to his maker. If you force not of this credit, but intend authority, gape after dignity, loue superiority, and delight to command, are not your hartes guilty of abhominable ambition, and testifie against you, that ye loue the honour of men, more then the honour of your Lord God? Let your glory be to know me; for to follow me is perfect worship. I am the glory of my people, and they are my countenance. Eccles. 24.

Liberty you loue; why then remaine ye the slaues of sinne? ye are content to be the Deuils bondmen and thral, rather then ye wil be my seruants; and to endure his heauy fetters, rather then sustaine my sweet yoke. Vse the liberty which I haue giuen you, captiuate not your spirits and free-wil, to the earthly inclination of sensuality. And why should you preferre gold and siluer before me, whereas I redeemed not you with corruptible mettel, but with the last droppe of my bloud? The earth is mine, ye are mine Luke 15.

husband-

husband-men and labourers; al goodes are mine, and ye are my Stewardes; is it much for you to render to me my owne, if I demande it? you are rich enough, if ye haue a good conscience; and most pestilent pouerty is in a wicked breast, wherein is no goodnesse. Better is piety then pretious stones, it is the word of life; and a Bay-tree alwaies flourishing. Better is a little with piety, then great treasures. Many seeking riches, turne away their sight from seing truth, and easily make shipvvracke of their soules; seeke not so eagerly, that which is an impediment to the entry of my Kingdome.

Ecclef. 3.

Pro. 30.

Rom. 15.

Ecclef. 27.

But for asmuch as you thinke your selues so wise, consider yet a little, and you shal see much more of your foolishnesse, which euery child may plainely discry, and conuict you of folly; what profiteth it you, that my Church hath power to forgiue sinnes, seing you haue no accesse vnto it? that shee prayeth for her children, both liue and dead, seing ye be none of hers?

50.

The great folly of Schismatikes.

What

What auaileth it you, that my Paſſion is a medicine to ſaluation, ſeing ye apply it not vnto you? that my holy Body ſanctifieth and prepareth to glory, ſeing ye neuer receiue it? What booteth it you, that the juſt ſhal ſhine like the Sunne, ſeing ye for your ſchiſme, ſhal be as vgly as fiendes? that to the righteous is prepared a Kingdome of glory; ſeing ye be vvicked, and deſerue torment in Hel? That there is a Heauen, ſeing ye ſhal not enter into it. Angels and Saints, ſeing ye ſhal neuer enjoy their company?

Finally, in vaine it is to you that there is a God, into whoſe reſt ye ſhal neuer enter, and whoſe face ye ſhal neuer ſee, ye haue mouthes, and praiſe me not aright; eares, but neuer heare the Canonical praiers, and voice of my Spouſe, eies ye haue, and neuer behold me your Sauiour, though moſt louingly I offered my preſence among men, that they may daily remember my Paſſion.

Al

50.
God wil
peruert the
wisdome
of Schis-
matikes.

Al this notwithstanding you thinke your selues wise, and that my Catholikes are improuident persons. Contend with them no longer, but contend with me. See if I turne not your deuises againſt your selues, and make the wicked fruits of your vaine conceipts, to light vpon your owne heades. Contend with me in wiſdome, and see whether you can more eaſily lay a foundation of felicity, or I ſubuert it; you gather together, or I ſcatter; you purpoſe, or I preuent; you determine, or I fruſtrate. Your truſt is in the ſecurity, which is promiſed and permitted vnto you, for your vnconſcionable conformity; as though they could aſſure you of proſperity.

Curſed is the man, which truſteth in man: Whence ye leaſt feare danger, I ſend out miſchiefe againſt you as a Sergeant, and my wrath as a Purſuiuant; no ſtrength ſhal be able to defend you, nor any place to hide you. I would haue deliuered you from them, but who ſhal reſcue wretched ſinners out of my hands. I diſpiſe ſuch, as to pleaſe men diſpleaſe

me,

me, and their bones I wil cruſh aſunder.
As I hate the ring-leaders and maſters of
falſhood, ſo abhorre I their diſciples and
confederates: You feare them, but it is I
which wil plague you; you dread to ſtep
in the hoare froſt, but ſnow ſhal ouer-
whelme you; ye feare drops, but ſtormes
ſhal ouer-take you; ye feare a cracke as it
were of thunder, but I wil ſtrike you with
my horrible boltes in deede. As with
the holy I am holy, ſo vvith the ouer-
thwart I wil be ouer-thwart, of al the e-
uil which you haue ſowen, ye ſhal reape
ſeauen-fold; for to the ſword I haue ordained thoſe, who paſſe from righteouſ- Ecclef. 16.
neſſe to the Tents of iniquity, Anathema Iud. 5.
to the land of Meror, for not aiding my
Iſraelites in their extremity of battaile,
and Anathema to thoſe, whoſe joyning
with my aduerſaries, and yeelding to
them, hath made my hoſt a pray, yet
want I not meanes to maintayne my
Church, and without you it ſhal triumph.

Vnprofitable trees, how long ſhal I
expect fruit in vaine? yeares and yeares
are paſſed; and alwaies I finde you barren.

H The

The Axe therefore shal be set to your rootes, and ye shal serue for fire, if ye were Roses as ye be cankers, yet being so intangled among thornes and briers, ye should goe together to the furnace, ye shal see my Catholikes in my Kingdome, and your selues be kept without dores as dogges; which of my Saints wil stand betweene you and my fury, whose communion you haue renounced, with whose impugners ye are associate.

What helpe can ye hope for of the Angels, whom ye haue contristated by auersion from their King? Your Guardian Angels ye haue chased away, by entring Schismatical Temples. They are ashamed to haue laboured so long in vaine about you, neither wil follow you into the Kingdome of darkenesse. At that day therefore, ye shal see my children glistering in glory, and shal say. *Behold these are they, whose course of life we esteemed ridiculous, and zeale to be meere madnesse, whom we thought to be miserable, and eschewed their company as ful of calamity, now with how great di-*
uersity

uersity hath *God deuided their felicity from our wreatchednesse* ? If I deferre til then you care not. Nay, the Iudge is at the gate, and his rodde sleepeth not; Though ye be flexible by fauour, yet wil I be iust, though ye dissemble with me, I wil not dissemble with you, nor faile of my threatning word. Ye shal know that I looke not downe on earth for nothing, nor in vaine behold the actions of the Sonnes of men. Ye doubt whether there by prouidence, but when I repay you in waight and measure, and subuert al your wise imaginations, then ye shal feele it.

Goe to the Synagogues of Sathan, sit with the malignant in their Church, and wot wel that you shal be judged for so doing. Passe this life as merrily as you can, but hope not for the life to come. Be not content with your owne euil, but peruert and hinder others also, (which is the proper office of the Deuil) rather then further them to saluation as Angels. Ye shal one day finde, that double sinnes are needlesse, for of one you shal be condemned. Feare of disgrace

H a, *spurs*

spurreth you to perdition, forgetting that
I gaue *Toby* fauour in the sight of King
Salmanasar, aboue al others, because a-
boue al others he honoured me most,
and least feared the Kinges displeasure,
in matter of conscience.

Dauid and *Ioseph* might also serue you
of example, that credit is not alway lost
by seruing of me, but seing ye so feare to
loose mens fauour, ye shal loose it, they
shal maligne you, abuse you, hate you
worse then Recusants. From your wealth
and fatnesse proceedeth often your iniquity, I wil make you leaner, multiply-
ing your miseries, and the third heire shal
neuer enjoy those thinges, for enjoying
whereof ye forsake me. I wil put a ring
in your nostrels, and a curbe in your
mouthes, your owne conceipts shal perish, and my wil shal preuaile. You are
jealous of your honours, and thinke you
that I wil not stand vpon mine. Because
you dispise me, I therefore defie you;
and as spittle I cast you out of my mouth.
You are none of mine, and I wil be none
of yours; I wil blot you out, and crosse
you

you as notes out of vſe are wiped out of tables. And when I behold your neceſ-ſities, I wil clappe my handes ouer you. You haue caſt me away as a burthenſome and vnprofitable God. But I wil ſhake you off, as a man would caſt filth from his coate. Ye haue ſet a time to your ſelues, beyond which ye wil not expect, and now tired with expectation, ye are quite deſperate. Me, who made the globles of heauen, wil ye limit? to me who am e-ternity, wil ye preſcribe an houre or a yeare? For this marke what I tel you; ye that ſay, *We ſhal neuer ſee good daies, but* Num. 14. *ſhal die in the wilderneſſe, and therefore now let vs follow the time.* Good times ſhal come, and ye ſhal neuer ſee them, but die in the wilderneſſe, and (which is worſe) in your ſinne; your fortune ſhal be like to the incredulous captaine, who ſaw the wonderful plenty and alteration, 4. Reg. 7. which he beleeued ſhould come to paſſe, but neuer enjoyed the benefit thereof, and ye likewiſe which ſay. *Good time ſhal ſhortly come, we wil not be to forward before we ſee them, but wil then be conuer-*

H 3. *ted.*

ted . Good time fhal come vvhen I
appoint : the prefixed number of my
Martirs being accomplifhed , when al
hartes haue beene fufficiently laide open,
when I haue tried out , and retried al diffemblers , fuch as I finde you to be : Yet
fhal not the fruit hereof, nor the joy be
fuch, as you promife to your foules, fome
of you fhal die before, others at that time,
vvhen they would moft gladly liue a
while , others fhal euen then haue their
hartes hardened in fome other finne , as
now in Schifme.

52.
An inui-
tation to
returne
from finne.

Repent therefore , repent and turne to
the Sheepe-heard of your foules : O ye
my fheepe ; turne vnto your Lord God
O ye children , why fet ye your foules to
fale for vanity , and fel your felues to the
Deuil for a vile price ? Why fuffer ye
creatures to draw you from your Creatour ? Adhere no more to gold, filuer,
and poffeffions, vvhere-with I often cloy
my flaues, and fmile at your childifhneffe.
Let not droffy mucke., nor dirty farmes
feperate you any longer from my church.
Wed not your felues fo ftraightly to the
world,

world, which passeth in a moment, and al that is therein, no otherwise then a cloude before the Sunne.

The riches that ye haue, others had before, and some must haue after you. Aske your Mannours and Landes, how many owners they haue had, and they vvil reckon vp vnto you a long Catalogue; none of whom could euer yet by wit, strength, or power, either retaine them stil himselfe, or assure them to his posterity, ye shal finde them bought, sold, changed, reexchanged, giuen, inherited, purchased, let out, morgaged, forfeited, vsurped, conquered, lost, recouered, by right, by wrong, by might, by law, with a thousand other alterations. If the sundry liues, and demeanure of such seueral possessors, and what these goodes did cause vnto them, were recorded. Ye should see substance and possessions to be nothing else, but the pray of extortioners, the obiect of rauenours, the eie-sore of great personages, the ready pray of a Tyrant, the nourse of vnthriftinesse, the wracke of youth, the carke of age, the source of al vice, the shipwracke of al soules : A burthen, which oppresseth al that vndertake it, a gate out of which enuy cannot be shut forth, a thorny bush which choaked al goodnesse and grace. Regard them not therefore, but haue pitty on your soules, spare your selues and sinne no more.

Ecclef. 30.

Returne, O my prodigal children, and I wil receiue you. How many hire-lings haue their fil in my house, while ye in a forraigne land deuour huskes with swine. Returne, and I wil cladde you with a new stole, and cast your sinnes in-to the bottome of the Sea. Let euery one of you hasten to saue himselfe, as being in a daungerous tempest, to him which doth perish, al the world perisheth. Why die you and liue not? Why spend you your talents, and not in purchasing heauen? Circumcise your hartes, that ye may vnderstand, pul your tailes out of your eares, and stoppe not reason with sensuality: ye are not beasts but men, vse the dignity of soules, of reason, of con-science, of free-wil. Follow me in simplicity

plicity of hart, and proue me if I shew not my selfe a good God vnto you and whether I wil forsake you, or yet suffer you to be tempted aboue your power, or any further then is necessary for your good, you shal see that nothing is better then to feare me, and nothing sweeter then my law; yea, I wil prouide for you by such meanes, as you would least expect. So shal ye be sure to tast happinesse at last, and to be blessed at your end. No man euer trusted in me and was deluded. Be not ashamed to defend truth and professe it. For this confusion wil bring you to glory. Be not a-fraide to striue euen vnto death for righteousnesse, I am your reward incomprehensible. Passe to the part of the holy flocke and liue with them, which liue and praise my name. The Synagogue of sinners is as a heape of stubble, and their end is a flame. What reward is it to be Catholikes, when times are Catholike, now in the time of impiety and infidelity, shew a good conuersation. With-draw your selues from those, whom malice and sinne hath blinded,

Eccles. 23.
Eccles. 1.
Eccles. 2.
Eccles. 24.

Eccles. 4.

Eccles. 17.

Eccles. 21.

Eccles. 18.

blinded, depart from their pollution, touch not their filthinesse, away from it, away from it; come not neare it on paine of your foules. Looke backe to the rocks from which ye haue fallen; for blessing is vpon Syon, and curse vpon Hebal; my spirit ouer Hierusalem, and my sword ouer Babylon: Become ye fellow Citizens of the Saints; enrole your selues in my family; be reconciled to me, and I wil be reconciled vnto you. My Messengers and Legates, I haue sent into al quarters to preach my peace vnto you, and offer you pardon. Consider and see; this is al that I your Lord God require at your handes, that ye leaue dissimulation, that ye loue me, and feare me aboue al, walking before me in a perfect and vpright hart. Doe this and liue for euer, ye shal be my children and I wil be your Father.

Shal

SHal this Embaſſage be of no regard?
   Sent from a God, and from a man beſides.
Who for thy ſake in loue he hath not ſpard.
  His head, his armes, his legs, his ſacred ſides,
    But al haue beene embrued in deareſt blood,
    To ſaue thy ſoule, and worke thy greateſt good.

Bond-ſlaue thou waſt, to hel and to damnation,
  No worldly meanes from thēce could ſet thee fre.
No price on earth, to ranſome thy ſaluation,
  But what alone muſt be performd by me.
    I ſpared not, what treaſure heauen did hold,
    To gaine for heauen, what to hel was ſold.

I tooke mans fleſh, deſcending for thy ſake.
  I paſt to hel, to free thy ſoule from thence.
What to require me darſt thou vndertake?
  At what Tribunal pleade in my defence?
    The world doth tēpt, thou yeldeſt, deuils thretē,
    Betwixt them both, thy Sauiour is forgotten.

Thou loueſt the world, & therefore loath to loſe it.
  Thou feareſt the power of helliſh damned crue.
Thy ſoule is mine, and thou durſt not diſpoſe, it.
  Little remembring what thou haſt to rue.
    Wilt thou refuſe me, now the time is thine?
    And then preſume, when that the day is mine?

                      Thy

Thy time is now, thou fighteſt for a crowne,
  I firſt beganne the conflict and the fight.
I wan the field, and put the Deuils downe.
  I ſhewd the way, how thou mighſt gaine thy right,
    Mercy is offered, whilſt this life doth laſt.
    Iuſtice doth follow, when this date is paſt.

Let loue enflame thee, firſt for thy creation,
  Thou art not able to content me truly,
Then what thou oweſt for thy wrought ſaluation,
  Is not in thee to make requital duly.
    Yeeld loue for loue, let not thy loue be plaſt
    Where loue turnes hate, when that this lif is paſt.

What loue, what terrour, al the world may yeeld,
  Al are but ſhadowes, glaunſing on a wal,
Or like the winde, ſtowping the corne in field,
  They haue ſhort time, of no regard at al.
    The loue of heauen, the dreadful judgemēt day,
    Theſe, theſe, are they, whoſe endes cānot decay,

Chooſe now of whether thou wilt haue thy ſhare.
  Of that, which endeth in a moments blaſt.
Or of thoſe treaſures, which I doe prepare,
  For my true champions which ſhal euer laſt.
    The world is gone, thy Sauiour ſhal remaine,
    Stand faſt to him, and heauen is thy gaine.